Praise for Dan Sherman's LinkedIn Training

"For over 20 years I've been guiding Fortune 500 companies with their marketing, and in that time I've never seen a more powerful tool for generating business and worldwide visibility than LinkedIn. My good friend Dan Sherman has now created what I consider to be an indispensable guide to using this powerful social media site to achieve all your professional goals. Read *Maximum Success with LinkedIn* today, and you will discover how to use the site to build any type of career or business that you want."
—Charlie Cook, Marketing Coach, Author, and CEO of MarketingforSuccess.com.

"It's a shame that so many people ignore LinkedIn as a viable career growth and business building tool. Dan Sherman's *Maximum Success with LinkedIn* unlocks the secrets of how to use LinkedIn so that you can use it for your great benefit. A worthwhile guidebook for your success."
—Jim F. Kukral, Author of *Business Around a Lifestyle*

"Dan's book is an intelligent, easy-to-follow guide for anyone interested in benefiting from social media. I couldn't wait to log on to my LinkedIn account to implement a number of Dan's creative suggestions."
—Ed Brodow, Author of *Negotiation Boot Camp*

"It is no accident that Dan Sherman is one of the world's foremost authorities on LinkedIn. He studies, innovates, and educates around LinkedIn far beyond pretty much anyone else on the planet. And in his phenomenally practical and readable book *Maximum Success with LinkedIn*, Dan makes that passion and skill available to us mere mortals. If you're looking to develop You, Inc., this book should be your business bible. As Dan brilliantly puts it, 'If you're not on LinkedIn, you're not in business!'"
—Rob Brown, Bestselling Author of *How to Build Your Reputation* and Founder of the Global Networking Council

"I'm all about results, and Dan Sherman delivers in his book, which offers doable advice that is easy to understand and put into practice. If you are someone who needs to know how to use LinkedIn more powerfully for the professional side of your life, his book is a must read! I highly recommend it to my clients."
— Sheryl Nicholson, CSP, International Speaker, Author, and Coach

"Dan Sherman has taken ev̲e̲r̲y̲t̲h̲i̲n̲g̲ ̲ bout how to use LinkedIn to build a w̲ career of your dreams, and he's put it ̲ a for you to use

in your job search. Dan shows you how to rise to the top of recruiters' searches and showcase your skills and talents and how to get the recruiters to contact you to discuss their openings. I have bought numerous books on how to best use LinkedIn for finding a new job, but I now recommend Dan Sherman's *Maximum Success with LinkedIn* only because it takes you from beginner to expert in no time at all. Buy it, use it, and I guarantee it will open up so many new job search options that it will leave you excited about working on your job search each day until you close on that new job."

—**Frank Welzig, Executive Career Coach and President of**
http://www.NewJobCoach.com

"This is one book you cannot afford to overlook! From beginning to end, *Maximum Success with LinkedIn* is a MUST READ. It outlines everything you need to know in order to propel your business miles ahead of your competitors and stay there."

—**Terri Bork, Author of** *The Google Places Bible*

"Dan Sherman is an expert on how to leverage LinkedIn to build your business connections beyond what you may have considered possible. In his book *Maximum Success with LinkedIn,* he generously shares tips and strategies for expanding your LinkedIn connections and turning them into bankable leads. I highly recommend hiring Dan to educate and enlighten you or your employees on the true power of LinkedIn."

—**Mandy Wildman, Money Momentum Coach at**
Monetize Your Vision Coaching

"I followed just a few of Dan's tips and took my LinkedIn connections from 400 to 1,400 from Friday to Monday with very little effort. I was actually out of town at a mastermind, so not spending much time at all online, but I still had a huge increase. I can't wait to see what happens when I really work at it! Thanks again for the training and the information you shared."

—**Joanne Eckton, Management Consultant and Professional Coach**

"Although my LinkedIn profile was at 100 percent complete, I knew I was not utilizing the power of LinkedIn the way I should be. I hired Dan for a one-on-one session to teach me how to optimize my profile, add applications, and learn the value of the paid version. Dan was excellent at staying on task and teaching me in 90 minutes what would have taken me 20 hours to figure out on my own. I'll use Dan's expertise for my clients in the near future. Thanks, Dan!"

—**Clint Babcock, Vice President, Tampa Bay Sales Development,**
LLC, a licensed Sandler Training® center

"I went to one of Dan's presentations on the power of LinkedIn and employed some of the tactics he taught about beefing up your profile. I own a fishing charter website, and now if you type 'fishing' or 'fishing charters' in the People Search, I am number one! Dan's tactics and methods for business growth generate immediate results."

—**Chad Nikolic, CEO, FishNCheap.com**

"Dan knows his stuff. I went to a recent class where Dan took people from 0 to 60 regarding to leverage LinkedIn for their business. They may have come in knowing nothing, but after two hours, they had everything they needed to know to effectively market themselves and to generate leads using LinkedIn."

—**Mark Guthrie, Chief "e" Architect and Owner, biz360.biz**

"My company just went through a rebranding, and so I came to Dan to learn how to post videos on my LinkedIn profile. He showed me how, and he also taught me how to join groups and which ones to join, which I had no clue about. His training will help my business tremendously."

—**Jan Tinder, Group Vice President, The Advantage Group**

"I knew nothing about LinkedIn before I came to Dan's training, and I was very skeptical about how I would use it to benefit my business. Dan knows LinkedIn inside and out, and now I'm totally confident that I'm going to get a lot of leads from the site in terms of people finding me, and because of my ability to find other people. I'm going to really start to connect with others and grow my business. If you want to learn LinkedIn, get in touch with Dan."

—**Robert Case, Commercial Lender, Signature Capital Lending**

"If you've not had the opportunity to hear and learn from Dan about LinkedIn, you're missing out on great information that can significantly boost your B2B and B2C business. Dan is an absolute expert when it comes to maximizing your presence on LinkedIn. I highly recommend Dan as a speaker, seminar leader, and consultant."

—**Andre Kasberger, Online Marketing Strategist**

"Dan convinced me and showed me how to use LinkedIn effectively. On previous occasions I found LinkedIn difficult to use and purposeless, so I canceled my account. Dan changed my mind, and within half an hour I had all the basic tools to effectively set up a profile and start collecting contacts again that were relevant to my business. Dan is fantastic! In fact, I happened to run into two of my contacts today, and we opened a productive dialogue. Without LinkedIn, those conversations would have never taken place. The net result is I will be doing business with these people in the next couple of days."

—**Philip Frommholz, Owner, Phil the Mover**

"Dan's presentation on LinkedIn was filled with the nuts-and-bolts information I needed to start improving my LinkedIn profile, which I expect will lead to many opportunities to connect with other professionals. I recommend his workshop to anyone, whether you are a beginner or a more advanced LinkedIn user."

—Joe "The Blog Guy" Jacobson, Owner, Step by Step Blog Building

"I attended Dan's LinkedIn class, and it was really helpful. I already had a LinkedIn account, but I didn't really 'get it,' and in fact I was a little put off by the whole thing. But Dan took us through using LinkedIn step by step, showing us how to optimize our profiles, the importance of groups and discussions, and so on. Now when I do a search on my specialty keywords, I'm on the first page. Great course, great value."

—Mark Liquorman, Microsoft Access Expert

"I signed up for Dan's LinkedIn class because he is a LinkedIn expert! Dan has taken the time to not only master LinkedIn, but he also is a patient teacher and has obviously provided training to attendees of all skills and experience levels. Dan Sherman is a great LinkedIn trainer. I can definitely recommend his classes to anyone looking to learn how to begin using LinkedIn or to optimize their profile and leverage this incredibly valuable business building tool."

—Amy Campbell, Marketing Consultant

"Though I have been an active member of the LinkedIn community for some time, I found Dan's training to be highly informative and valuable. Dan presents his subject matter in an engaging and easy-to-understand manner. If you are looking for ways to leverage LinkedIn to grow your business, you must contact Dan Sherman."

—Lee Silverstein, Executive Career Coach

"Dan provides an outstanding, detailed synopsis not only of the many facets of LinkedIn, but also of how to get found, how to find others, and how to broaden your net of exposure. Dan's training really opened my eyes to a lot of areas of LinkedIn to help expose my business, create partnerships, and find clients. Highly recommended."

—Jay Adams, President, Alpha Omega Telecom

"Just finished Dan's LinkedIn training, and I definitely feel that I'm walking away with a lot of information that will help me. I wasted a lot of time in the past on the site, and now I feel like my time will be spent more fruitfully. I'm excited to get on LinkedIn, try some things, and practice."

—Victor Amuso, Software Developer, ParableSoft

"I attended Dan Sherman's LinkedIn training, and I learned exactly what I needed to use LinkedIn to take my business to the next level. Dan is really a LinkedIn expert. Not only is he very involved on LinkedIn, but he is also a very great teacher. He really helps you no matter what your level of LinkedIn expertise. I strongly recommend Dan if you need a LinkedIn expert to help your company."

—Paul Belshaw, Owner, Belshaw Accounting and Tax Services

"I wanted to learn to use LinkedIn to grow my business. That's when I discovered Dan Sherman, and my search was basically over. I've learned more—and learned more quickly—from Dan's courses than from anyone else. With many years of marketing experience under his belt, Dan is a true pro. He not only knows how to apply tried-and-true marketing principles to the new world of Internet marketing, but has also immersed himself in the details of LinkedIn. And, unlike so many other 'experts' in these areas, Dan really knows how to teach important principles and techniques to newbies and veterans alike."

—Luke Melton, Graphic Designer, Latitude 28 Design and Marketing

"Until I took Dan's LinkedIn course, I had no idea what it could do for my business. His class was informative, thorough, and easy to understand. Dan provides hands-on instruction that works for both the novice and the seasoned user. He has an incredible, in-depth knowledge of LinkedIn, as well as other marketing strategies. I highly recommend his book and classes with complete confidence."

—Terie Hynish, Unit Leader at PartyLite

"I have personally worked with Dan and attended his excellent LinkedIn seminars. Dan excels at staying on top of new technologies, and he is a great teacher and coach in several areas, including social media marketing and especially LinkedIn. I highly recommend Dan."

—Tony Rockliff, Chief Executive Officer, BestInternetMarketingSecrets.org

"I am so glad that I attended Dan Sherman's LinkedIn seminar, and I can't wait to put into practice all that I learned from him. He is extremely knowledgeable and proficient in the world of social media—so much so that I only wish we had had more time together. I will definitely be attending future LinkedIn courses of Dan's and would highly recommend that others do the same."

—Lisa Keeling, Business Consultant

"I attended a LinkedIn class with Dan Sherman and found the information very compelling, so much so that I'm going to go home right now and start updating my connections and my profile all in an effort to increase my business, my sales, and my bottom line. I recommend you learn from Dan."

—Don Fisher, Multimedia Business Consultant

"I thought that LinkedIn was just about jobs and my résumé, and that's all I had on there. Before I took Dan's training, I never had any idea what it could do for my business, not only for marketing to other online marketers, but also to my community of wholesale clothing stores, manufacturers, and Zumba enthusiasts. I found lots of ways to find groups and companies, and how to market my business. I learned a lot from Dan."

—Vijay Harkishanani, Entrepreneur and Zumba Instructor

"Dan Sherman is truly a wealth of information on LinkedIn. He is a dynamic public speaker who can take business owners from a place of very little social media marketing knowledge to a point where they are ready to begin the very next day, promoting their personal and business brands throughout the social media world. He has extensive knowledge of all phases of LinkedIn and social media marketing. Dan can teach you step by step so you are not overwhelmed with the idea of using technology to market your business, and that is so important for business owners as well as entrepreneurs today. I highly recommend Dan Sherman."

—Dr. Kytka Hilmar-Jezek, Bestselling Author

"Dan's knowledge and skill in the area of LinkedIn and social media are exceptional. I found that he gets results swiftly and conveys his know-how with simplicity, which is a rare huge plus. I highly recommend Dan to any company owners or entrepreneurs needing and expecting to work with a pro to help them acquire a continued high volume of Internet traffic."

**—Joe Yazbeck, President, Prestige Leadership Advisors,
and Author of *No Fear Speaking***

"I recently attended one of Dan's LinkedIn seminars and was blown away by the insightful information he was able to share. I realized I had not been using LinkedIn to its full potential for maximum exposure, not only on the LinkedIn site but search engine optimization (SEO) benefits as well. I've immediately implemented the changes on my profile, and I would recommend that everyone do the same. If you are in the business of building connections and being found, you won't realize the full potential until you take one of Dan's classes. Thanks again, Dan!"

—Rae Catanese, Blogger and Realtor

"My husband and I had the pleasure of attending Dan's LinkedIn seminar at Barcamp in Sarasota this past weekend. Dan really impressed upon us the value of LinkedIn and showed us how to maximize our LinkedIn accounts to generate business and potential clients. Dan is truly the LinkedIn expert and knows LinkedIn like no other. I highly recommend that any businessperson take Dan's class and learn about LinkedIn. I would even go as far as to say, it could make the difference between whether or not your business can survive and thrive! Thank you, Dan!"

—Julie Larson, Web Designer and Internet Marketer

"I have heard Dan speak several times about LinkedIn, and I was really impressed with his knowledge and his ability to share this knowledge with beginners like me. I was blown away by his knowledge base. Dan is an asset to any business big or small that wishes to make a presence in the social marketing arena. I would say hire him today."

—Jan Stammer, Owner, Circle of Independence

"Dan is truly the LinkedIn expert. Dan explained the process and organization for this site clearly and concisely. I am very excited to be participating on LinkedIn now. Get your business moving more effectively with good connections. Hire Dan, the LinkedIn expert, so you can get more business. Thank you, Dan!"

—Susan Higley, RDH, LMT

"I just finished Dan Sherman's training on LinkedIn. I learned how to save thousands of dollars in consulting every year, and that's just one of the benefits I got out of it. I highly recommend his training."

—Jim Thornton, Founder, Leadership for Continuous Improvement

"I had the pleasure to meet Dan through one of his many great webinars about efficient use of LinkedIn for professional branding. Dan's online training was of great value and filled with new learning, suggestions, and techniques even for advanced LinkedIn users. I will personally be looking forward to other webinars from Dan and strongly recommend attending."

—A. Albeshelani, Manager, Production Management at Nuance Communications

"Thanks, Dan, for excellent online training and a very good use of my time. Your well-organized LinkedIn training was informative and interactive, and it even made me better aware of several 'hidden' aspects of LinkedIn functionality. I highly recommend that anyone using LinkedIn listen to this session. What a wonderful resource LinkedIn offers once you get to know its hidden features."

—Ken James, Television Technologist

"I enjoyed listening to Dan's BRILLIANT online training on LinkedIn. I use LinkedIn every single day, and I thought I knew all there was to know about LinkedIn. Sequentially and strategically, Dan swiftly cuts through the nonsense and gets to the point, giving you the ammunition needed to fire up your profiles."

—Kamlesh Darji, Life Optimization Coach

"When we needed a LinkedIn expert to contribute to our internationally read marketing blog, we reached out to one of the best in the business, Dan Sherman. He's now our go-to expert on all subjects related to LinkedIn, including how to use the site to build your business and create a worldwide brand. The response to Dan's posts have been great, as our readers really appreciate his practical and easy-to-implement advice. Thanks, Dan, for helping our clients become LinkedIn Superstars!"

—Lauren Johnson, Marketing and Affiliate Manager

"I was fortunate enough to book Dan to speak at the organization I run, called Tampa Bay Computer Society, on using LinkedIn to grow your business, and he was sensational. The strategies he taught our members will help them gain more customers and more sales in a short amount of time. Dan is a LinkedIn expert, and his ability to explain LinkedIn in a way from which everyone benefits is fantastic. Both veteran Internet marketers and newbies alike were really impressed and grateful. I strongly endorse Dan as a LinkedIn trainer to any company or organization looking to create rapid success using LinkedIn."

—Dave Dockery, Founder, Tampa Bay Computer Society

"I've attended two of Dan Sherman's LinkedIn training sessions, and I look forward to more. Dan has taught me a great deal about how to achieve my goals using LinkedIn. Dan is a LinkedIn expert who knows how to explain the site in clear detail, so that anyone can immediately put to use his advice and expand their presence."

—David Mitchell Blood, Green Entrepreneur

"Dan is not only a LinkedIn expert but also an extremely engaging trainer. I've viewed his online training ('10 Ways to Find Your Perfect Job on LinkedIn') several times, and I plan to play it again. Yes, it's that good. Thanks for the work you do, Dan. It helps me do my work better."

—Christine Osborne, Encore Navigator

"I had the pleasure recently to work with Dan to moderate his online training '10 Ways to Find a Job on LinkedIn.' I agree that Dan Sherman is truly a LinkedIn expert, and the LinkedIn training he provided was very well received. Dan's approach to LinkedIn training is clear and concise, and he is very genuine and sincere about helping each individual maximize the power of LinkedIn. His LinkedIn training warrants reviewing and watching again, as he has proven himself to be the LinkedIn expert that I was looking for. He was able to help so many, and I highly recommend taking advantage of his special offers."

—Mark Lynch, Senior Director of Business Development, ILostMyJob.com.

"If you are looking to take your personal brand and value proposition to the next level, pick up Dan's book *Maximum Success with LinkedIn*! I had the pleasure of consulting with Dan, and I have found his contributions refreshing and high-impact. Many market themselves as experts in the field of business coaching, but I have encountered very few who are as insightful as Dan Sherman!"

—Jason Alford, Health Insurance Executive

"Dan Sherman is definitely the 'LinkedIn expert.' He is very passionate at what he does, and he has the willingness to help others succeed professionally with LinkedIn. After attending his one-hour webinar, I was able to take my LinkedIn profile to the next level. He taught us how to transform our profile to a career magnet by adding value with only five action items. He taught us the techniques for finding work in the hidden jobs market, how to grow our network, and how to create our own brand promise (my favorite). Ever since, my knowledge on the usage of LinkedIn has grown, and I feel more confident. But more important, my profile represents who I am, and I am proud of it. I would recommend Dan Sherman for any of his webinars and career consultation programs."

—Abadis Ruiz, MSM

"I read Dan's book and was extremely impressed with his in-depth knowledge of LinkedIn. I immediately contacted him and set up a private consulting session. Dan helped me optimize my profile and showed me a number of techniques for finding consulting work and much more. I plan on studying his six hours of training videos online, and I will be setting up additional one-on-one training sessions with him in the future. I highly recommend Dan. He is knowledgeable and personable, and his LinkedIn training is a great value. Consulting with Dan in this manner was a very efficient use of my time, and I believe most of you will agree. Hire Dan now!"

—Rob Darling, Former White House Physician

"Dan has been an excellent service provider who knows his industry inside and out. Dan's services have already given me an increase in leads in just one day of implementing his techniques! Dan's services go many levels deep, and I look forward to implementing more of his strategies. His years of experience have culminated in a fantastic type of service and level of service. I highly recommend Dan to anyone looking to set themselves apart from the crowd."

—Mark Pearson, Realtor

MAXIMUM SUCCESS

SUCCESS

═══ WITH ═══

LinkedIn

SECOND EDITION

Dominate Your Market, Build a Global Brand, and Create the Career of Your Dreams

DAN SHERMAN

New York   Chicago   San Francisco   Athens   London
Madrid   Mexico City   Milan   New Delhi
Singapore   Sydney   Toronto

Contents

Contents

Foreword

As the former CEO of Guerrilla Marketing, I have answered a lot of questions about what *guerrilla marketing* really is. Being a guerrilla is all about using unconventional ways of reaching conventional goals. When it comes to guerrilla marketing, it has always been about the unconventional ways of capturing leads and converting prospects into sales.

Being a guerrilla marketer has a lot to do with hard work, creativity, and finding the most affordable ways to generate leads and sales. That's why I love this book that Dan Sherman wrote on LinkedIn and why I am so thrilled to see the second edition in our hands today! I consider Dan to be one of the world's most credible authorities on LinkedIn and its huge, sometimes hidden, powers.

Jay Conrad Levinson, the father of Guerrilla Marketing, was the creative director at the Leo Burnet Advertising Agency. There, he developed such iconic brands as the Marlboro Man, Tony the Tiger, Morris the Cat, the Jolly Green Giant, DieHard Battery, Charlie the Tuna, and the Pillsbury Doughboy. Jay went on to teach marketing and advertising at the University of California, Berkeley. The common question he would get is, "How does an entrepreneur or everyday business professional market and advertise with little to no budget?"

After all, Jay was known for working with big companies and brands that had huge budgets. He did some research and realized that at that time (the early 1980s), there was no book or method that helped people increase sales primarily from their hard work and creativity. That led him to write *Guerrilla Marketing* in 1984, which eventually sold 21 million copies in 62 languages around the world.

Guerrilla marketing methods change and evolve over time because what was once unconventional sometimes becomes conventional, just as what was once conventional can become obsolete or forgotten. Often that obsolete method of marketing can be revisited and reintroduced to the marketplace once again as "guerrilla." For example, take direct-mail marketing. It was once very effective, but it became a less effective marketing tool from 2008 to 2012. However, because email deliverability has become more difficult, we see direct-mail making somewhat of a comeback for marketers who really know how to do it right.

Of course, now social media has become more important than direct mail or electronic mail. And the most important social media platform for businesspeople by far has become LinkedIn. If you work it hard with a level of creativity and consistency, you can have huge results. And you can do it for FREE! It might just be the best guerrilla marketing weapon out there! And with LinkedIn continuing to evolve, I don't see that changing anytime soon (hence this second edition of *Maximum Success with LinkedIn*).

Many of the challenges that exist in other marketing vehicles and platforms simply don't exist in the LinkedIn world. For example, ads in snail mail became "junk mail," telemarketing became a huge social faux pas and eventually illegal, and much of email was eventually labeled "spam," and it ran up against similar laws and restrictions. Every single one of these challenges developed because these platforms existed in a world where a high percentage of people did not want to be contacted by people they did not know. That, of course, is what makes LinkedIn special! The LinkedIn community is made up of people who inherently want to network and connect with other businesspeople. That's why people in your LinkedIn network are called "connections."

LinkedIn is for businesspeople, and it exists for the sole purpose of connecting together businesspeople from around the world. Although there are rules and etiquette involved in using LinkedIn, the overall themes are business, networking, introductions, connections, referrals, and collaborations.

Unlike many other social media platforms, LinkedIn does not have pictures of cats and kids and other distractions. LinkedIn is kitty and kiddy free! Don't get me wrong: I have a few pets and eight kids, but it's nice to have a place that is business appropriate that welcomes straight-up business dialogue!

In my last book *Cracking the Icon Code: Learn How to Earn an Icon Status and How to Net 6 Figures from Your Image, Expertise, and Advice,* I show readers how to gain the social proof that will position them as icons in their industry. My book tells its readers how to monetize their knowledge and experiences. Earning icon status has a lot to do with getting testimonials and endorsements, as well as sharing your accomplishments publicly.

LinkedIn understands the power that comes with having an icon status, and it specifically provides ways for you to easily get and share this "social proof." To that end, it has useful features like *recommendations* and *endorsements*. Additionally, there are places to put your biography, including the names of books you've published, and there are ways for you to celebrate your other accomplishments appropriately. The next closest thing to a LinkedIn profile would be to create a website for yourself, which many people do, but only at greater expense and more work, and only with the hope that people will somehow find it.

Your LinkedIn profile truly has the potential to position you as an icon in your industry. On my profile, I have dozens of recommendations and close to 1,000 endorsements . . . and they're all in one spot for people to see! Thanks to Dan Sherman, people like you and me can truly capitalize on LinkedIn's full potential.

Infusionsoft, a CRM software company, received a $54 million investment from Goldman Sachs in 2013. When I worked in a yearlong contract with them in 2008, they were just taking off. People would always talk about how great the software was, but how much better it would be if it just did this "one more thing,"

. . . and then they would say what their "one more thing" was. Well, Infusionsoft worked hard to implement those good ideas, and before you knew it, the software became quite robust. However, its users also started to say that it was getting too complicated.

Ironically, in an effort to make the software better by giving people more features and benefits, Infusionsoft created a challenging situation in which its needed much more training and faced other issues as well. I learned quickly that you can't have a software system that simultaneously does a lot of things and is also a system that you can just sign in and use. To find this balance is what really makes an online platform an actual success, and that's what LinkedIn has truly done.

That said, just as we use only 10 percent of our brains, many LinkedIn users use only 10 percent of its capability . . . if that! That's why there is the need for an expert and a book. That's where Dan Sherman comes in. He is the unbiased LinkedIn expert who will give it to you straight as a person who has actually mastered the program and who practices what he preaches: he uses LinkedIn almost hourly. Dan is what I call a truth-teller, giving it to you straight and making complex things simple.

Now for the most important advice I could ever give you about your success in business. The number one most important thing a businessperson can ever have is a list of contacts and clients. There was a day (before the Internet) when it was said that if your whole business was burning to the ground and you could run back in and save only one thing, you should fight the flames for your "golden Rolodex" of contacts and clients.

You must build a list of prospects, and what I call suspects, to call upon. You have to have whatever information you need to contact your business contacts, referral partners, and past clients. You need to know who knows the people you need to know. To avoid these list-building activities greatly reduces your chances of business success.

The simple fact of the matter is that people don't buy when you are ready to sell, but rather when they are ready to buy.

The same can be said about when clients refer business to you. So it's our job to stay in touch and dwell in the forefront of everyone's mind so that when they do need your products or services or when they are in a position to recommend you, they think of you first. You can't do that without regularly talking to "your" people. With LinkedIn, you can easily stay in touch with your list of clients and prospects. LinkedIn is your golden Rolodex, and Dan Sherman is your guide to mining the richest place online. Enjoy!

David T. Fagan
Author of *Cracking the Icon Code* and coauthor of *Guerrilla Rainmakers* with Jay Conrad Levinson
http://www.DavidTFagan.com
https://twitter.com/davidtfagan

Author's Note

Anyone with at least a casual acquaintance with the Internet knows that it is a constantly evolving, rapidly innovating space in which to work and play. New developments in technology and changes to websites happen minute by minute. That's what makes the Internet so exciting. In this book, I've given you all the latest information on LinkedIn that was current at press time. As the inevitable changes take place on the site, I will be providing regular updates to the book through the following website:

http://www.mhprofessional.com/sherman.

Preface to the Second Edition

I'm excited about LinkedIn. I truly believe in its potential to uncover hidden opportunities for every working man and woman in the world. People who take the time to explore LinkedIn can find opportunities to grow their business, gain worldwide publicity, land the perfect career, develop a network of referral partners, meet mentors who will take their career to the next level, locate investors for their ideas, and much more.

I tell everyone I meet about LinkedIn, and often I'm greeted with phrases like, "Well, I have a profile, but I have not done much with it," or, "I received some invitations but never joined . . . couldn't figure out what it was about."

Why people have avoided using LinkedIn is understandable for three reasons. One, the constraints on their time limit how much people can take in, and unless people truly see the benefit, they are not going to get involved. Two, because LinkedIn is a social network, businesspeople might dismiss it as a waste of time, another place to play Angry Birds, chitchat about the weather, and dish the dirt on who got dropped from *American Idol*. Three, LinkedIn has a label as being exclusively a site for posting your résumé and looking for a job.

I wrote this book to convince you that while LinkedIn is a social network and it's great for finding a job, it really is an all-purpose, high-powered professional networking site where you can accomplish all of your business goals. I want all businesspeople and job seekers to stop what they are doing, log on to

LinkedIn, and start making the connections that will take their career—and their life—to the next level.

After reading this book, you will know everything you need to know to make the most of LinkedIn, and then it's up to you to put the largest professional networking site on the planet— and the ultimate personal branding platform—to work for you. I hope you find this book inspiring and educational and that you put these techniques to work right away.

While it can and will change your life, LinkedIn, at its most basic, is a tool (albeit an amazing one). It should be used in conjunction and in harmony with all the business disciplines out there that are available to make you more successful. That's why here, in the pages of this second edition of the book, you'll be reading words of advice from experts in such fields as sales, public relations, inbound marketing, video production, leadership, networking, and so on. This book is intended to give you a holistic view of personal and business success with LinkedIn functioning as the vibrant, dynamic core element.

As with any Internet-based resource, LinkedIn constantly evolves. Since its inception, LinkedIn has continually revamped its look and feel, and it has added brand new features and removed others. This second edition has been completely updated with all the new changes to the site's navigation and with all the brand new features that contribute to its being the go-to site for anyone who has business goals to achieve and fulfilling careers to pursue.

To your LinkedIn success!

Acknowledgments

To begin with, I'd like to thank all the guest writers in this second edition who graciously lent their voices and their wisdom so that you can obtain a truly comprehensive marketing education by the end of the book. Some of these writers are super-successful LinkedIn users; others are highly regarded consultants in key fields necessary for professional success. All are wise and talented, and they have proven, real-world strategies to share within these pages that will certainly contribute to the achievement of your business goals.

Thanks go out to Clint Babcock, Kipp Bodnar, Eric Blumthal, Yvonne and Hank Charneskey, Kelly Diedring Harris, Judy Hojel, Chris Krimitsos, Nile Nickel, John Patrick, Lee Silverstein, and Joe Yazbeck. Special thanks go out to David T. Fagan for his insightful foreword in which he rightly observes that LinkedIn may very well be the most powerful Guerrilla Marketing weapon ever invented.

And now, I must give thanks to the hardworking professionals of McGraw-Hill located around the globe. In every aspect of book production, sales, and support, they have exceeded my expectations. I appreciate their dedication and their support of my efforts to help shine a light on a tool that can be used by business professionals to create a better future for themselves. I'd like to send out special thanks to these McGraw-Hill superstars: associate publisher Mary Glenn, my editor Casey Ebro, Ann E. Pryor in publicity, Laura Yieh in marketing, Maureen Dennehy in production, and Yin Chan in special markets.

Introduction: Love at First Click

My involvement with LinkedIn began because of a habit. It's a habit that I freely admit to. I'm not ashamed of it, and I don't want to cure it. In fact, I like this habit: I'm a reader.

I love to read. Fiction, nonfiction, whatever I can get my hands on. To me, libraries are like temples full of the most amazing knowledge and entertainment right there for me to enjoy—and they're free! My library is one of my favorite places. You will find me most weekends trudging out of my local library with an armload of books.

I loved to read as a teen as well, and when I went off to college, I majored in English, which meant I got to indulge in my habit for four solid years, reading the best literature the world has produced. Reading and writing papers on what I read . . . that was indeed the life. This could be why I graduated with honors, even though my minor was in backgammon and it seems I spent an inordinate amount of time participating in that addictive game.

Today I enjoy reading all kinds of books. I enjoy fiction—I'm a Clive Cussler and Michael Crichton junkie—but I tend to gravitate to business books. I've devoured everything Richard Branson, the daredevil CEO of Virgin America airline (and one of my first-level LinkedIn connections) has put on paper. I have studied books about the creation of Starbucks, Apple, McDonald's, the Republic of Tea, and other corporate success stories. I've devoured motivational books by Tony Robbins, Brian Tracy, Jack Canfield, and Joe Vitale. Anything that would inspire me and help me grow professionally has landed on my reading list.

My love of reading also extends to magazines, and for as long as I can remember, I have subscribed to and read faithfully six magazines: *Forbes, Fortune, Inc., Fast Company, Entrepreneur,* and *Wired.* Every month I read them cover to cover, and I always find something of value to add to my business education. My files are bulging with torn-out articles from these magazines about new trends, products, websites, or companies I need to research.

And so it happened on that fateful day in 2007 when the latest copy of *Inc.* landed in my mailbox. I opened it breathlessly in anticipation of reading yet another fantastic tale of entrepreneurs shooting for the moon, living their dreams, starting the next Apple or Microsoft. I was not disappointed, for in that issue was the story about a four-year-old website that was taking the business world by storm, a site that was connecting the world's professionals into a massive online networking database.

The site was called LinkedIn. I read every word in that article, and I felt a strange tingling in my body . . . no, it was not the onset of a cold. It was the realization that what I had waited for my entire professional life was here. I immediately jumped on my Dell laptop, opened an account, filled out a profile, and started inviting friends and creating groups. From day one I became a fanatic and never looked back.

Internet Databases Are in My Blood

I think the reason I had such a strong affinity to LinkedIn was that I was no stranger to Internet databases that help people create connections to propel their careers forward. In fact, I used to sell them.

During the boom years of the Internet bubble (the late 1990s and early 2000s), I was the director of marketing at two Internet companies in Silicon Valley: Personic and BrassRing Systems. Both firms sold applicant tracking software to human resources departments at large companies, in a category then called *application service providers* (ASPs). We sold a *hosted service,* meaning that the software sat on computers in our facilities while the end users, human resources staffers, simply logged on and utilized the program to find the best candidates for open positions from the résumés they had collected. Today this kind of software is known by newer names, including *software as a service* (SaaS) and *cloud computing*.

Having been a firm believer in the idea and the primary cheerleader at two companies selling hosted databases in the recruiting industry, the concept of LinkedIn was a no-brainer: you log on, and there are all your contacts. No muss, no fuss; no software to install, debug, or maintain.

Fast forward to today, and I have become a social media trainer teaching business owners how to make the most of LinkedIn, a social media website praised by Nielsen Online as "the world's largest audience of affluent influential professionals." For me personally, LinkedIn has brought many rewards:

- I have a network of 30 million businesspeople I can ask questions of and from whom I can get advice.
- I get consulting offers and media requests regularly because of my daily presence on the site.
- I have built a personal brand as a social media expert through my interactions on LinkedIn and with my groups.
- I get training offers from groups and companies that wish to learn how to learn to use LinkedIn.

In short, I use this amazing site to create the kind of life I always wanted. And now I want to show you how to use LinkedIn to get anything you want, for it truly is a remarkable "manifesting" device. Whatever you need, you can produce it on LinkedIn.

How to Create a Yacht

I love reading positive thinking books like Rhonda Byrne's *The Secret*, Esther and Jerry Hick's *The Law of Attraction*, and Joe Vitale's *The Attractor Factor*. I agree that you attract to you that which you think about. And to me, LinkedIn is a real-life, wish-granting dream generator that will send to you whatever you hope to create.

Let me share with you one example. A good friend of mine lives here in my hometown of Tampa, Florida, and she loves to go boating. Now, Tampa is a boat-crazy town. Every weekend people take to their boats and set sail into the crystalline waters of the Gulf of Mexico, but my friend had no boat, nor did any of her friends.

But she had LinkedIn, she loved it, and she was good at using the site. She had started a LinkedIn group for power users in Tampa who also loved LinkedIn and were dedicated to building large personal networks on the site. One day she decided she wanted to throw a party for her group, and the party should be on a yacht. Not a small yacht, either. Something grand.

So she logged onto LinkedIn, and she did an investigation in the Advanced People Search. She used the keyword "yacht," typed in the Tampa zip code, and hit the *Submit* button. The results returned three yacht brokers in her network. She reached out to the brokers and told them about her group (of which I am a member), how they were influential decision makers, movers and shakers, and so on, and how the yacht brokers would benefit by aligning their business with her group of LinkedIn power users.

One yacht broker liked the idea, and so they met in person. That's how it came to be that the first party for her LinkedIn group was held on a 50-foot yacht on the Gulf. The broker was the party's sponsor, and he got to display one of his yachts for sale while my friend reciprocated by getting the word out through LinkedIn and other social media sites about his company and all the wonderful floating pleasure palaces he had for sale.

That's just one tale of many. There are so many people who are finding jobs, partners, investors, mentors, employees—even yachts—on LinkedIn. So let's get going, and I will show you how you too can find whatever you want and achieve all of your goals on LinkedIn.

Chapter 1: Social Media Is Not Your Father's Marketing

Before we jump right into LinkedIn, it's important to lay down a few ground rules about marketing yourself in social media. It will help you approach LinkedIn the right way and get the best results. I want to help you avoid being "that guy"—the one person who is shunned by people at networking events because he shows up and immediately starts tossing out his business cards like he's dealing Texas Hold'em in a Vegas card room. You need to approach marketing on social media with some finesse and restraint.

Let's start at the beginning. I've been in marketing well over 20 years, working in Silicon Valley, as I mentioned, and also for large corporations like Charles Schwab. I've been in the advertising game since I graduated from Tufts University in the Boston suburbs with a degree in English and got a job at an advertising agency as a copywriter.

The changes that social media has brought to the world of advertising and marketing have been nothing short of earth shattering. No longer are marketers held hostage to TV, radio, and newspapers as the only ways for them to present their wares to the world. With the push of a button and the click of a mouse, you can send your marketing message via video, post, tweet, update, blog entry, and more around the world in an instant.

In short, marketing has been revolutionized. What does this have to do with you? Well, you are marketing a product called You, Inc. You will notice on LinkedIn that the site revolves primarily around people, not companies (there is a section for building a company profile that I'll discuss later). As you market You, Inc., on social media sites like LinkedIn, you need to pay heed to the new rules because marketing today is a brave new world.

We used to have traditional marketing, or interruption marketing, which meant that marketers would break into your Steelers game or *CSI* episode and bark at you with some ridiculous commercial (this still happens, but technology has invented many ways, like TiVo, to avoid them). Now we have social media marketing, which is in essence a conversation. Specifically, on LinkedIn, social media marketing is a dialogue you have with the people you want to influence to, among other things:

- Hire you
- Work for you
- Invest in your company
- Be your mentor
- Partner with you

So you need to think soft sell, not hard sell. You can equate marketing on social media sites like LinkedIn to a backyard barbecue. Now, you would never walk up to a stranger at a barbecue and say, "Hi, can I sell you some insurance?" You get the point. Social media is all about engaging people in conversations, getting them interested in you first, and then seeing if there is some common ground for doing business as a next step.

Honesty Is King

Essentially, in social media it's just like a party where you let people get to know you and then invite them to learn more about you by visiting your website or blog, where you provide more information on how you can help them. Marketing on social media sites like LinkedIn means being real, authentic, and honest. People buy from those they know, like, and trust. In social media, you have the opportunity to let people see how much you know, and you let them make up their own minds as to whether you're someone they need to do business with.

The old saying (attributed to many people, including Zig Ziglar, the granddaddy of sales training) is, "People don't care how much you know, until they know how much you care." With social media marketing, you show people that you care about them by being interested in them, asking questions, and offering help. Then you move on to creating a business relationship.

Fortunately, LinkedIn has extensive ways for you to create situations in which people can get to know, like, and trust you. It's a great place to become a valuable resource to people by expressing your expertise through group discussions, through status updates, and by presenting your knowledge in videos, blog posts, PowerPoint slides, PDFs, presentations, and more that you add to your profile.

Social media is a "pull" medium as opposed to a "push" medium. You use LinkedIn's powerful features to show professionals from around the world your expertise and to pull them into your sphere. It goes without saying that it's not the place for the spam or trickery that sometimes is associated with a certain rogue element found in the Internet marketing world (that is, the folks who have you click on a link purporting to take you to a cool site, but you wind up on a male enhancement drug advertisement). LinkedIn is a place where you can build your brand as an expert and have people knocking on your door . . . and what's simply amazing is that it's free! Yes, there are premium accounts, which we'll cover, but I would say that 90 percent of the world can achieve their goals with the free basic account.

With that disclaimer about marketing on social media out of the way (be nice, play fair, don't be pushy—not too hard, right?), let's take a closer look at marketing You, Inc., on LinkedIn.

LinkedIn: Your Personal Worldwide Database

There are plenty of social media sites to join, but none will have the immediate impact that LinkedIn will have on your professional career. You can play Farmville and Mafia Wars on Facebook or watch Lady Gaga and silly cat videos on YouTube, but you can achieve tremendous success on LinkedIn, and that's why it's growing at an astounding rate. It's at 300 million members and counting in 200 countries and territories worldwide.

The best thing about LinkedIn is that it has the most affluent, most well-connected users of any social media site. Executives from all Fortune 500 companies are registered on LinkedIn, and 66 percent of LinkedIn's members are decision makers or have influence in the purchase decisions for their companies. LinkedIn holds the record for the highest average household income over all other social networking sites at over $109,000 per member!

While you can plant imaginary crops or wink at potential mates on other sites, LinkedIn is all business. There are no distractions. On LinkedIn you will find only professionals who are focused on just one thing: networking to create success for themselves and their businesses. LinkedIn is no longer a secret; with its IPO in 2011 valuing it at over $6 billion, everyone now knows about LinkedIn. Recently even America's president joined the LinkedIn phenomenon by using it to hold an online town meeting to talk about his economic proposals.

Who's Having Success with LinkedIn?

LinkedIn helps professionals across the board. Many people at first considered it a job-hunting site, but it is so much more than that. The range of people that it helps is extensive:

- Consultants who want to connect with prospective clients and build up their brand equity as experts

- Business-to-business marketers who are creating awareness of their new product launches or service offerings
- Sales professionals who do research on prospects before contacting them, finding out about their personal interests, school affiliations, and whom they might know in common in an effort to create better rapport
- Job hunters who are expanding their circles of business contacts to create a better chance of finding that perfect job, and who are keeping themselves top of mind with potential employers
- Small businesses who are staying in front of customers and reaching out to prospects
- Entrepreneurs who are seeking funding and getting the attention of investors in their ideas
- Recruiters who are looking to find staff for their companies and sorting through the world's largest pool of talent

Basically, anyone in business can get a boost from the global networking capabilities of LinkedIn. I tell my consulting clients flat out: if you are not on LinkedIn, you are not in business.

LinkedIn offers you the platform to achieve all your business goals, including these:

- Driving more traffic to your websites
- Getting media attention
- Promoting your events
- Finding the perfect work
- Interacting with professionals from around the globe you would never have been able to contact before
- Obtaining free advice from top consultants on urgent business issues

Understanding the LinkedIn Levels

Any discussion on how to leverage LinkedIn should begin with its overall structure. Your connections on LinkedIn are made up of the people you invite to join your network and, by degrees, all the people in the networks of those directly linked to you. Say you invite Sally who works with you into your network. She becomes your first-degree connection. You and Sally might have other first-degree connections in common, since you may both have invited other colleagues into your networks.

Now Sally is in your network as a first-level connection, and all first-level connections can be contacted with a free, direct message. Your second-degree connections include all the people who are first-level connections with Sally. For example, if Sally worked with John at another company and they are first-level connections, now John is your second-level connection. (You can ask Sally for an introduction to John and send John an invitation to connect. If he accepts, he becomes a first-level connection with you.)

Let's say that you haven't yet invited John into your network. Sally is a first-level connection, and John is a second-level connection. Your third-level connections are all the first-level connections of John, your second-level connection. Say you wanted to meet Mike, a third-level connection who is connected on a first level with John. The process is that you would send an introduction request through Sally to John to meet his connection Mike. You create a message asking Sally to send it to John to send it on to Mike. In most cases, your first-level connection Sally will be happy to forward the introduction request on to John and Mike.

Why is that? It's primarily because LinkedIn exists entirely for networking. People understand why you are there, and they will most often send on your requests. I know that I send on 100 percent of the introduction requests I get. I feel fine doing it because I know that the people getting the request have the complete right to accept it or ignore it. It's really up to them if they want to make the connection. So I and many others forward all requests. Now, as you will learn later, there many communications methods available to you on LinkedIn for you to reach other professionals with whom you are not first-level connections.

*   *   *

Now you know the basic rules for marketing yourself on LinkedIn, and how the site is structured. The sky's the limit. Now is your opportunity to use the world's largest professional network. Starting with the next chapter, you will learn how to build your foundation for success on LinkedIn: a powerful, user-friendly and customer-focused profile.

Chapter 2: The LinkedIn Profile: Your Miniwebsite

Creating a Powerful Profile

If you are like many people, you've gotten an invitation to connect on LinkedIn. If you don't have an account yet, simply go to http://www.linkedin.com and sign up for an account. All you need to do is enter your name, email address, and a password. LinkedIn will send you a confirmation email, and you click it to confirm that it is indeed your email account. Then log into LinkedIn using your email and password, and you are ready to go.

You might be tempted to start looking for contacts to invite as connections, but hold off on that just for a little while. You have a different goal at first, and that is 100 percent completeness of your LinkedIn profile. LinkedIn even has a grading system that tells you how close you are to fully completing your profile. When you go to *Profile > Edit Profile*, LinkedIn will present you with suggestions on completing your profile, and it will show you a circle on the right side measuring your progress. Initially the circle will have very little blue color, but the more you add to your profile, the more blue your circle will become until LinkedIn anoints your profile with the "All-Star" designation (see Figure 2-1). Having an All-Star profile brings with it many benefits. These include your showing up in more

Figure 2-1. When you have made your profile 100 percent complete, you will receive the "All-Star" designation. A fully filled out profile brings many benefits, including higher rankings in LinkedIn searches.

searches for your expertise and your informing the world that you are taking your networking on LinkedIn seriously—and people should take you seriously as well.

Here is how Mike, an engineering recruiter, described in a group post the benefits of reaching LinkedIn's pinnacle of profile completion: "I never realized the advantages of being an All-Star until I was contacted by several Fortune 500 firms. This may be of better use than most people think. Develop a great profile, and constantly tweak and enhance it. At some point you may be shocked at the results! True story."

To get to All-Star, you need to add the following:

- A current position with a description
- Industry and postal code
- At least two past positions
- Your education
- At least five skills

- A profile summary
- A profile photo
- At least 50 connections

When you've completed these basics, you can start to add other worthwhile enhancements, such as recommendations and PDF documents, but you will never really be done with your profile. Your profile is your miniwebsite on LinkedIn, to which you can constantly add your latest achievements and that contains content that separates you from the crowd and demonstrates your expertise. It's where everyone will come once they have discovered you in another area of LinkedIn, such as groups, and it's where you want to impress them! So work on your profile every day to make sure it does the best job it can of representing who you are and what you can offer.

I recommend you spend a lot of time creating a fantastic profile. Yes, you do need to spend time networking in the various functions of LinkedIn, but remember that it's your profile where people you want to impress will ultimately end up once you meet them. Since your profile is so important, we are going to spend the next several chapters on creating a world-class profile. Let's start with the basics.

How to Make Your Profile Rock!

Your home base on LinkedIn is your profile. It's where everyone goes to see who you are once they've seen your LinkedIn group posts or status updates. Don't confuse your profile with a résumé because it needs to be and can be so much more. It's actually a miniwebsite that you can customize to create a multidimensional marketing tool for yourself as a service provider, a job seeker, an entrepreneur seeking funding, or something else.

First of all, make sure that everything you do on your profile is client and user focused. When you first meet a prospective client, you don't rattle off all your accomplishments that you've memorized by rote; you don't blurt out where you worked and how amazing you are; you don't whip out your diploma.

No, the first thing you do is figure out how you can help that client, what problems you can solve, and what results you can help them achieve. Since LinkedIn is for making connections, and for the majority of professionals that means clients and business partners, you need to design your profile to create that *client-focused* benefits-oriented approach. Your profile should answer your potential client's or partner's question, "What's in it for me?" So focus on the benefits you will provide and how you will provide them.

Another thing to keep in mind is that we have become a race of time-pressed, multitasking, instant-gratification-seeking humans. We have drive-through coffee stands, banks, pharmacies, and even weddings in Vegas; movies on demand on every device imaginable; and quick response (QR) codes on every item in the department store so we can pull instant data and reviews. And when it comes to reading, we are all scanners. We want the pertinent facts fast and without a lot of work. We want easily digestible bites of information. We prefer *Dilbert* over *War and Peace*.

That means your profile should be scannable by someone in a hurry (which is all of us). Avoid big blocks of text. Get in, get out, and your reader will thank you.

Designing the Perfect Information Box

On your profile, the first thing people read is the large information box on the top of the page with a light gray background. Let's first work on that to make sure your first impression is a perfect one.

Use a Professional Photograph

LinkedIn is all about people connecting with people, and we do business with those we know, like, and trust. Here you want a professional headshot, and a nice pleasant smile goes a long way toward making your profile inviting to read. Avoid the cutesy route that works okay on Facebook where you show your golden Labrador or cute three-year-old child; stay away from pictures of two people (it's nice that you have a significant other . . . but this profile is about you); and don't use a cartoon or something silly. And even though QR codes are all the rage, avoid the temptation and show us your smiling face.

To add a photo, click on *Profile > Edit Profile.* Click on the camera icon, and on the next page click on *Choose File* to browse your hard drive and upload a photo from your computer.

Create a Great Professional Headline

When people find you in searches on LinkedIn or read your discussion posts in groups, they see a little box with your name, your photo, and your headline (directly under your name).

Don't be like most people, who have the default setting where LinkedIn just takes your current job title and makes it your headline. Boring! This does not give people a clue as to why they should connect with you, or do business with you, or how you can help them.

Make it a benefit-oriented headline. Show what you can do to help people. There are two ways to do that. One, if you have several different skills, write a list of words naming those skills. Capitalize each word, and separate them with a straight up and down line—it looks neater than dots or asterisks (you make the line by holding down the shift key and the backward slash: \). Here is how I have my headline:

Dan Sherman
McGraw Hill Author of *Maximum Success with LinkedIn* | LinkedIn Corporate Sales Training | LinkedIn Job Search Programs

Another approach to your professional headline is the "benefit statement" approach. This is when you put into a sentence how you can help people, especially if you are only focused on one area of expertise, for example:

- Top Graphic Designer Makes All Your Promotional Materials Pull Customers In Like a Magnet
- Expert Webmaster Creates Sites That Engage, Enlighten, and Convert Your Prospects into Raving Fans

If your target market is localized, then make your headline localized as well. Get specific. Think niche:

- Helping Small Businesses in Boise Get the Most from Their IT Investment
- Assisting Home Buyers in Orlando to Find Their Dream Home Fast and Efficiently

You get the idea. Turn yourself into a direct response copywriter when writing your headline, and tell the world what benefits you offer. One strategy you can use is to look at the profiles of other professionals who do what you do and see what they've put in their headline. If you see something great, follow their lead. Make your headline concise, compelling, and value driven, and you'll stand out from those who just use the default first job title.

To change your headline, go to the top menu bar, click on *Profile > Edit Profile;* click the pencil icon by your headline, and then fill in a professional headline for your profile (see Figure 2-2).

Customize Your Website Section

Here is another place where you can customize your profile to make it benefit oriented. You can list three websites here, and LinkedIn gives you the choice of standard names for the sites in the drop-down menu, such as "My company" or "My blog." At the bottom of the drop-down menu is "Other." What you want to do is select "Other" and then put in some kind of benefit-oriented statement.

Make it a call to action by offering something in the name of the site that gives people a reason to go there. You can use

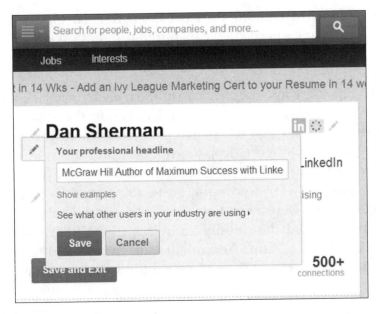

Figure 2-2. In the Professional headline section, you have the opportunity to write a headline that describes the benefits you offer to anyone wishing to do business with you.

"Download a free real estate report" or "Get a lead generating system" or "View 10 Free Social Media Videos." By using something catchy, you will get more people to go to the site, where they can then connect with you, join your mailing list (and get into your sales funnel), or sign up for a free 30-minute consultation—whatever is the next logical step for your prospects. Job seekers can send readers of their profile who click on a website link to an online portfolio or any site where their work and expertise are on display. Entrepreneurs can direct potential investors to a site with their start-up information and goals.

Here is what I am using in my website section:

- **LinkedIn Training.** Takes readers to my main site, where they can learn about my online and on-site LinkedIn training classes
- **Sell More with LinkedIn.** Leads people to my website, where they can sign up for one-on-one LinkedIn sales coaching

- **LinkedIn Training for Real Estate Agents.** Takes people to a site where they can purchase my LinkedIn video training course for real estate professionals

To change your website descriptions, click on *Profile > Edit Profile.* Then click on *Edit Contact Info* beside the small Rolodex card image. Click the pencil icon next where it says *Websites;* choose *Other* in the drop-down menu, and add your call to action; and remember to click *Save Changes* and test your links! (See Figure 2-3.) To test them, go to *Profile,* and look at your profile as if you were a first-time visitor. Try out the links to make sure you entered the website addresses (the URLs) correctly. (Don't forget the "http." You might want to copy and paste the website addresses right from the top address bar on the sites.)

Figure 2-3. To create interesting descriptions for the websites listed in your main information box, click *Edit* next to *Websites* and then on the edit screen select *Other* from the drop-down menu and add a descriptive term.

List Your Twitter Account

If you have a Twitter account, add it here. Click on the pencil icon next to *Twitter* right above *Websites,* and you will get a box where you can add your Twitter account and tell LinkedIn how you want your tweets displayed.

Customize Your Profile Link

When you first sign up for LinkedIn and get your profile, the public link that you use to send traffic to your profile will be cluttered. It will say something like, "linkedin.com/in/diysik49393." You'll want to clean it up and make it simple by changing it to your first and last names. Then you can put it on your business cards, in your email signature, on your website, on other social media sites—anywhere you want in order to drive traffic to your profile. Once you see how robust you can make your profile, you might even decide that you don't need a separate website; you can drive all your traffic to your LinkedIn page.

If the name you want is taken, try adding a middle initial or using different variations of your name. Another approach that I use and many people have also used is to turn your public profile link into a personal branding website address—that is, a tag line that shows people what you can do for them. Here are some examples:

linkedin.com/in/atlantaplumber
linkedin.com/in/greenthumb
linkedin.com/in/expertcoder
linkedin.com/in/orlandorealtor
linkedin.com/in/socialmediatrainer (This is the one I use.)

You don't have many characters, but you have enough to be creative. Make something you will want to put everywhere.

To change your public LinkedIn address and adjust your public profile settings, click on *Profile > Edit Profile*. Next, at the bottom of the box with your photograph and headline, in the small LinkedIn *in* block showing your existing profile website address, click *Edit*. This takes you to a page where you can customize how your LinkedIn profile looks when found in the search engines.

You can check and uncheck boxes for what you want displayed. On the right side you will see *Customize Your Public Profile*.

This is where you can select what you want the public to see. I have everything checked because I want everything to show, but you can customize yours. In the lower right of this page, you will see *Your Public Profile URL.* Click on *Customize your public profile URL.* You will then get a box in which you can put what you want after the "linkedin.com/in" in your public website address. Then click on *Set Custom URL* (see Figure 2-4).

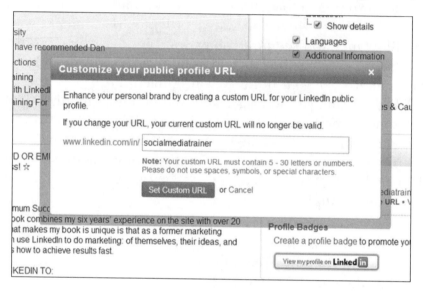

Figure 2-4. You can customize your public profile URL with your name or a branding term to create a short and memorable web address to use for directing people to your LinkedIn profile.

Lastly, on the bottom of the information box, you will see a blue button that says *Improve your profile.* Clicking on that will prompt LinkedIn to offer suggestions on information you might want to add to your profile. To the right of this button is a gray button with a down arrow; when you click on that, you'll be given five options: *Ask for a recommendation* takes you to the page where you can request recommendations from your first-level connections; *Create profile in another language* allows you to create a profile in over 40 languages; *Share profile* opens a dialogue box where you can tweet your profile or post it to Facebook; *Export to PDF* instantly gives you a copy of your profile in a PDF format; and *Manage public profile settings* takes you back to the page where you customize your public profile.

Creating the Ad for You, Inc.

Now that we've finished with the information box, there is much more to do to make your profile a complete advertisement for the brand known as You, Inc. The following are all parts of your profile that you can customize. You can then arrange them in any order simply by hovering your mouse over the two-sided arrow on the right of the section's title, waiting until you see the four arrows or cross-hair symbol and the instruction *Drag to rearrange profile sections*, and then dragging sections to wherever you want in your profile.

Your Summary

This is one of the most important parts of your profile. It's the place to let people know what's in it for them should they decide to partner with you, hire you, and so on. You have 2,000 characters with which to show people why connecting with you is the smart thing to do. Let me show you my summary so you can see one type of format you can use (see Figure 2-5).

ABOUT DAN SHERMAN
I am the McGraw-Hill author of *Maximum Success with LinkedIn*—a guide to the world's largest professional networking site. The book combines my 7 years' experience on the site with over 20 years as a marketing executive. What makes my book unique is that as a former marketing executive, I focus on how people can use LinkedIn for marketing themselves, their ideas, and their personal brand. I show readers how to achieve results fast.

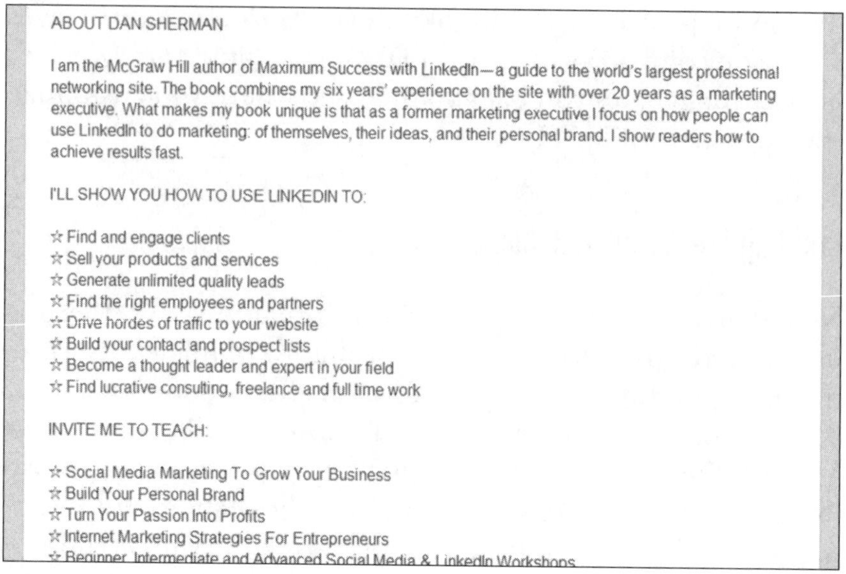

ABOUT DAN SHERMAN

I am the McGraw Hill author of Maximum Success with LinkedIn—a guide to the world's largest professional networking site. The book combines my six years' experience on the site with over 20 years as a marketing executive. What makes my book unique is that as a former marketing executive I focus on how people can use LinkedIn to do marketing: of themselves, their ideas, and their personal brand. I show readers how to achieve results fast.

I'LL SHOW YOU HOW TO USE LINKEDIN TO:

☆ Find and engage clients
☆ Sell your products and services
☆ Generate unlimited quality leads
☆ Find the right employees and partners
☆ Drive hordes of traffic to your website
☆ Build your contact and prospect lists
☆ Become a thought leader and expert in your field
☆ Find lucrative consulting, freelance and full time work

INVITE ME TO TEACH:

☆ Social Media Marketing To Grow Your Business
☆ Build Your Personal Brand
☆ Turn Your Passion Into Profits
☆ Internet Marketing Strategies For Entrepreneurs
☆ Beginner, Intermediate and Advanced Social Media & LinkedIn Workshops

Figure 2-5. On the Summary Page in Edit Profile, you have the opportunity to write a compelling ad for yourself describing in detail who you are and what kind of value you can provide to other LinkedIn members.

I'LL SHOW YOU HOW TO USE LINKEDIN TO:
* Find and engage clients
* Sell your products and services
* Generate unlimited quality leads
* Find the right employees and partners
* Drive hordes of traffic to your website
* Build your contact and prospect lists
* Become a thought leader and expert in your field
* Find lucrative consulting, freelance, and full-time work

INVITE ME TO TEACH:
* Social Media Marketing to Grow Your Business
* Build Your Personal Brand
* Turn Your Passion into Profits
* Internet Marketing Strategies for Entrepreneurs

* Beginner, Intermediate, and Advanced Social Media and LinkedIn Workshops
Learn more tips by joining "Link Success with Dan Sherman." Join Tampa Bay Marketing Professionals on LinkedIn. Download my LinkedIn training brochure below; view a testimonial video in my Experience section.

Need a speaker for your group on social media and LinkedIn? Contact Dan Sherman by visiting his site at http://www.linkedsuccess.com.
I am an open networker and accept all invitations.

The Reasons Behind My Format Choice

Since we are all scanners, I believe the summary should be easy to scan. That's why I chose the outline format: because it's easy to read quickly, and it's what I recommend you do. Essentially, in your summary, you should tell people the following:

1. Who you are
2. Whom you help
3. How you can help them
4. How to get in touch with you

Start off with a few sentences that describe who you are and sum up your professional qualifications. Then use the headline and bullet format as I have done. You will see that I introduce myself, and then I go right into what I can do for you, how I will do it, and in what modes I can help you. I also clearly point out what I can speak about should you desire to hire me. Everything is neat, concise, and to the point, and it can be easily consumed.

I also use the summary to tell my readers about some of the multimedia aspects and resources I have in my LinkedIn profile, where they can learn more about me, such as my video, my brochure, and my list of publications. No one is a mind reader. If you want your potential clients and partners to get the full picture of what you offer, show them where to look in your profile. I also advertise my two LinkedIn groups where people can join and share ideas on how to get the most from LinkedIn and learn from others' ideas on marketing strategies. This encourages more people to join my groups, thus expanding my circle of influence.

You'll see that I include some very important contact information in my summary. "I am a LinkedIn open networker" (which you will sometimes see abbreviated as LION) means that I want to grow my network as big as I can to give me as much exposure as possible to potential opportunities for consulting, speaking, reaching the media, acquiring new partners, and so on. That's why I include the statement that I accept all invitations.

Be an Open Versus a Closed Networker

Let me clarify: some people use LinkedIn and restrict themselves to connecting only with people they know. For me, that doesn't work. I want as big a network as possible, since I don't know who knows someone who knows someone who can give me my next big opportunity. LinkedIn says to connect only with people you know, but that does not work for me.

I want invitations from everyone to grow my network, and I assure them I will accept all invitations. (Maybe one in a hundred I don't accept because they have a goofy cartoon for a picture or a headline that seems like it's a fake profile or a phishing scam. In that case, I just click on the *Ignore* button.)

Include Your "Call to Action"

Also, in your summary, remember to include a call to action. Your summary states what you can do for them. Don't make them hunt for a way to contact you and shower you with Benjamins! As the movie title said, *It's All About the Benjamins!* Include your phone number or email—however you want to be contacted.

You'll see on my LinkedIn profile that I have my phone number. I'm a speaker and coach, and I want to make it as easy as possible for people to do business with me. Give whatever you are comfortable giving, but in all cases make it easy for people to do business with you by giving them lots of contact points.

Promote More than One Kind of Expertise

What if you have several kinds of businesses and you help people in many ways? You can try a variation of the summary outline I've suggested by having blocks of information that reference each of your skill areas.

For example, let's say you have three skills. You are a graphic designer, website builder, and copywriter (hey, you're pretty talented; we should talk!). I recommend you start with an overall statement, such as this:

Who I Am
Joe Smith is a talented communications professional with many years of experience helping business owners generate more sales and profits with superior branding and promotional materials.

Then you would have a section for each skill, noting whom you help and how you help them.

Graphic Designer

Whom I Help
I help small businesses with their graphic design needs [and so on].

How I Work with You
I can design your business cards, letterhead, [and so on].

And so on for each of your three skills. You are limited in the summary to 2,000 characters, so if you put multiple skills and companies in there, you will have to keep each one short and punchy. If there is a specific place where you want readers to go to learn more about each skill set, then put a call to action in each area. So, in the above example, if you have a site just for graphic design, include a call to action with a website address just for that one area (there is no place for a hyperlink in the summary, but there are many places for them in the rest of the profile). Do the same for each of your *skill blocks*.

*   *   *

Some final thoughts on the summary. As you spend time on LinkedIn, you will see profile summaries that are simply people boasting about how great they are and what they've achieved. No one cares! (Except a mom.) Tell people what you can do for them. As we say in sales, your customers are tuned to one station: WII-FM (What's in it for me?).

Second, I don't expect you to have a complete *Webster's Dictionary* in your brain. That's what spell check is for. So write your summary in a word processing program, spell check it, and then copy and paste it into LinkedIn. That way your spelling is accurate, and you can pull symbols into it. (I used bullets that I got from MS Word. There are other symbols you can use too if you like. I've seen musicians use the notes icon.) Remember: you get only one chance to make a good first impression! A profile with lots of typos will most likely defeat any purpose you have on LinkedIn no matter what you are trying to achieve.

Filling Out Your Work Experience

Did you ever go into a job interview, and the interviewer said something like, "So, tell me about yourself"?

One of the first things LinkedIn will ask you to do is fill out your work experiences. In this section you have the opportunity to tell potential clients, partners, hiring managers, and investors what you're all about and what you've been up to all these years. If you're just out of college, even though you don't have a lot of experience, there are plenty of options for information to put here. You see, they don't be to nine-to-five jobs. They can be any of the positions or activities in which you obtained experience relatable to the work world. For those of us more "seasoned" (I love that term—makes us sound like lamb chops, right?), there's lots to talk about. For our work Experience section, we can relate the journey we have been on, or as the Grateful Dead said, "What a long, strange trip it's been."

One question is, do you put every place you have ever worked? The answer is, for the most part yes, and there are good reasons why, as you'll soon learn. However, you should exclude jobs that really do not contribute to your professional career or that make it easier for the people from those jobs to find you, or jobs that detract from your credibility. Like the summer you spent fitting people with penny loafers in a shoe store, or getting a tan as a lifeguard, or manning a Tilt-a-Wheel at the Jersey shore. Those jobs you can leave off because they don't make you more desirable as a service provider or more employable, and no one from those jobs will be looking to connect with you.

Other than jobs that don't elevate your professional status, put every decent company you have ever worked for on your profile. Adding a great company, even though you were on a lower level or even an intern, adds credibility to your profile. You're associating with a great brand name, and it gives other people who worked there and are looking at your profile a personal connection with you and a reason to trust and like you. You've got something in common.

Another reason to list all your relevant jobs is that recommendations must be associated with a position you listed in Work Experience. You can't have a general recommendation that says something like, "She's an all-around great person." Recommendations are crucial to building your brand on LinkedIn, and they are social proof that you are the wonder kid you say you are. Every position you list gives you another opportunity to include a rousing recommendation from a colleague, boss, satisfied client, business partner, and others.

Lastly, a great reason to include well-known companies where you have worked in your Work Experience section is that LinkedIn automatically adds the logo of that company on your profile. Since many of your profile readers are visual in nature, they can scan your profile and see well-known logos of top companies, and that credibility then extends to you. As an example, I proudly worked eight years at Charles Schwab, and the blue Charles Schwab logo is on my LinkedIn profile. Even though I am no longer working in financial services, having the logo of a top billion-dollar company on my profile adds to my reputation as someone with a solid corporate background and solid business know-how.

Adding Non-Full-Time Jobs

You can and should include volunteer positions, as this gives viewers of your profile a chance to see that you are giving back to your community and you're a well-rounded individual. For new graduates who have very little job experience, posting volunteer jobs shows that you have been actively involved in different industries, that you are a team player, and perhaps that you have held some leadership roles.

Listing and describing volunteer jobs is also handy when you are filling out your profile should you currently be unemployed and looking for work. Saying that you are the president, membership chairman, or volunteer coordinator of a local charity as your *Current Position* tells hiring managers that you're not just sitting on your sofa eating Oreos and watching *Mad Men*. You're active in the community and polishing your people skills. Another great option for this same situation is to start a LinkedIn group and to list your current role as "group manager, ABC LinkedIn Group." It shows that not only are you active and social media savvy, but you are also a thought leader in your field.

Take some time crafting the job description; don't be tempted to just put in your titles and leave it at that. You never know which accomplishment of yours will be the one that puts you ahead of the competition in the eyes of a potential client or employer. Fill your descriptions with keywords, the skills and job titles that people will be searching on in LinkedIn to get the expertise they need. If you know a certain programming language or you're an expert in a graphic design program, put it in. Use care crafting the description, since it tells the story of who you are as a professional and gives you the chance to use lots of keywords. (Keywords are the terms that people use to search LinkedIn when they are looking for experts.)

Even part-time work can be listed in your work experience, especially if it has to do with the role that you want to be branded for because you can use a lot of keywords in the job description. For example, I want to be branded as a LinkedIn expert. So, in my profile I list several consulting assignments in my past work Experience section where I was a LinkedIn trainer at different corporations and professional groups. Since that term is what I want to be branded as and found for, I include several of these, even though they were short-term positions.

Arranging the Order of Jobs

Go to *Profiles > Edit Profiles*. Under the information box with your name, headline, and location, click on + *Add a current position*. A box will come up where you put your company name, title, location, time period, and description. If you want the job to show up in your current work Experience, click on the box that says *I currently work here*.

Basically, if you click that box near the position saying "I work here," it shows up near the top of your Experience section, and if you don't, it shows up lower. For keyword optimization, you want several job titles in positions you hold now and those you've held in the past to include keywords that you want to be found for. To add your past jobs, click on + *Add a position* and don't click the *I currently work here* box, and put in the start and end months and years you worked there. If you are unemployed and searching, it's okay to leave your current job in the Experience section as long as you add an end date to the job to alert recruiters and hiring managers that you are available.

To change the order of the jobs that you currently hold (for example, let's say you list some current part-time jobs, a volunteer position, and a consulting assignment), it's easy to arrange them in the order that you want readers to see them. In the *Edit Profile* mode, simply hover your mouse over the two-sided arrow at the top right of any job where you have indicated you currently work, look for the words *Drag to reorder this current position,* and drag and drop it.

Adding Sections That Make Your Profile Shine

Now that you have the basics covered, you have the opportunity to add lots of sections that you can use to really tell your story and give readers a glimpse into your professional as well as volunteer activities (see Figure 2-6). The following are sections you can include:

- Certifications
- Publications
- Courses
- Honors and Awards
- Organizations
- Projects
- Patents
- Test Scores
- Languages
- Volunteer Experience and Causes

Everyone has a different background, and the sections you add here will help tell your complete unique story on LinkedIn.

Go to *Profile > Edit Profile,* and look on the right-hand side at the choices listed there to see what sections you want to add

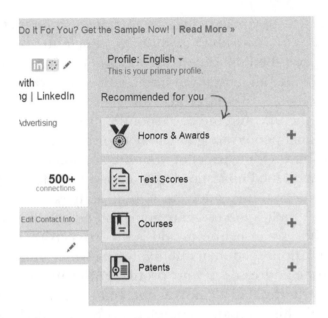

Figure 2-6. You have the option to add informative sections to your profile by going to the *Edit Profile* mode and looking on the right-hand side. These sections not only add depth and dimension to your profile but give LinkedIn users a way to order your products and services.

that will make your profile stand out. Simply click on the plus sign (+) to the right of the section you wish to add.

I use several optional sections, including Publications. That is where I put information on my books and my online courses. What I love about this section is that the title of each item is hyperlinked, and then there is a space to describe the publication or course. So people who read about my books and want to learn more can click on the title, and away they go to http://www.Amazon.com. Those who want to buy more courses click on those titles, and they are brought to the web pages where they can submit their order.

If you have an article on the web that shows you are an expert, if you've published a story in an online magazine, if you have a book listed on http://www.Amazon.com, if you have an online course to sell—if you have literally anything written on the web or available via the web that you want people to have instant access to, add the Publications section and link to it. It will give your profile depth, and it will brand you as an expert. To add website addresses to your profile, just click on + *Add* in this section, add the title and the corresponding website address, and describe what people are going to read or learn about.

If you have a white paper on your site that you want people to read, first add the Publications section to your profile in the *Edit Profile* mode, and then add your website address and a description of the publication users are going to find on your site.

Another great section to add is the Projects section. Like the Publications section, it offers you the chance to add unlimited website addresses to your profile. For example, I worked with a client who had a construction company, and he wanted to highlight his company's completed projects and show them to prospects visiting his profile. So we added the Projects section, then added each project description and hyperlinked them to photos he had previously uploaded to Flickr, a free photo sharing site. This way, his prospects could actually see the great work his firm had done. The Projects section is a great way to provide proof in living color of what you have achieved in your career.

I use the Projects section to link to my YouTube channel. As a speaker, it's helpful for me to make available demo videos of my presentations in order to convince companies to retain me as a trainer, so I use the Projects section to link to short, two-minute segments taken from longer corporate training sessions that I've done. If a prospective client is interested in seeing how I am on stage, I can direct them to my LinkedIn profile.

Another optional section I am using is Volunteer Experience and Causes. I encourage you to add this section to your profile. After all, one of your top priorities when developing your profile should be to help readers see you as a credible, interesting person with whom they want to do business.

Showing your involvement in local and national charities tells another part of your professional story, and this may be appealing to some of the people you are trying to create relationships with.

The Volunteer Experience and Causes section is really three topics in one:

1. **Organizations you are looking for.** Here is where you let the world know how you'd like to donate your time and talent.
2. **Causes you care about.** You can choose from a list LinkedIn provides or enter your own specific cause.
3. **Organizations you support.** Here you type the name of the organization you are supporting, and LinkedIn will look through the list of organizations in its database and find the one you want to include on your profile. This is why you should make sure your favorite charitable organization has a company profile on LinkedIn.

Letting People Know About Your Multiple Personalities

As we end this chapter, I want to make a confession: if a genie granted me one wish, I would choose to go back and relive every day of my four-year stint as an undergrad at Tufts University. It was truly amazing. I was the lead singer and keyboardist of the hottest rock band on campus, I had a large group of rowdy and fun friends, and every night offered a new opportunity to indulge in what many college students have as their undeclared major—namely, Advanced Partying. My nighttime escapades were widely known and were reflected in the nickname I had on campus; I was called "The Bat" because I came out only at night.

What I'm getting at is that we all have many personas, and since one of the key benefits of being on LinkedIn is that people can find you for opportunities, you want to take some time and think about your personas. What variations on your name should people be typing into the LinkedIn search to find you? If you have some aliases, add them as the bottom line in your summary, like this: "AKA The Bat." Don't assume that others know how to spell your name or that they know your name has changed. Add an AKA at the bottom of your summary in these cases:

- Your name is difficult to spell. Include all common misspellings.
- You got married. Include your single name.
- You got divorced (hey, it happens!). Include your former married name.
- You have an alias or nickname that you are known by.

By putting an AKA in your summary, you cover all your bases for being found for exciting new opportunities on LinkedIn. And one more thing: if someone terrific happens to find you because you used this strategy, and he asks you where you learned this neat trick, tell him, "The Bat told me."

* * *

Now you've laid the groundwork for an amazing profile. But there's more to do. Let's continue with the next thing you must add to your profile in order to give you the advantage over your competition: social proof, or recommendations.

Chapter 3: What Goes Around: Giving and Getting Recommendations

Your profile is your work of art, your *Mona Lisa*, your *David* statue, your Sistine Chapel ceiling. Everything on it has been placed there by you to build your brand as the go-to person in your field, the expert unequaled in the modern world.

Everything was created by you, except one important section that can help determine your success on LinkedIn: Recommendations.

Recommendations are proof that you are as good as you say you are in your profile. Fortunately, LinkedIn gives you the chance to get recommendations from a wide variety of people, so you'll never be at a loss for testimonials to add to your profile to create what has become so crucial in today's transparent Internet world—namely, social proof. You can tell people how great you are, but no one is really going to believe it until someone else (besides a close relative or your sweetheart) is there to agree.

It reminds me of the famous *New Yorker* cartoon that summed up the perils of trusting what you see online. Two dogs are in front of a computer, and one is typing away and says to the other dog: "On the Internet, no one knows you're a dog."

Put another way, on the Internet, you often don't know what you're getting. Because so many people have been burned by believing what they read online, there is now a wariness and distrust of anything on a website. Thankfully, the Federal Trade Commission (FTC) has jumped into the fray, and it has created laws to protect consumers from merchants who display fake testimonials and fake blogs. However, the Internet is so vast it's impossible to police every single company.

Social proof goes a long way to calming the fears of people, and it's easy to add it to your LinkedIn profile. It can come from a variety of places: you can ask colleagues past and present, bosses past and present, people who reported to you, business partners, professors, people who did work for you—literally anyone with whom you've worked in the past. What makes recommendations believable social proof is that the names of those making the recommendations show up as hyperlinks next to their recommendations so that they can be easily checked out and their praise corroborated.

Social Proof Is the Key to Success

So, why are recommendations so crucial to your success? First of all, recommendations form a key element of your profile, and the number of recommendations you have received for each position is noted under each one. When someone is choosing between two people for work or consulting, if one person has lots of strong recommendations in his or her profile that detail specific accomplishments and goals met while the other person has none, the hirer will probably give the person with recommendations the first shot at the opportunity. LinkedIn is all about seizing the moment, so you've got to be ready with a killer profile, including recommendations.

I had an experience recently when I was presenting to a marketing company that was interested in hiring me for LinkedIn training, and it was also interested in partnering with me as a trainer to its clients. As I spoke, I pulled up my profile on the large 50-inch plasma TV mounted on the wall, and I scrolled through it including my recommendations (which number around 150). The president of the company looked at it and said, "Wow. Lots of recommendations! That's good." I knew I had scored some points, and I indeed got the training job and signed that company up as a referral partner.

Second, when LinkedIn users search for certain skills, they use keywords, and the words in recommendations are "keyword searchable." That's why you might offer to help write them, as we'll see in a bit.

Third, the number of recommendations you have helps determine how high you show up in rankings when people do a LinkedIn search. Because of LinkedIn's search algorithm, all things being equal, you appear higher above other people's profiles who have the same keywords if you have more recommendations.

Consider Which Contacts You Might Get Recommendations From

Now's a good time to start thinking about all the people who can contribute a recommendation and help you with this crucial aspect of your profile on LinkedIn. But not everyone can write you a recommendation—just those who are LinkedIn members and are directly connected to you (in other words, your first-level connections). That's why it's important to connect with anyone you've ever worked with who might contribute a recommendation.

So, if you know people who would write you a great recommendation but haven't made the plunge and established themselves on LinkedIn, you may consider sharing some of the benefits of being on the site, showing them how to sign up and connect with you, then asking for the recommendation. You'll be doing them a favor and getting some more social proof for your profile.

If there is someone already on LinkedIn who you feel would give you a great recommendation but you're not first-level connections yet, then take that step and invite that person to connect. Once you do, you can request a recommendation.

You want to receive quality recommendations, and a great idea is to mix up the kinds of relationships presented for each of your positions. Request recommendations from someone:

- You reported to, or who was higher up in the organization
- Who worked with you in the same department
- Who worked in another area of the company at your level
- Who reported to you
- Who was a client
- Who was a vendor

Get Recommendations from First-Level Connections

Simply go to your profile on LinkedIn, and click on the gray button with the down arrow near the bottom of your information box. Select *Ask to be recommended,* and then follow these steps:

1. **Choose what you want to be recommended for by picking out a position from the drop-down menu (see Figure 3-1).** This is why it's so important to fill out your Work Experience section completely with all the positions you've held. It gives you a wider range of positions to get recommendations for—be they part time, full time, or volunteer.
2. **Decide whom you'll ask.** Click on the blue LinkedIn box on the right, and a box will display with your first-level contacts. Put a check by the name of the person you want to ask. I recommend asking just one person at a time even though you have the ability to "group ask" up to 200 people at once. Getting recommendations is just too important a task to create a mass mailing that might not have the same effect as a highly personalized request.
3. **Create your message.** The system provides a very vanilla, watered-down request. Erase that bad boy immediately! You are building the crucial part of your profile; don't take shortcuts by just sending what someone at

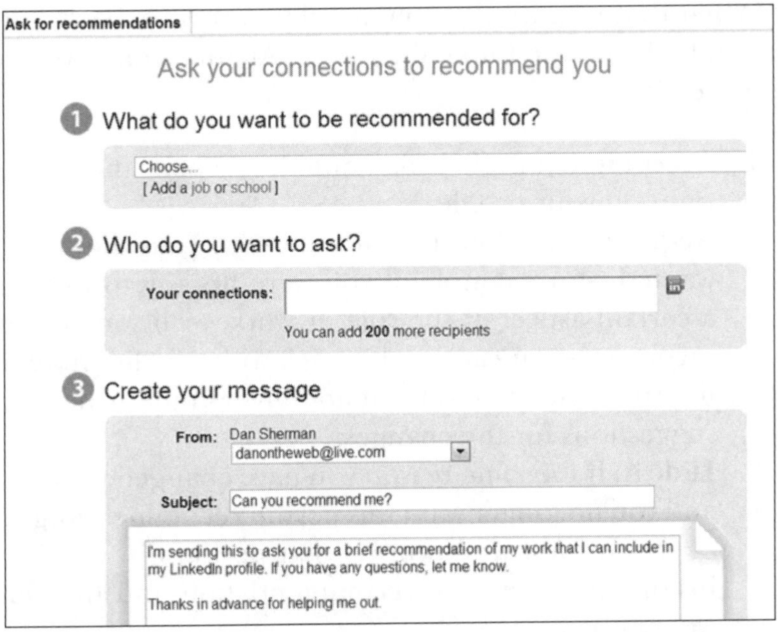

Figure 3-1. The Request Recommendation form gives you a way to add social proof to your profile by enabling you to write to your first-level connections and ask them to provide a testimonial for the work you did together. Be sure to customize the message to your connection.

LinkedIn wrote. Besides, you are asking for someone's time, so the least you can do is write a short note. Create a very specific request based on what the two of you did together. For example:

It was great working with you on the Bruce Willis *Great Moments of Sensitivity in Cinema* retrospective. Who knew there were so many? It would mean a lot to me if you could recommend my work on the project.

Consider sending your connection a list of three bulleted items of what you'd like covered in the recommendation. It will make it easier for her because she won't have to wrack her brain remembering what you worked on together. Plus, you will get a recommendation back that presents the key skills and abilities you are highlighting as part of your brand.

When that treasured recommendation comes back, you'll get notified in your LinkedIn inbox. At that point, you will have a few choices:

1. **Accept it.** If it is what you wanted, accept it, and it will go right on your profile.
2. **Request a revision.** If it did not come out the way you wanted—for example, if you were hoping to highlight a certain aspect of the role or work, or if something is incorrect—you can send it back with a polite note asking the writer to modify it and giving him or her some suggestions for the changes.
3. **Hide it.** If for some reason you have changed your mind and you no longer want this person recommending you, or if you want to downplay that position in your work history, just hide the recommendation and the world will never see it.

One way to ensure that the recommendation you get is the one you want is to provide a little assistance. Like you, we're all a little busy. The person you want the recommendation from may have too much on his or her plate to sit down and play Shakespeare for you. That's okay. You can write the recommendation for that person just the way you want it to appear, with all the great keywords you want to be found for, and you can send it to him or her. That person can use it all or edit it and send it back. I have done this, and it does work. People are often glad to give you recommendations, but they don't have the time to write them, and they are appreciative of the fact that they can recommend you without working up a sweat.

I recommend that you discuss this with your contacts ahead of time to see if they are open to helping you in this way. Next, write them a note through LinkedIn that says something like this:

Dear Alice,
As we discussed, I'm really interested in adding your recommendation to my profile, and it would mean a great

deal to me if you can help me. I would really appreciate it if you could include some examples of the results you realized by working with me. I wanted to make it as easy for you as possible, so here is a possible draft. Of course, feel free to edit this one or create your own. I appreciate your help.

Rather than send a draft, what I do sometimes is send people a few bullets that they can then put into their own words. You see, they don't know exactly what you are trying to build your brand as—they're too busy building theirs! So I keep a bullet point list on my computer, and I send the list off when people say they will write a recommendation for me but they want to know what to say.

One thing to keep in mind when you ask for recommendations is that you're actually doing your contacts a favor when they send you one. That's because now their name shows up on your profile, giving them added exposure to your network. Since my profile is viewed quite often, I use that as a small bargaining chip when I approach contacts for a recommendation.

Want More Recommendations? Write Some!

What if you're just starting out in the working world, and you don't know anyone who would recommend you? Or what if you are just starting out on LinkedIn altogether? What's the best way to prime the pump? Start writing recommendations for anyone you can think of. Write 5 or 10 a day and get the ball rolling!

Go through your contacts by clicking on *Network* on the top toolbar, which will bring up your first-level contacts. Begin by sorting contacts by location to find people in your area whom you know. Click on *Filter by,* and select your area from the drop-down menu, or write it into the box provided. Chances are that you worked on something together that you can recommend them for. Then make a list of anyone you worked with or had a positive experience with. It could be a mentor, teacher, colleague, employer, vendor, customer, or someone you served with on a volunteer committee if you don't have a lot of job experience.

Then once you know whom you want to recommend, open up their profile. On the bottom of their information box is a blue button that says *Send a message,* and it has a down arrow on the right. Click the arrow and select *Recommend,* and the recommendation form will display. Pick the job you are recommending them for, your relationship with them at the time, and then write very specific recommendations that are genuine (see Figure 3-2).

Put some thought and energy into it. Begin by looking at their profile first, and checking out their professional headline and summary. You'll see just what they are promoting as their brand and what keywords they are using to be found. Incorporating

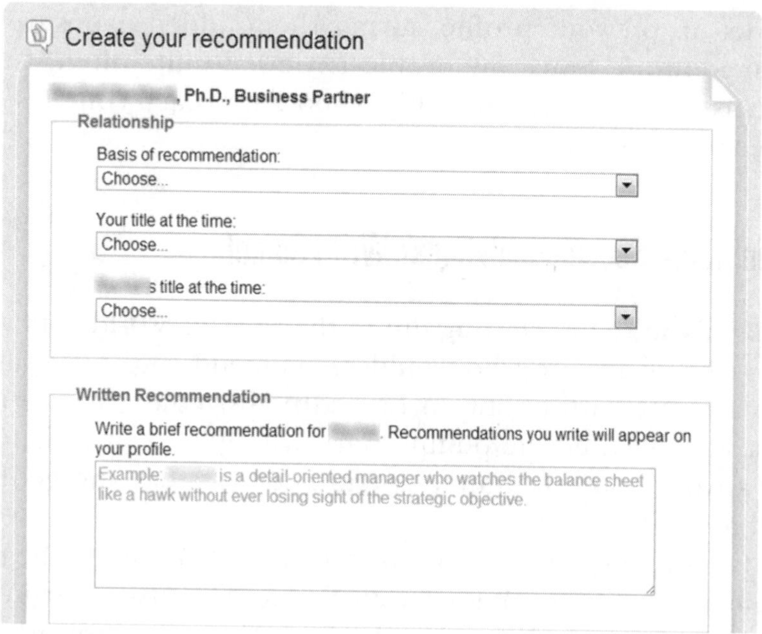

Figure 3-2. The recommendation form offers you the chance to offer a sincere testimonial for your contact's work. Writing unsolicited recommendations is a good idea and can lead to unexpected benefits.

that information into your recommendations will likely prompt them to accept because your recommendations will help them optimize their profile. Another reason why it's a good idea to check their profile first before you write is that they might have changed their career focus and desired branding since the last time you worked with them.

Start off your recommendation with a strong endorsement that sums up your impression of the person. For example, "Joan was a strong leader in our department whose hard work and creativity helped us exceed all our goals." Then back up your recommendation with some details, and close with an endorsement about how anyone would be lucky to work with her in the future. You don't need to write a book—only about 10 sentences max.

When you send off your unsolicited recommendations, you are going to make their day! Don't forget, you also benefit when they accept your recommendations because your name is now on their profile hyperlinked back to you, and you get added exposure and potential additional traffic back to your profile. You might even be one of the two featured recommendations LinkedIn positions at the bottom of each person's job. Write a great recommendation to ensure that the recipients accept it.

But that's not all. Do this often. I do this on a daily basis, and I see great things happening. Over half of the time, the recipients are so appreciative that they write a recommendation back, adding to my social proof.

Often the recipients are so grateful that they ask for some words from me so they can write a great recommendation back (and I'm prepared!). One time a fellow trainer picked up the phone and called me to thank me, offered to return the recommendation, and then suggested we meet up and come up with some partnership ideas. The other day another trainer emailed me to say thanks for an unsolicited recommendation and asked me to call him, and we got together and he is now sending me business. I try to write at least one unsolicited recommendation a day because of the return recommendations, potential business, and exposure on LinkedIn that it gives me.

Know the People You Are Recommending

Sooner or later you are going to get a recommendation request from someone you don't know. Recently I got a request from someone asking me for a recommendation based on the fact that we were both on LinkedIn. Fail! I just ignore these. Remember, it's your name hyperlinked to your profile next to the recommendation, and thus it's your reputation on the line. Guard your brand wisely on LinkedIn, and give recommendations only to people you know, those whom you've had a positive experience with and who you feel can do good work for others.

I'm an open networker, but that does not mean I'll recommend just anyone. I will connect with them, but I will recommend only people I know.

Manage Your Recommendations

You have complete control over which recommendations you show. Simply go to *Profile > Edit Profile;* scroll down to the Recommendations section; click on the pencil icon on the right-hand side; then click on the *Manage visibility* hyperlink. This will take you to the page to manage your recommendations (see Figure 3-3).

Now, click on the link *Manage* under any position. You will get a screen displaying all your recommendations for that position. You can click on the box that says *Show* to show or hide recommendations. Under each recommendation, you will also see a hyperlink that reads *Request a new or revised recommendation from* . . . . That link takes you back to the Request Recommendation screen where you can send out a new request.

Scroll down to the bottom of this page, and you will see another section labeled Pending Recommendation Requests. Here you will see recommendation requests you made for this position that have not been answered, describing whom you wrote to and what date your request was sent. There's a hyperlink by each request that says *Resend* that you can use to send it again. At the very bottom of this page is a helpful hyperlink that says *Request endorsements from connections who haven't yet recommended you for this position,* which takes you to the Request Recommendations page.

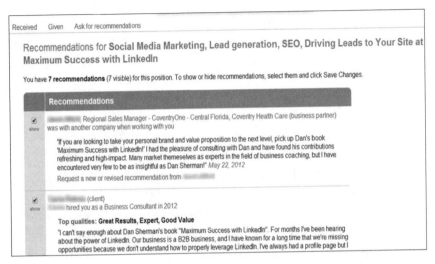

Figure 3-3. The Manage Recommendations screen gives you the opportunity to manage your recommendations for every position. You can show or hide a recommendation or request a revision, and on the bottom of the page you can see pending recommendation requests that have not been responded to and resend them.

Everyone networks at different speeds, and everyone uses LinkedIn according to his or her own needs. I find that it's okay if a week or two has gone by after you made your request to remind people by resending the request from the Manage Recommendations screen. Sometimes they are too busy when the request first arrives in their inbox. When I resend the request, I often get the person to write me something on the second attempt. You have to work at it, but it's worth it.

Get the Social Proof You Need

I hope you see that asking for and making recommendations regularly is a worthwhile endeavor because it is something that will add greatly to your success on LinkedIn. To sum up this important task:

- Don't hesitate to ask for recommendations. If you don't ask, you don't get.
- Do great work in everything you do, so everyone is glad to recommend you.
- Strike while the iron is hot. Once you complete a great project for someone, ask the person to recommend you on LinkedIn while it's fresh in her mind.
- If someone you want a recommendation from is not tech savvy and not on LinkedIn, make the effort to get him onboard and connected with you. He will benefit in the long run.
- Givers gain. Give out recommendations freely. You can keep track of how many you've sent out by going to *Profile > Edit Profile*, clicking on the pencil icon next to Recommendations near the bottom of your profile, and clicking on the *Manage visibility* link. Then on the Manage Recommendations page, click on the *Given* link on top to see all the recommendations you have sent out.
- Lots of quality recommendations in your profile separate you from the pack and give you credibility. Make it a part of your daily routine to give them and ask for them.
- Seek out recommendations for school, nonprofits, and volunteer work if you are just starting out in the work world.

*   *   *

That's it for this crucial part of your profile. Definitely add beefing up the Recommendations section of your profile to your daily list of LinkedIn tasks.

Now let's really spiff up your miniwebsite on LinkedIn by adding all kinds of presentations, documents, and videos that will turn your profile into a 24/7 broadcasting tool for the You, Inc. brand.

Chapter 4: It's Show Time!
Adding Multimedia to Your Profile

"There's No Business Like Show Business" is the title of a song and movie from the 1950s that celebrates the excitement and glamour of a life in show business. I agree that there's nothing like show business, and when it comes to your LinkedIn profile, there is a way to add some excitement and glamour without ever taking a Greyhound to Hollywood. Why be boring and one-dimensional when you can put on a show?

To start the transformation of your profile from dull to dazzling, go to *Profile > Edit Profile* on the top menu. Now, look for the "media box," a box with a plus sign (+), which shows up in the top right in three sections of your profile: your Summary section, your Experience section (for every position listed), and your Education section (see Figure 4-1). This media box is the key that will turn your profile into a multimedia wonderland. The great part about using this media box to add multimedia to your profile is that your LinkedIn miniwebsite works for you 24/7—spreading your articles, videos, and presentations to everyone who wants to know more about you—while you are busy doing other things.

Let's take a look at some of the options you have for uploading files to your profile. This should open your eyes to how you can make your profile one of a kind to reflect that fact that you are, well, one of a kind!

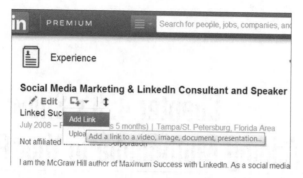

Figure 4-1. The media box (a box with a "+") located in your Summary, Experience, and Education sections allows you to turn your profile into a 24/7 multimedia marketing tool for the brand of You, Inc.

Add Video to Your LinkedIn Profile

We live in the entertainment age, when increasingly people are accustomed to being "spoon-fed" their information. While I happen to love to read, I surmise that most people would pass on reading a description of a galaxy far, far away in favor of sitting on the couch with a bucket of Orville Redenbacher and watching a squadron of P-38 Starfighters zipping courageously through space to battle an evil empire. So, how can you turn this to your advantage?

The answer is to add video to your profile. The media box in the *Edit Profile* mode has a drop-down menu, and when you click on it, you will see the option to *Add Link* or *Upload File*. To add video, we are going to work with the *Add Link* choice. Here is where you can add the hyperlink, or web address, to a video posted on the web.

What if you don't have any videos on the web? Well, have you heard of YouTube? It's one of the many video hosting sites available to you where you can create your own free channel and upload unlimited videos from your computer, tablet, or phone. Other free video hosting sites approved by LinkedIn include Vimeo, Vevo, Viddler, and blip.

My preference is to go with the big kahuna, YouTube, the stunningly successful Google acquisition. If you are new to

YouTube, just visit the site and click on the blue button in the upper right that says *Sign in*. You will then be asked to create a Google account that allows you to take advantage of not only YouTube but all of Google's other services such as Google+ and Google Docs.

Now with your Google account, you can create your free You-Tube channel where you can upload videos. Then, to add videos to your LinkedIn profile, simply click on the *Add Link* option from the media box, copy the hyperlink address of the individual video into the space provided, and press *Enter* (see Figure 4-2). To see what video formats LinkedIn will accept, first click on the link *Supported Providers* to see a full list of accepted video portals.

Now the ball is in your court. What kind of videos would you like the world to see? The options are unlimited. Right now I have video testimonials on my profile from clients who have taken my LinkedIn training. The videos provide that all-important social proof in a way that trumps words on a screen. Prospective clients for my LinkedIn courses can see and hear the joy and elation of business professionals who never knew what LinkedIn can offer and who have learned to use it to achieve success. Video involves more senses than words on a screen, so my prospective clients give these testimonials more attention. Prospective clients can get a sense of the emotion of my customers, and they can see and hear their satisfaction.

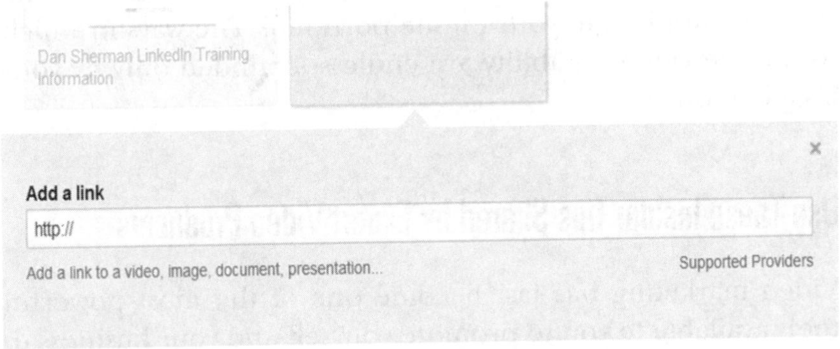

Dan Sherman LinkedIn Training information

×

Add a link

http://

Add a link to a video, image, document, presentation...   Supported Providers

Figure 4-2. Clicking on the *Add Link* option in the media box in the Summary, Experience, and Education sections allows you to add video and multimedia to your profile.

If you don't want to put up testimonials, then put up a video of you talking about your area of expertise. Set up a small camcorder and record yourself, or have a friend interview you while filming you.

This is great if you are a consultant or entrepreneur—you can create a 60-second commercial for yourself. In the first 30 seconds, you can tell people who you are, then whom you help and how you help them. In the next 30 seconds, you can explain how to reach you and connect with you to see if there is a possibility of working together. A video will bring your profile to life, add that show business spark, and allow your personality to shine through. It's back to the old adage: people do business with those they know, like, and trust. A video is a great start in allowing people to know the real you.

If you are a job hunter, you'll want to create a video résumé and really stand out from everyone else looking for the same position that you are. Talk about what you are looking for, what you bring to the table, and how you could benefit any organization that hires you.

If you are a company owner, show off your facility with a guided tour, or show how you make your product, or introduce your employees and let them talk about the products.

If you are a real estate agent, how about a guided tour that proudly displays the beautiful properties and amenities in the area in which you work? If you are a graphic designer or architect, why not link to your online portfolio? The ways in which to use the video capability are endless, bounded only by your imagination.

Use These Insider Tips Shared by Expert Video Producers

Video marketing has fast become one of the most powerful tools available to you to promote yourself and your business to the world. Now that you've learned how to add videos to your LinkedIn profile, your mind must be spinning with ideas for videos to create.

With visions of Steven Spielberg–like masterpieces, you run and grab your video camera, and you get ready to shoot your LinkedIn video . . . and then fear sets in. You realize that even though you are clearly an expert in your field, you never went to film school or interned on a Hollywood studio lot, so you don't know if you can shoot and upload a video that presents your ideas successfully.

Fortunately, shooting a LinkedIn-worthy video is not that difficult, and it doesn't require a *Titanic*-sized budget. With a video camera and your imagination, you will be able to create a video you can be proud of. And to guide your new endeavor, I asked two media experts how people on a limited budget—and with less than James Cameron–level movie-making skills—can create a solid video they can upload to LinkedIn and other websites.

Hank and Yvonne Charneskey of VonHenry Media are award-winning documentary film makers who work regularly with business owners to help them translate their ideas and passions into video in order to gain more publicity and clients. Here are their top 10 tips for making your own videos that will work 24/7 for you online, bringing you the results you need for your career and business:

1. Keep your videos simple. Present only one idea per video.
2. Plan your talking points before you shoot your video. Use 3- by 5-inch cards as references to keep you on track.
3. Wear plain clothing. Do not wear white clothing, bright clothes, or bold patterns.
4. Choose an uncluttered background. Having clutter in the video will distract from your message, as viewers will be looking at the various things, not at you. Also, pick a background that contrasts with your hair color so you are distinct in the video.
5. Use indirect natural light. Shoot with your back to a window, or shoot your video outdoors.
6. Choose a filming location that has nonreflective sound qualities. Try to minimize echo as much as possible.

7. Turn off phones, air conditioning, TV, and other noises in the background. Ask someone to watch your kids and your dog while you shoot your video to ensure that there are no interruptions or off-camera noises.

8. Use a tripod for your shoot. Shaky videos are unprofessional, and they distract from your message.

9. Allow three seconds of silence to pass before you begin speaking on camera. Wait three seconds after you've finished speaking as well. This makes editing much easier.

10. You can do it yourself, but if you want to take your videos to the next level, consider enlisting the aid of a local production company. Check with your network for recommendations, call your local chamber of commerce, ask others in your circle of friends and business partners, and get some names of qualified video professionals. Then reach out to them, explain your project, and get at least three quotes. You may be surprised at how affordable hiring a professional is for your video. Also, you will benefit not only from their professional equipment but from the knowledge they've gained helping professionals like you in terms of knowing what works well in a business video.

The husband and wife team of Hank and Yvonne Charneskey, owners of VonHenry Media, produces documentaries and industrial, commercial, and educational videos and films. Their expertise is in providing exceptionally captivating projects that reflect their cinematic approach to videography. Visit their website at http://www.vonhenry.com.

Add Promotional Literature to Your Profile

Let's look at the other option in the media box, the *Upload File* link. You can add documents to your profile and turn LinkedIn into a round-the-clock fulfillment center for You, Inc. By uploading documents, you provide your profile viewers with readily available information that can help you achieve your business and career goals. When you click on the *Upload File* link from the media box, you can browse and select the file you wish to add (see Figure 4-3).

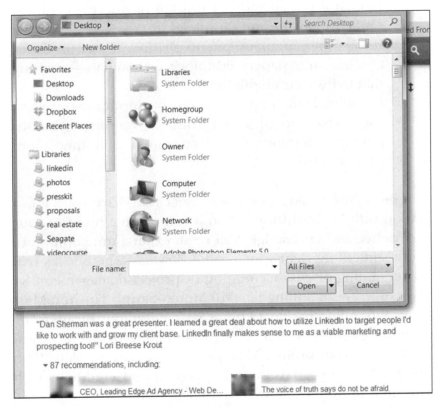

Figure 4-3. Clicking on the *Upload File* option in the media box opens up a box with the files on your hard drive, which allows you to select the one you want to upload.

What should you upload? Be creative!

- If you're job hunting, turn your résumé into a PDF, and make it available (first erasing any information you don't want on the Internet). You can also include testimonial letters from those not on LinkedIn. If you can't get them to join and write the testimonial for your profile, turn their letters into PDFs, and add them using the *Upload File* option.

- If you're a consultant, upload a PowerPoint about your company or a company brochure. I currently have my company brochure on my profile, and I never have to mail it out anymore. I just tell prospects to visit my LinkedIn profile and download it.
- If you own a company, put up pictures of your products, articles, white papers, customer testimonials—anything that helps your credibility
- If you're launching a start-up, put up an overview of your project to get angel investors, venture capitalists, potential employees, and customers salivating about your venture.

The ability to add documents lets you share your information with LinkedIn users, and it can provide proof of your experience and knowledge. You're an expert. You know more about something than your profile viewers—whether it's real estate lending or cost accounting or project management. So you can write something like "10 Money-Saving Tips You Must Know When Purchasing a Phone System for Your Business" or something similar, save it as a PDF, and allow people to download it from your profile. That way, you are creating value first, thereby building a favorable impression and credibility with anyone with whom you want to do business.

* * *

Take a look at what you have to offer, and see what you can add to your profile to increase your value to your viewers, which will in turn increase your marketability and your credibility. In the online world, content is king. What kind of content can you offer your readers that can help solidify your brand and establish you as an expert? Look through your articles and presentations, and then turn your profile into a miniwebsite that promotes You, Inc.

Now let's look at even more sections you can add to your profile to truly set you apart from the competition.

Chapter 5: The Finishing Touches: Creating a Rocking Profile

At this point we're almost done adding the sections that make up a world-class profile. Here are some additional important areas for you to fill out to make your profile the best it can be.

Skills & Expertise

There is a section called Skills & Expertise where you can list a whole range of your abilities. Go to *Profile > Edit Profile,* look for Skills & Expertise in your profile, then click *Edit.* Start typing a skill into the open box, and LinkedIn will suggest a skill from a drop-down menu. If it does not suggest a skill, that's okay; just add the skill you want to display. For example, I have many LinkedIn skills, including LinkedIn group management. That was not in the suggested skills, so I added it myself. When you have added a skill, be sure to click the blue button that says *Save* at the bottom of the screen (see Figure 5-1).

Listing your various skills is another way to demonstrate your value to potential partners and clients, so make sure you add as many as you can up to the 50 allowed. Also remember that everything on your profile contributes to your being found in LinkedIn searches. When you add skills with your keywords, you increase your chances of being on top when people search for your expertise.

Figure 5-1. The Skills & Expertise menu in *Edit Profile* mode allows you to add up to 50 skills to your profile. It's also where you can manage whether your endorsements are displayed to the public.

Another aspect of the Skills & Expertise feature you'll want to know about is called Endorsements. Remember how I said in Chapter 3 that it is important to get social proof to create a successful brand on LinkedIn? Well, the Endorsements feature allows LinkedIn members to endorse each other's skills and expertise. Endorsing someone's skill is like giving a recommendation; however, there is no text, and it is much simpler and faster to do.

To endorse a fellow member's skills, simply scroll down on that person's profile to his Skills & Expertise section. Look at his list of skills, hover your mouse over the plus sign by the skill, and you will see a hyperlink appear that says *Endorse.* Click on it, and the text will change to *Endorsed!* and you will have endorsed him for that skill, and your smiling face will then appear as an endorser right there on the profile. So not only do you help your friend gain more social proof, but you also gain branding and exposure by having your photo on his profile.

In addition, when someone who is not a first-level connection clicks on your photo, a window will pop up with your name, professional headline, and two buttons that say *View profile* and *Invite to connect*. This will allow more users to visit your profile and see what you are all about, and it will also allow them to invite you to become a connection. But if someone who is one of your first-level connections clicks on your photo in someone else's Skills & Expertise section, she gets different choices: a *Send a message* button and a *View profile* button.

Just as you learned in Chapter 3 about requesting recommendations, you should also add asking for endorsements to your LinkedIn strategy. Here are some guidelines to follow:

> **Endorse others first, and endorse honestly.** You can start by endorsing the people who are in your network first, before you ask for endorsements (remember: givers get!). You'll be helping your friends see where their strengths are. But don't go overboard and endorse every skill they have listed. Put some thought into it, and highlight the areas of expertise you are really willing to vouch for. Those you endorse will be notified about your kind actions, which means they might turn around and start endorsing you.
>
> **Begin with your most trusted friends.** Notify the people you know best and trust the most about the endorsement feature. Tell them that you have endorsed their skills, and ask them if they would pick a few skills of yours to endorse. Pick out the people you know well, and in this way you can slowly begin to add endorsements.
>
> **Leave spam in the can.** In a situation like this, you never want to blast out an email to everyone you're connected with and ask for endorsements. Mass mailings are considered spam on LinkedIn, and they are typically ignored.

Just as you focus all your communications on LinkedIn, target your requests to just the people you want to reach.

Languages

The world is shrinking, and people who speak many languages are in high demand. Make sure you add your languages by going to *Profile > Edit Profile,* and then going to Languages and clicking on *Edit.* You will then see a screen where you can add your languages, and choose your level of expertise among these choices:

- Elementary proficiency
- Limited working proficiency
- Professional working proficiency
- Full professional proficiency
- Native or bilingual proficiency

Education

Go to *Profile > Edit Profile* and fill in the places you went to school by clicking on + *Add education.* You can also add your dates attended, degrees, fields of study, grades, and activities and societies that were a part of your school days. It's important to add your school for numerous reasons (see Figure 5-2). When searching for ways to build your connections, LinkedIn will display all the students who were at your school at the same time as you were, and it will give you the opportunity to connect with them. This will enable you to get a jump start on building your connections. If you don't fill out your school, you will miss out on this valuable way to begin adding connections.

Also, if you don't have a lot of work experience, filling out the Education section can help. LinkedIn gives you the ability to add recommendations to your profile right from the Education section. Perhaps a professor will agree to write a recommendation that will give you a chance to complete

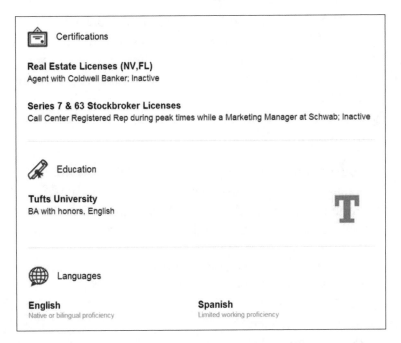

Figure 5-2. Adding and completing various sections will enable you to have a complete profile that represents all your achievements and abilities. Shown are sections for Certifications, Education, and Languages.

your profile. I would focus on adding colleges and vocational schools here if you can and list your high school if that is your only option.

Remember too that the Education section provides you with the small box and plus sign (+), or the media box, enabling you to add videos and presentations to this section. Adding this type of material would be very helpful if you recently graduated and you are now job hunting and wish to show off some of your accomplishments and achievements.

Advice for Contacting You

This is a key section that you will also find by going to *Profile > Edit profile*. Next to where it says *Advice for Contacting (Your name),* click the blue *Edit* hyperlink by the pencil icon. Click on that to bring up a box where you can give additional information to your profile visitors on what you'd like to discuss and how you want to work with them. I use this section to promote my LinkedIn training business, so it's another area where you can establish and promote your brand and tell the world how you can help them. Here's mine as an example:

> Do you want to find your perfect career? Or how about increasing your sales? Contact me to show you how to leverage LinkedIn to achieve all of your goals. Email me at dan@linkedsuccess.com. I help:
>
> - Sales and marketing professionals
> - Real estate agents
> - Entrepreneurs
> - Business owners
> - Job seekers
> - Executives in career transition
>
> I can help you with:
>
> - Driving more traffic to your site
> - Building a sales funnel of targeted clients
> - Finding the ideal career with LinkedIn
> - SEO
> - LinkedIn marketing
> - Lead generation
> - Internet marketing
> - Information product creation
> - LinkedIn training
> - LinkedIn consulting
> - LinkedIn keynotes
> - LinkedIn coaching
> - LinkedIn training for real estate agents
> - LinkedIn training for CPAs
> - LinkedIn training for business owners
> - LinkedIn training for sales professionals

- LinkedIn training for marketers
- LinkedIn training for all professionals
- LinkedIn network development
- LinkedIn profile enhancement
- LinkedIn search techniques
- LinkedIn job search strategies

If you want to make more in-depth choices about how and why people contact you, there is a way. Click on your photo at the top right of any screen to reveal the Account & Settings menu. Select *Privacy & Settings* from the drop-down menu. From the left-hand menu, select *Communications,* and then *Select the type of messages you are willing to receive.* Here is where you can tell LinkedIn what kinds of messages you are open to receiving, such as introduction requests, OpenLink communications, and InMails. You can also select the types of opportunities you want to receive, such as expertise requests, consulting offers, and business deals. Under Opportunities, I have selected all options because I want to stay open to everything (see Figure 5-3).

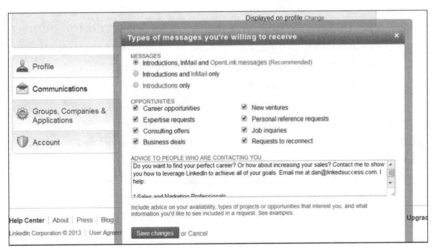

Figure 5-3. In your Settings under *Communications,* you will find a menu that allows you to select options for the types of messages you can receive, what types of opportunities you want to be contacted for, and a text box where you can write a note to other professionals describing what opportunities you are seeking to find on LinkedIn.

You can change this section as often as you want as your priorities change and you seek different opportunities. Remember to click on the blue *Save Changes* button when you are done editing this section.

Personal Details

Finally, there is also a section called Personal Details to fill out. Go to *Profile > Edit Profile,* find the section, and click on *Edit.* This is where you can put as much or as little as you want regarding your birthday and marital status. It's up to you what you want to put out there; I put my birthday (no year).

You have the option to add your birthday and marital status, then restrict who can see that information. Clicking on the padlock icon near birthday and marital status reveals settings to select who can see that information, such as your first-level connections, your entire network, or the general public.

* * *

Adding sections will help to make your profile a complete marketing tool for You, Inc. By doing so, you make your profile much more complete and useful to your readers.

Now, let's turn our attention to one of the main buzzwords you hear about in Internet marketing, and that's *keywords.* You want to discover what the keywords are that people are using to find someone with your talents and abilities, and then you can add them to specific places on your profile. Follow along as you learn exactly how to do that.

Chapter 6: All About Keywords: Optimizing Your Profile to Be Found

Everyone has a brand. I am talking about You, Inc. What do you want to be known for? What's your specialty? What sets you apart? Once you make that decision and have it written down in a few words, then you can create your LinkedIn profile in such a way that when people are searching for someone with those skills, your profile is number one or at least on the first page.

Wouldn't it be great for people to find YOU rather than your always making calls and contacting other people to achieve your goals? In this section, you'll learn how to make that happen, and I'll start off by using myself as an example.

I want to be known as a LinkedIn expert. Now, I have 30 million people in my network, and when I do a simple search (by selecting *People* from the drop-down menu on top of any screen and entering "LinkedIn" into the search box), I get over 319,000 results for that term, and my profile appears as number five on the first page. As a result, I get speaking opportunities and consulting requests just by people finding me.

Bear in mind that your search results will be different. If you searched for the keyword "LinkedIn" but I am not in your network, I won't show up, of course. But within my network, I do. And that means more people will click on my profile, visit my websites, download my brochure and articles, and so on.

The reason I show up first is that I optimized my profile by adding the term "LinkedIn" in several key places. Now we'll cover exactly how to ensure that you appear on the first page of LinkedIn search results so that you will become known as the expert, you'll gain credibility and authority status, and you'll get the sale or job or whatever you are seeking.

Four Required Places for Your Keywords

The first step is to pick your keywords. What do you want to be found for? Next, optimize your profile by putting the keywords in the four main places that will help you show up as number one for the keywords that describe your brand or expertise. Once you make these changes in your profile, you should see some instant results in how you appear in LinkedIn search results.

When you're ready to optimize your profile, here are the four places to put your keywords to instantly move up in LinkedIn search results.

1. Headline

As discussed previously, you can make your headline a benefit statement like this one:

> I Provide the Most Comprehensive and Affordable IT Training in the State of Nevada

Or if you provide several benefits, include them with initial caps, and use the shift and backslash key (\) to make a straight vertical line, as in the example below:

> Web Designer | Graphic Artist | Programmer | Author

Both styles work because they both tell people how you can help them. Just be sure that you include your brand or keywords in the headline because that is one of the key places LinkedIn considers when ranking you in search results. You will see in my profile that I have written "LinkedIn" several times in my headline.

2. Current Work Experience

The second place LinkedIn looks is your current work experience, so make sure your current job titles have your keywords prominently displayed. I have "LinkedIn" in my current job titles, and so that helps me with rankings.

I see many people with CEO or president as their job title. If you are required by your company's policy to have that description in your LinkedIn job title, or if you simply prefer it that way, then please leave it alone. But if you are very interested in coming up first in LinkedIn search results, you'll need to change that to a more meaningful keyword—that is, to what you do rather than what you are called.

3. Past Work Experience

Just as you describe your current jobs, you want your past jobs to have your keywords in the job titles so that LinkedIn moves you up in the rankings. So maybe you're thinking that you don't have a past "job" that had that keyword. Simple fix: the things you list as "jobs" don't have to be full-time, nine-to-five jobs. If you have worked as a consultant or a volunteer in a particular field, or if you have worked in any way that you can list as a "job" on LinkedIn and that you can describe using one of your keywords, you are all set.

On my profile, I have included as past jobs some short-term LinkedIn consulting and speaking work. That enables me to use the term "LinkedIn" in my past experience, which moves me up in the rankings. You should try to list several past jobs with your keywords in the position titles.

4. Summary

Here is where you get to give your commercial for your brand, for You, Inc. Remember to make it value driven and benefits oriented, stating how you help people and how can they reach you and hire you. You can also add a little bit about you personally in this section. People want to do business with people they know, so adding some personal thoughts is helpful.

Your summary is where you need to add keywords for your branding to make sure you show up high in the search rankings. Don't "stuff" keywords, meaning don't put in an overabundance of your keywords so that your summary is not readable as sentences. Work them in so that your summary still reads correctly and flows well. You have 2,000 characters to use, and I suggest you use them all.

Researching Your Competitors

Go ahead and make these changes today. To begin the process, I strongly suggest you do a little research first. Go to the search box at the top on any screen, select *People* from the drop-down menu, and search for one of your keywords to see if you show up on the first page of the results. Then, add keywords in the places as I suggested, check again, and see if you appear on the first page of the results.

When I did this with a local sales trainer, we searched one of his main keywords, and he was nowhere to be found. When we added "sales trainer" in the four places I mentioned, his profile immediately came up number five. I also recently helped a computer expert who wanted to be found in LinkedIn searches by showing him where to put his specialty, Microsoft Access, in the four key places. He told me that before he did this, he did not appear in search results, but afterward his was the first profile when that term was searched on.

One tip: when you are doing competitive research, check out the profiles of the people who appear in the first few positions for your keyword. You'll see the keyword you searched for highlighted, and you can see just why they showed up ahead of you. How many times do they have the keyword in their headline? In their summary? In their past and current jobs? You can actually count them up, and that will create a benchmark.

Follow their lead, and add your keyword into your profile in the places they have it on theirs with some of their methodology. If you keep tweaking your profile, you'll soon end up ahead of them in the search results.

Your goal is to be number one for your search term. Then you will be contacted for consulting, speaking, or other types of work when people are searching for your specialty (see Figure 6-1).

Figure 6-1. To see where you come up in LinkedIn searches, type your keyword into the top search box on any screen after you select *People*. Your goal is to be on page one in search results for your expertise.

Advanced Optimization Strategies

Keyword placement is really important to appearing high in the search rankings, but other factors also come into play. You'll get ranked higher if you have more recommendations and more connections, so you need to be working on these as well as your keyword optimization. Having a paid account also aids in getting ranked higher. So if you can get a premium account, I would recommend it.

Another advanced keyword strategy is to go to one of your favorite job boards and find four or five job listings that really appeal to you. Cut and paste one description at a time into a *word cloud tool,* which creates a visual representation of the words used in the text (a well-known word cloud tool is http://www.wordle.net). The resulting word cloud will show you the most important words in that job listing, and after you have done a few of these, you will see keywords repeated over and over that recruiters and hiring managers may be using to search (see Figure 6-2). Add those keywords to your profile, and you will stand a better chance of being found when someone is searching for those skills and traits.

Figure 6-2. A word cloud created from an Internet job posting helps you see a variety of keywords that are most important to employers. By adding these keywords from several job postings to your profile, you increase your chances of being found by hiring managers and recruiters.

Other Places to Optimize Your Profile

The four areas I've mentioned are the most important places to put your keywords in order to be ranked high in search results. But you can also optimize your profile by having keywords show up in the following places:

- **Recommendations.** It's helpful to have your keywords in recommendations you get because that contributes to your profile's optimization. That's why it's a good idea to write up some bullet points containing your keywords for people to use who agree to recommend you. You can even write the whole recommendation for them and put in your keywords.
- **Websites.** You can optimize the section where you are allowed to put three websites. Put in a "call to action" to describe your site, and use your keywords. The names of all three of my websites (that is, LinkedIn Training, Sell More with LinkedIn, and LinkedIn Training for Realtors) have the term "LinkedIn," which is one of the main keywords I want to be found for.
- **Public profile website address.** You can optimize your public profile website address. Go to *Profile > Edit Profile*. The last line item in your main information box is "Public Profile" by the small LinkedIn "in" icon where you will see the hyperlink *Edit*. Click on that, which will take you to the Public Profile page, and find the box on the right called *Your public profile URL*. You can add a keyword to the end of your hyperlink address.
- **Groups.** Join groups with your keywords in the title because some of your groups show up in your profile. You can join up to 50 groups, so you can have many with your keywords in their name.
- **Skills.** Add your keywords in the Skills & Expertise section. Add them automatically by going to *Profile > Edit Profile* and going to the Skills & Expertise section, clicking on *Edit*, and entering your skills.
- **Interests.** Here's another great spot to optimize your profile that I see very few people using as a strategy. I use it to get found in searches on LinkedIn, and it's very

effective. In the Interests area in the Additional Info section, you have a text area where you can write quite a bit about what your interests are.

You should definitely put your keywords in the Interests area in your profile, but here's an additional idea. In my profile, I list LinkedIn because it's a huge interest, and using the term helps me with optimization. But in this area I also put the names of all the social media and LinkedIn experts I follow and those who have high brand name recognition. I'm interested in them, so it makes sense. But by having their names on my profile, I also get found when people are searching for them.

Perhaps someone is looking for a social media speaker, and when she searches for an expert by name, I come up. If I'm available to speak and the other person is not, I can put myself in contention for the opportunity. If you're interested in this strategy, search on your keywords in the People Search, find the name brand experts who appear on the first page, and then add their names as your interests.

Where NOT to Optimize Your Profile

As you look around on LinkedIn, you will run into profiles where people have endeavored to add information into their name field. For example, people sometimes add how many connections they have and/or sometimes their email address:

Billy Bob Thornton 20,000 Connections Wildman@BBT.com

I recommend you do not put anything extra in the name field, such as keywords, phone numbers, or email addresses, because it is against the LinkedIn Terms and Conditions (T&Cs), and you really want stay on their good side. I'll tell you a story to demonstrate.

Once, I had to contact LinkedIn customer service with a question. At the time I had optimized my name field as shown below:

Dan Sherman | Speaker and Trainer

I got a note back from customer service, not with an answer to my request, but with a strict warning that I was in violation of their T&Cs with my name field. So I had to change it and then write back with my question, which they then answered, but it was a delay for me. Now, many people optimize their name field or even add their phone number, email address, or status as a LinkedIn open networker (LION), as discussed in Chapter 2, but for me my name is branding enough.

I'm confident in my name as my brand. I don't need to embellish it, and I want to stay on the right side of the LinkedIn rules. I'm sharing my experience with you so you can make your own judgment call on this.

Moving Sections Within Your Profile

Working on your profile is an ongoing process. You are never quite done because there are always ways to improve the content and optimization. One strategy you can experiment with is moving entire sections around until they are in the order that best suits your needs.

We touched on this briefly before in Chapter 2. But I want to go over it again because it's really important to modify your profile so that it fits your career goals, and not just leave sections in their default positions.

Once you have built a very robust profile with lots of sections and applications, decide what it is that is most important for people to see when they land on your profile. You can move entire sections, like the Summary, Experience, and Languages sections, simply by hovering your mouse over the two-headed arrow by the heading of the section, waiting until the four-arrow, cross-hairs, gun-sight-like symbol appears, and dragging and dropping the copy to your heart's content.

Personally, I put Projects right after my Summary because I like having my speaking videos front and center. I've seen people put their Advice for Contacting (Name) first because they want their contact information to be prominent; others put their Experience first to showcase their career accomplishments; still others lead with their Summary. It just depends on your LinkedIn goals. What do you want your prospective client, partner, investor, customer, or manager to see first? Whatever order will best position you to your target audience, that's how you should arrange your sections.

* * *

Now that you have added sections and applications and completely filled out your profile, you've created your own little piece of real estate on LinkedIn of which you can be proud. It truly displays all that you are capable of offering to the world, and you want everyone who might potentially do business with you to stop by and partake of all the information. Only people who are in your network can see your complete profile—so how do you grow your network to its maximum effectiveness?

Coming up, I'll explain how to create a first-class network that will be the cornerstone of your LinkedIn strategy.

Chapter 7: Your Virtual Rolodex: Grow Your Network by Adding Contacts

As a professional speaker, I am always looking for ways to improve my skills, and for a long time I was a member of the largest speaking organization, the National Speakers Association. One year our national conference was held in Orlando, and one of our presenters was Harvey Mackay, the famous author and successful company president. He was promoting his new book on networking, *Dig Your Well Before You're Thirsty*. A master networker, Mr. Mackey urged all of us to make sure that no matter the state of our current work situation, we should always be adding contacts to our database so that we have the people we need when we're ready to reach out for partners, employers, advisors, investors, and anyone else who could assist us.

To me that is the beauty of LinkedIn. By getting involved on the site, you are actively building a huge database of professionals around the globe who can provide assistance to you when the need arises. Whether you are just starting out on LinkedIn or have been active for a while, you can see how well you've dug *your* well by going to the top toolbar and clicking *Home > LinkedIn Home*. In the right-hand column, you will see: *Your LinkedIn Network*. You will see the number for your total first-level connections, another number revealing how many total people are in your network (first-, second-, and third-level connections combined), and how many new people have joined your network recently. (Refer back to Chapter 1 for the discussion on understanding the LinkedIn levels.)

The Magic Number Is 500

Check your first-level connection number and see what is there. If it is not a robust number, not to worry. There are plenty of ways to grow your connections. Your first objective is get out of the single digits and get to at least 500. This is because the number of your LinkedIn connections is prominently displayed in the top information box on your profile that people scan first when they come to learn about you. If you have fewer than 500 connections—say, 100—people will assume that you are not a well-connected person. This may label you as someone who does not have much value to them when they are deciding whether to add you to their LinkedIn network or even to hire you or work with you.

Until you get to 500, you are not going to be perceived as a very active LinkedIn user, and consequently you won't be seen as a strong potential connection or a "player" in the LinkedIn world. But once you get to 500, LinkedIn stops counting on your profile and puts "500+." That means whether you have 501 or 5,001, it will still say "500+." You want every aspect of your profile to reflect well on you. Try to get to 500 as soon as you can so you're "in the club."

Adding connections brings other benefits. When you connect with more people, it extends your second- and third-level connections until you are literally connected with millions of professionals around the globe (around 65 percent of LinkedIn users are in the United States, and the others are spread out worldwide). That means there are millions of people who can find you, hire you, offer you publicity opportunities, partner with you, invest in your firm, and help you with any business goal you have. Without a large network, you won't have many people who can reach you, read your profile, learn about you, or work with you.

Having a large network makes you a desirable connection and someone whom people will want to add to their network. That's because when they connect with you, they increase their network of connections. Your first-level connections become their second-level connections, your second levels become their thirds.

To Connect or Not to Connect

The debate concerning whether to connect with people you don't know versus connecting only with people you know sometimes takes on the seriousness of Hamlet's monologue in Shakespeare's tragedy that begins: "To be or not to be." You'll find proponents on both sides. But in my mind, there's no argument. I'm firmly in the camp of the "open networkers," and I believe you should connect with everyone you can. It simply expands your network and your opportunities. With a larger network, you can look at more profiles and contact more people, and more people can contact you. Massive connecting speeds up and enhances all your networking goals.

If you connect only with those people you know, people in your city, or those you grew up with, you'll be stuck in that same circle, and you won't be exposed to new opportunities. A great example of opening up your opportunities happened to me recently when I connected with a networking guru in England. He was able to read my profile, and he saw that I'm well versed in LinkedIn. So he invited me to an interview on his podcast on the subject of networking.

I did the interview, and now people in England are aware of me and my products and services, and they are buying my online courses. Had I turned down his invitation connection because I did not know him, I would not have had the opportunity. This is just one of many examples from my experience. I get consulting requests from Japan, Czechoslovakia, and India as well as from all around the good ole' USA because I am an open networker and I work to broaden my network with people from around the world whom I don't know.

How to Get More Connections

Let's get to the heart of this: whom do you invite, and how? First, you should know that LinkedIn allots all new users 3,000 invitations to use for connecting with people, and it limits us to 30,000 users in terms of how many first-level connections we can have. The 3,000 is flexible because when you run out of invitations, you can write to customer service by clicking on the *Help Center* hyperlink on the menu at the bottom of any page and request more. The 30,000 is fixed; I have not seen them waive that yet (and yes, I do have contacts with 30,000 connections).

In my experience, I have been allotted more invitations four times. I am very careful to stay on LinkedIn's good side, meaning that I follow the rules, and I write them a nice note requesting more invitations. The reallocations have varied; before I got a premium account, I would be given an additional few hundred new invitations each time. Once I got a premium account, on my fourth request, I got 3,000 more invitations to use.

What if you invite someone and the person never responds? Can you take it back? The answer is yes. Just go to *Inbox > Invitations,* and click on the *Sent* tab to see all of your sent invitations. Click on any invitation you want to withdraw to open the message; then click the *Withdraw* button. The person will not be notified that you've withdrawn the invitation, but you won't get the invitation back.

I recommend that you invite only people you know to connect, or those who you are sure are open networkers (that is, they say so in their profile, or you found them via an open networking group). When you send an invitation to connect with someone, the person has the choice to click on *Accept* or *Ignore.* If she clicks on *Ignore,* LinkedIn gives her a choice to click on *I don't know [name . . . you!]* or *This is spam.* You don't want people clicking on the spam option because their doing so will creates a black mark on your account. Get too many of them, and LinkedIn starts to restrict your ability to invite more contacts. So if you want to invite people you don't know to connect, or people who are *not* open networkers, send them a message first and introduce yourself. In the message, explain why you want to connect and why it's in their best interest to accept an invitation from you. If the person says, "Sure, let's connect," then you have the green light. If you don't hear back, move on to other potential connections.

How to Start Inviting Contacts

The place to begin is on the top toolbar. Click on the icon on the top right of the screen that has a plus sign (+) and an outline of a person. You will notice *See who you already know on LinkedIn* and a place to put an email address, such as a Gmail, Outlook (formerly Hotmail), Yahoo!, or AOL address (see Figure 7-1). When you put in your own email address and click *Continue*, LinkedIn searches your email database and finds all your contacts. It identifies which people are already on LinkedIn by matching their email address with their LinkedIn account.

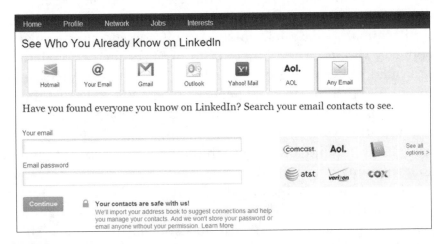

Figure 7-1. On the Add Connections tab is the area to enter your email address and see whom you know who is already on LinkedIn. Also in this tab you are able to import desktop emails and invite someone by using his or her email address.

You will see a small blue box next to those who are already on LinkedIn. Go ahead and invite your email contacts who are already on LinkedIn. Do not have any concerns over spamming or losing control because LinkedIn will never automatically invite people in your address book. You need to do it.

You can also import an email list from programs such as Outlook or Apple Mail. Click on *Any Email* below the envelope icon. When you do, you will see a section called *More Ways to Connect.* There you will see two hyperlinks. Click on *Upload contacts file,* and you can browse your hard drive and upload a file. Click on *Invite by individual email,* and a box will open where you can type in email addresses or cut and paste a list.

When looking through the list of your current contacts, I recommend that you do not invite anyone to join you who is not on LinkedIn already. To invite someone who is not using the site already is really a waste of an invitation because that person is not going to know what LinkedIn is, and he or she will ignore you, thinking that the site is some meaningless thing. (If they only knew!) It involves some time on your part to explain to people not on LinkedIn why they should join, so do this on an as-needed basis (for example, when you want a recommendation).

Personally, I have had mixed results convincing my email contacts who don't use LinkedIn to use it. Some people have indicated to me they are very cautious with their privacy, and they refuse to join any social network at all. Others say that they have a job and don't need a job-hunting site (cue Mr. Mackay). So, since there are so many people using LinkedIn to connect with, I don't spend any time trying to convince people to join so I can connect with them.

If you do feel like making the effort, as in the case in which you want a recommendation from them, you can enlighten them on the fact that LinkedIn lets you stay in contact with people even when they have changed jobs; it helps you find an amazing array of opportunities through your extended network; it is the most powerful personal brand builder out there; it's a free research database to help you find anyone you want to meet; and it's free and easy to join. Explain the benefits, and if they remain unconvinced, you should just move on.

Let's continue with adding connections. Go to *Home > LinkedIn Home,* and in the right-hand column you will see *People You May Know.* Click on the hyperlink + *Connect* under the first person you see, and that will take you to a page with four tabs on top: *Add Connections, Colleagues, Alumni, and People You May Know.*

The Add Connections tab takes you to the page we have already discussed in "How to Start Inviting Contacts." This is where you enter your email address, and LinkedIn lets you know which of your current contacts are already on the site.

Click on *Colleagues,* and everyone who worked at each company you listed in *Experiences* (your job history) during the time you were there will appear. This gives you a very easy way to build your connections, since you may know them and they are on LinkedIn right now.

Tab over to *Alumni* and that brings up a screen displaying all your school classmates who attended the school when you were there. That's why it's important to add where you went to school in the *Education* section. Again, these will be people you may know who are already on LinkedIn, and they are good to invite.

The final tab to the right is *People You May Know.* Take a look through, and see if LinkedIn has identified people you know who are on the site already. If you know them, invite them. If you don't recognize any names, ignore this.

Click back to the page showing the four tabs, and you'll discover a way to monitor your sent invitations. On the very far right is a hyperlink that says *View Sent Invitations.* Here is the page we discussed before where you can manage your sent invitations and can withdraw or resend some if you wish.

Remember, the larger your network, the more powerful LinkedIn becomes in terms of helping you achieve whatever business goal you have. If you have only 100 people in your network because you are happy about knowing each person and his or her family in depth, remember that these 100 people have probably referred all the business opportunities, prospects, and friends that you are going to get from them. So it pays to widen your connections as far and wide as you can.

Creative Ways to Get More Connections

Once you've gone through your email databases, schools, and past jobs, you should have a base on which to build your first-level connection database. The more connections you have, the more people get added to your network on a daily basis through second- and third-level connections.

Building your connections should become part of your daily routine. Here are some strategies for how to get more first-level connections on LinkedIn.

Networking

When you come home from a networking event with a stack of business cards, don't just chuck them into a shoebox. These are people you can add to your database on LinkedIn. The morning after the event, take your cards, look up each person on LinkedIn, and see who is not yet a first-level connection. Now you can send each person a personalized invitation, and if LinkedIn prompts you to add his or her email address, you've got it right there on the card. By doing it the very next morning, you will be top of that person's mind and he or she won't have forgotten you.

In terms of the personalized invitation, understand that LinkedIn will give you a standard message you can send that says, "I'd like to add you to my network." Whenever possible, you should strive to personalize your connection messages. It will make the people receiving them feel much more appreciated. Each one will know that he or she is not just another number in your database but a living, breathing human being different from any other on the planet. So go ahead and remind those people how you met, what impressed you about them, and how you might work together. For example:

> Hi Joe,
> It was great to meet you last night at the big charity event. Great entertainment, huh? How about those fire eaters and jugglers? I enjoyed our conversation about the correlation between start-up creation and Moore's law. Let's have coffee soon and see how we might be able to share leads. And please connect with me here on LinkedIn. Thank you.

On the Web

If you have a personal blog or website, you have a great place to put a hyperlink to your LinkedIn profile. Use your public profile hyperlink, which you can insert by going to *Profile > View Profile* and copying the link in the bottom of your main information box.

When people click on the link, they are connected to your profile, and they can read all about you and how you help people. Since every profile has a button that says *Connect*, you can get more people connecting with you. So make sure you have links to your profile on all your online sites, including other social media sites like Facebook and Twitter, with a call to action near the LinkedIn address stating, "Connect with me on LinkedIn."

Do you send a lot of email? Put your public profile hyperlink in the email signature so that everyone you write to can connect with you.

Do you have an email newsletter? Many of us do, and it's the perfect place to ask for connections. I hear great things about iContact, but you may use Aweber, Constant Contact, Mail Chimp, or some other program. Put a link to your LinkedIn profile where you can write an inviting message such as:

> I would love for you to connect with me on LinkedIn. I am building my network, and I would be very happy to introduce you to anyone in my network who could be of assistance to you.

On Your Business Cards

Make it easy for people to find and connect with you on LinkedIn. Include your public profile LinkedIn address on your card so that people you meet at networking events will be able to easily invite you to connect.

During Your LinkedIn Networking

Another way to meet people to connect with you on LinkedIn is something that will happen naturally. As you network with other professionals in LinkedIn groups, you are constantly meeting like-minded people. It is a natural occurrence that you will strike up online conversations with these people and agree to become first-level connections. The more active you are on LinkedIn, the more this will happen, adding to the size of your personal database.

When you meet someone in the LinkedIn groups you want to invite, you can click on his name and you'll be taken to his profile. From there, simply click on *Connect*. Then write something on the page in which you request a connection, reminding him about your interaction on LinkedIn and why you want to connect.

Open Networkers: The Key to Hyper Growth

Now we come to the secret weapon for creating a huge network on LinkedIn, and that is by joining open networking groups. The first one you should join is TopLinked, the largest. Go to the top search box, select *Groups* from the drop-down menu, then type in "TopLinked," and it will be the first group that appears. You will see TopLinked (Open Networkers) (see Figure 7-2).

Go ahead and join the group. Once you do, look at the first discussion titled "Post all connection invites as comments." In this discussion is a hyperlink that says *Click here for TopLinkedIn .com*. This link will take you to TopLinked, a group of open networkers on LinkedIn. When you on are on the TopLinked page, you will have two options: a free account or a paid account.

For my first three years on LinkedIn, I had the TopLinked free account. By signing up for one, you get Excel spreadsheets every week with about 2,000 email addresses of open networkers—people who have agreed to be on the list, so they are safe to invite even though you don't know them.

I suggest you sign up for the free account first. When you get the lists, which will show up in the email account you used to register with TopLinked (not your LinkedIn inbox), save them on your computer in a place like your desktop where you can easily find them. (All you need to invite someone to connect with you on LinkedIn is her email address.)

Then open up LinkedIn, and click on the person with a + icon in the upper right of any screen to go the Add Connections page. You will see *Any Email* under an envelope icon, so click on that. Toward the bottom of the next page, you will find a

Figure 7-2. By joining the TopLinked group, you can connect with other open networkers and dramatically increase the size of your LinkedIn network.

hyperlink saying *Invite by individual email,* and when you click on that, you will see an open text box with *Type email addresses below, separated by commas.*

Now it's up to you how proactive you are about adding contacts, but as a general rule, I would say it's best to invite only 50 people a day. What I do is copy 50 emails at a time onto my Notepad on my PC (if you are on a PC, click on the *Start* button on the lower left of the desktop and click on Notepad), add commas after each name, and then copy and paste the list into the *Enter email addresses* box. This method will grow your network fast.

Getting a Paid Open Networking Account

If you want to grow your first-level connections even faster, you can pay to get a paid TopLinked account and add your name to the *Invite Me* list. The charge is either $9.95 per month or $49.95 a year. I chose the $49.95 for the year because it is quite a savings. When I set my account up, I paid using my PayPal account, so it's a recurring payment that I make once a year. Sign up for an account at https://www.Paypal.com—it makes purchasing products and services online a snap, and it's secure. By doing this, your name goes out to the thousands of open networkers on LinkedIn who invite you to connect.

If you want to be even more proactive in the connection building area, go to the search box on top, select *Groups* from the drop-down menu, and type in *Open Networker* in the keyword search area. You will see other groups like *Open Networker.* Join this group and as many of the other open networking groups as you want. I have joined many of these groups, and I have even added myself to a second list called the *Invites Welcome* list, which costs me an additional $19.95 a year. Because of these two lists, I get about 30 invitations from open networkers a day, which helps me grow my network fast.

As you spend time on LinkedIn, you will see that people advertise the fact that they are open networkers with the abbreviation

LION (LinkedIn open networker). They'll sometimes even put it in their name field, such as "Betty Smith | LION." Or they will put it in their professional headline under their name.

I don't put LION in my name field or my headline. First, it is against the terms of LinkedIn to add anything to your name field but your name. Second, there are lots and lots of LIONs on LinkedIn, and I don't feel it's special enough to warrant taking up precious space in my headline. That's why I let people know I'm an open networker within my profile summary.

By taking advantage of TopLinked and the other open networking groups, you can rapidly expand your network. If you have only a few connections, your total reach will be small. Once you get up to thousands of connections, when you check your network statistics on your LinkedIn home page, you'll see that your network has millions and millions of people. That means millions of people who can find you, read your profile, and present opportunities to you. Go forth and grow your network!

Removing a Connection

As you can see, I am strongly in favor of growing your network of first-level connections to gain more access to opportunities. But if you are one of those who feel nervous about connecting with people you don't know, there is an easy out for you should you decide to no longer connect with someone. I know of people who have removed first-level connections, but I've never had to do it, despite having over 20,000 connections.

So if you find yourself ready to say "See you later, alligator" to someone, LinkedIn makes it very easy to remove a first-level connection from your account, and she will not be notified that you have done so. Simply go to that person's profile, and click on the down arrow on the blue *Send a message* button. Select *Remove connection* at the bottom of the menu, and that person is history.

What if you want to purge a lot of first-level connections at one time? That's easy too. Go to *Network > Contacts;* click *Filter by* and select *Connections only;* check the box next to the connections you wish to remove; then click *More* above the first contact, and select *Remove from Contacts.* All those contacts will be removed, and no one is notified.

As I mentioned, I have never felt the need to remove anyone, but you may be more interested in being an open networker now that you know how easy it is to remove a connection.

* * *

One of the benefits of growing your network into the thousands is that you will inevitably end up with millions of professionals in your network of contacts. That means you'll have lots of people you can connect with and a dizzying array of opportunities.

In the next chapter, let's discuss finding the people you want to meet and getting in touch with them.

Chapter 8: Your Social Influence Circle: Searching for and Contacting People

We've spent a good bit of time dealing with how to optimize your profile with keywords so you are found for opportunities. Now that you have created a profile that will show up high in LinkedIn search results, and you've made sure it's value oriented so that when people visit it, they will want to learn more about you, let's talk about the proactive side of LinkedIn: finding and contacting people.

First, expand your thinking about the people you can find on LinkedIn. Don't think of it as only a place to find customers, although that may be your primary focus here. You can also find partners to work on projects who may be interested in lead sharing. For example, a great person to connect with is what's called a *center of influence*, someone with connections and a client base similar to the prospects you want to reach.

Here's how it works: if you're a financial advisor, you might connect with a lawyer or banker in your location and see if you can create a mutual lead-sharing system. Whatever your occupation, look for noncompeting professionals who have the same kinds of clients you do. Contact them and set up a meeting where you can propose creating a potential lead-sharing group. Then perhaps once a month you can get together and share leads. You don't need to be in business alone. With LinkedIn, you can share other people's connections or clients (OPCs).

There are so many different types of helpful connections you can make on LinkedIn. For example:

- Look for service providers for your business. I have hired consultants to help me on a project basis after being impressed with posts they made in groups.
- Find people who can help you with a project, either part-time or as full-time employees.
- Locate an expert who can advise you on a critical part of your business.
- Connect with people in your industry, and set up a phone call to talk shop and see if there is any basis for a joint venture.
- Find speaking gigs for yourself, or find speakers for your events.
- Search for employees, investors, vendors, partners, suppliers, donors for your cause, board members, and strategic influencers.
- Locate a reporter who covers your industry and needs a quote from an expert for her story.
- Find a joint venture partner to collaborate with and use synergy to grow profits.
- Create an advisory board with top thought leaders.
- Find a mentor who can illuminate your path to your business goals and who can possibly open some doors for you.

Remember that everyone is on LinkedIn to network and do business, so don't be afraid to reach out when you have a need. Contact those people whose posts in groups impressed you the most. Click on their profile, find their contact information, and give them a call or send them an email.

Using the Advanced People Search

In addition to meeting people in groups, you can also use the very powerful Advanced People Search. In the top search box, select *People* from the drop-down menu. Leave the search box empty, and then click on the word *Advanced* to the right of the magnifying glass to bring up the Advanced People Search form (see Figure 8-1).

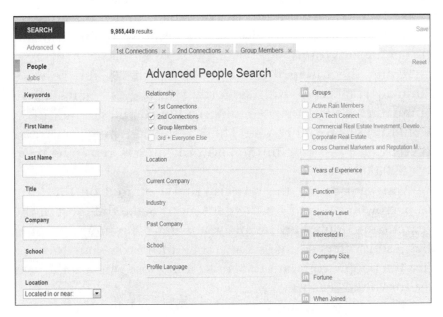

Figure 8-1. The Advanced People Search is your ticket to exploring the LinkedIn database and finding exactly the right people to connect with in order to pursue opportunities. With a premium account, you get many more options to sort the search results (premium sections are indicated by the gold "in" box).

Begin your search with keywords. What keyword will your intended targets have in their profile? If your keyword is made up of several words, put the words in "quotation marks" so that LinkedIn does not return profiles with the words in different areas of the profiles.

Let's say you sell to human resources managers. You could type "human resources" into the keyword box . . . but that would bring up thousands of people. So you use the whole Advanced People Search form to narrow your focus by filling in the location, the industry, and the relationship to you (choose first, second, or third level or your whole network).

Having a premium account will give you more options to narrow your search. You can get granular by selecting their seniority, company size, where in the Fortune 1000 they are ranked (according to size of company), and what kinds of contacts they want to receive. You can even search individually through your groups.

Using the whole form, I could search for the keyword "human resources," with seniority selected as "manager" in companies with 51 to 200 people, within 50 miles of me, and it would bring up 100 results. Those results are much narrower than when I just type in the keyword "human resources" and get 690,000 results!

You want to use the various criteria offered on the form to narrow down your list. If you want to make the most of the search function, then by all means get a premium account because it offers so many more ways to narrow your focus to just the people you want to contact and those who are the easiest for you to reach.

That's targeting just keywords or occupations. But let's say I wanted to target a certain company. If I wanted to sell my product to a human resources executive at Disney, for example, I would go to the Advanced People Search form and type in my keyword "human resources," type in "Disney" in the company box, and select *current* from the drop-down menu (because I only want to reach people in this search who currently have that job), and hit *search*. My results come up as 783 HR people in Disney, so I would want to refine that a little bit by location. I add in the zip code for Disney in Orlando, which is 32380. That brings it down to about 300, which is more manageable.

Of course, my search results are going to be different from yours, since we all have different networks. But the overriding fact is clear: the more people you have as first-level connections, the larger your total network will be and the more people you can search for. That's why I recommend being an open networker. If you have just a few people in your first level, you will not be getting the same number of profiles to look at as in the results that I get.

Saving Your Searches

If the search you did creates a helpful database of prospects, potential partners, or other people you are looking for, LinkedIn lets you save the search. Click on the *Save search* on the far right of the screen (see Figure 8-2). LinkedIn then gives you the option of getting an email notification daily, weekly, or monthly when someone new who meets the search criteria pops up in your network, and those notifications cover first-, second-, and third-level contacts as well as groups. With a free account, you can save up to three searches, while premium accounts let you save even more. Your network grows every day, so you should run your saved searches often by clicking on *Save search*, which brings up your saved searches, and selecting the search that you wish to run to see what new names pop up.

What you've done is create a perpetual prospecting machine for yourself. When LinkedIn notifies you of new people meeting your exact criteria, you can read their profile and get in

Figure 8-2. After you've done a people search, such as this one for sales managers, you can click on the *Save search* link in the upper right to save the search criteria and return and run the search over and over again to capture new names.

touch with them and let the magic of networking begin! Know what keywords you want, experiment until you find the right ones, and build your database of prospects as big as you can.

Making a Personal Connection

Once you have identified the people you want to meet, whether they are people you find in the groups or the Advanced People Search just described, you want to—as the old phone commercial used to say—"Reach out and touch someone." Take a look at their profiles for clues on how and with what method they want to be contacted.

Look at the Advice for Contacting [name] section. Sometimes a person will put down her phone number and email address in that section, or perhaps that information will be in her summary. If you have a number or email address, use it with discretion. If the person is a first-level connection, you have the opportunity to message her directly. In the information box at the top of her profile, look for the blue button that says *Send a message*. Click on it, and a dialogue box will appear where you can craft your message, and then press the blue *Send Message* button.

When sending someone a message on LinkedIn, be sure that you first read his profile. Then craft a personalized message explaining what you discovered in his profile that leads you to believe he would benefit from an association with you. Thank him for his time in reading your message. Be brief and to the point so that you're respectful of his time. Always remember to add what's in it for him if he decides to get back to you or accept an invitation to connect with you.

For example, you might write this note:

We are first-level connections, and I read your profile and was impressed with what you are doing in the areas of [fill in the blank]. I want to explore how we can work together because I feel I have a solution that might greatly enhance your ability to achieve your goals [add here what he will gain—that is, save money, save time, increase profits].

Would you be open to connecting here on LinkedIn? Also, can we set up a brief telephone call?

The worst thing you can do is make this assumption: "Oh, this person will never want to talk to me." Why would you think that? Whenever I make an assumption that someone does not want to have a conversation with me, I think back to the old chestnut from sales training: "The word *assume* stands for *making an ass out of u (you) and me.*"

Here's an example. I was giving a LinkedIn training session, and a student in the class was a commercial mortgage broker new to the site. He challenged me by saying, "Dan, I've got all these first-level connections. What the heck do I do with them?"

"Why don't you write to them?" I countered.

"Oh, they will never respond," he said.

"Try it," I told him.

"What do I say?" he asked.

I told him to tell the people what it was in their profile that made him want to write and ask to please have a conversation with them.

"This won't work," he insisted, rolling his eyes, but he played along. Right then he sent a direct message to a commercial real estate agent in another state where he wanted to do business, and he told the agent he felt there were some great opportunities in his city, and he asked if he would be open to a phone call. Within seconds the real estate agent responded with his phone number and asked my student to call him immediately. The look on my student's face was priceless.

Can I promise this type of results every time? Of course not. But that's what LinkedIn is for: connecting with people. You won't know until you try.

When you do make that personal connection, it's important to keep notes on your newfound relationship. Of course, the market is saturated with customer relationship management, or CRM, software programs that help you manage business relationships, so you have plenty to choose from. But you also have the ability to keep notes on relationships right within LinkedIn.

Right beneath the information box on the profile page of a first-level connection, you will see a heading with a small black star and the word: *Relationship.* Within the box below, you have four options:

- Note: Here you can write a note about your contact.
- Reminder: Here you can tell LinkedIn to remind you to get back in touch or take some action in an hour, a week, a month, or on a recurring basis.
- How you met: This gives you a place to jog your memory as to how you met and who introduced you.
- Tag: This opens up a drop-down menu where you select how you want to categorize the contact in order to facilitate further communications.

Contacting Non-First-Level Connections

If you and someone else are not first-level connections and there is no contact information available in the other person's profile, the next step is to look at her information box and see if she is an OpenLink member. (All premium account holders have the option to be in OpenLink.) You will see a small circle of colored dots to the right of that person's name. That means you can send her a message directly without being a first-level connection.

If she is not in OpenLink, look at the bottom of the information box where you will see a gray button that says *Send [name] an InMail.* InMail is the internal LinkedIn email system whereby you can contact anyone on LinkedIn who is in your network and is a second- or third-level connection. That's the good news. The "bad" news is that using InMail costs money! LinkedIn is a public company, and it has to please its shareholders!

If you have the basic free account, you can buy InMails for $10 each. The benefit of InMails over cold calls is that they include a link to your profile so the recipient can read your profile and respond to you knowing who you are. If the recipient doesn't respond in seven days, you get the InMail credit back, and you can InMail someone else. A premium account includes InMails: sales executive ($74.99 per month billed annually) gives you 25 per month, while the sales professional account ($439.99 per month billed annually) gives you 50 a month. Recruiters and power users love the plans with lots of InMails so they can reach out to lots of potential hires and contacts, but anyone can take advantage of those premium plans. InMails roll over to the next month if they are unused.

What's great about InMails is that they are instantaneous. They go right into the person's LinkedIn inbox. If you have not passed out on the floor after seeing the prices, then go ahead and purchase a premium account and include InMails in your LinkedIn prospecting and networking strategy. But if you are shocked and dismayed, don't worry. There are other avenues for reaching non-first-level connections including getting an introduction from a first-level contact.

Reaching Second-Level Connections

The introduction feature shows you who in your first-level connections is connected to your target person. Let's say your target is a second-level connection. In the information box in his profile, you will see a gray button that says *Send [name] an InMail* and on the right of this button a drop-down arrow (see Figure 8-3). Click on it, and you will see a link that says *Get introduced.*

When you select that link, the Introduction Request form will appear, giving you a list of first-level connections who can introduce you to your target. Scan the list for someone you know personally. She will be the person you will ask to send your introduction to your intended contact (see Figure 8-4). Click on her name, and she moves to the top of the form between you and the person you want to meet.

Figure 8-3. When you see a second-level connection you want to meet, you can send him an InMail or you can see how you are connected to him. Click the down arrow on the gray button in his information box and select *Get introduced* to see the names of first-level connections who can potentially introduce you.

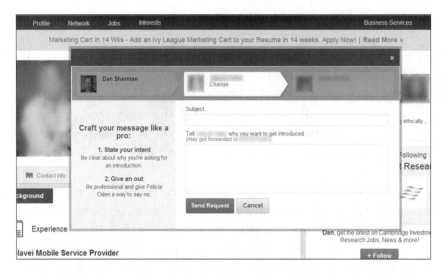

Figure 8-4. On the Introduction Request form, you can select the first-level connection you want to help you reach a second-level connection and explain the reason for your request.

The names are hyperlinks, so if you click on the name of the person you know, you are taken to her profile so you can refresh your memory on how you know her. Then go back to the profile of the person you want to connect with. You will see a link that says *Get introduced through a connection* on the top right. Click on that, and LinkedIn will display the Introduction Request form. You will see your first-level contacts who are connected to the person you want to meet. Pick the first-level contact you want to ask to make the introduction and click on her name.

Fill in the subject of your request, then tell your first-level contact why you want to be introduced. I recommend reading the profile of your target connection, discovering what his goals might be, and explaining why connecting with you will help your target contact achieve his goals.

Before you send off your message, you can check how many introductions you have left. The number you have depends on what kind of account you have. Basic free account holders get 5 outstanding introductions a month, executive account holders get 35, and the top of the heap sales professional members get a whopping 50. You can always check the number of your remaining InMails and introductions by clicking on your picture in the upper right of any page and selecting *Review* next to *Privacy & Settings*. When someone you have asked to be introduced to accepts and you make a connection, that introduction is then freed up for you to make another introduction request.

Reaching Third-Level Connections

What if the person you want to reach is a third-level connection, a friend of a friend of a friend? It works the same way, but your chances of a solid connection go down a little bit, since your introduction request must pass through two people. But it is still possible.

Everyone on LinkedIn is there to network, and it really is very little work to pass on an introduction. I always pass on any introduction I get, since I know the final recipient has the option to expand his network and meet someone new or pass, depending on his current needs.

So if you land on a third-level connection's profile and it's someone you want to meet, don't despair. Click on the down arrow on the gray button in her information box that's next to *Send [name] an InMail.* Then click on the *Get introduced* link to reveal the Introduction Request form. LinkedIn will display a list of your first-level connections who can start the introduction process. Click on the person you want to start the introduction process. You will then see the place to put the subject of your request and a note to your first-level contact explaining why you want to be introduced. The introduction request will go to your first-level connection, who will pass it on to a connection who will pass it on to your intended target connection.

In the process of reaching out to a second- or third-level contact, your first-level connection will get your request and then can add a message of his own before he passes it on . . . hopefully something nice that will encourage the final recipient to act on your request. The request will show up in your first-level contact's inbox. Since you get only five introduction requests a month with the free account, you may wish to follow up with your first-level connection so that the request does not languish in his inbox. I send any request I get immediately on to the next person, but everyone is different and has different demands on his or her time. So be sure to follow up if you can. Remember everyone networks at different speeds.

The nice thing about the introduction feature is that it's respectful of your first-level contact's time. You are not calling her and interrupting her with your request; she can review it and deal with it when she is working on her LinkedIn mail. She can write a nice introduction for you, and if she does, the person you want to reach is more likely to connect with you. A request to a third-level contact is more complicated, but it is still heads above a cold call. I have found that even though LinkedIn is a gigantic network with over 300 million people, there is an unwritten code of respect and openness to each other.

There are so many ways to reach the people you encounter on LinkedIn, such as accessing contact information they provide in their profile, or using InMail, introductions, and messages to OpenLink members. It should be no problem to reach anyone in your network if you really want to.

Contacting Groups of People

Up until this point, we've been talking about identifying individuals we want to connect with and sending them a targeted message. As we say in marketing, it's the "rifle" approach. What if you want to use the "shotgun" approach and send the same message to many people on LinkedIn?

Before you do, you should be aware that any mass promotions in any medium—be it direct-mail postcards, emails, or mass messages of any kind—have a low return rate. You're very lucky to get a 1 percent response rate from any kind of campaign of this nature. However, it's an accepted strategy in marketing, and it can be useful to you as long as you have realistic expectations.

The other consideration is that in its infinite wisdom, LinkedIn has put in some controls over how many mass messages you can send in the system. Think about it: I have 30 million people in my network (that's first, second, and third levels). If I and other people were allowed to message millions of people every day with a push of a button, well, pretty soon the site would be overrun with mass mailings and turn into a swampy and spammy mess.

So LinkedIn allows you to send mass messages, but it limits you to contacting 50 first-level connections at a time. To do so, click on *Network* on the top toolbar, then select *Contacts*. Click *Filter by* and select *Connections only*. Then check the box by the connections that you'd like to message. If you choose the *Select all* feature, you will be selecting only connections on that page. Once you have checked off the connections you want to message, find the *Message* link with the envelope icon above the list of contacts.

Click on it, and you will be given a text box in which to send a message to up to 50 first-level contacts. Here's an important tip: before you click on the blue *Send Message* button, unclick the box that says *Allow recipients to see each other's names and email addresses* so your contacts don't get upset that their personal information is being shared, and your message looks more targeted and professional (see Figure 8-5).

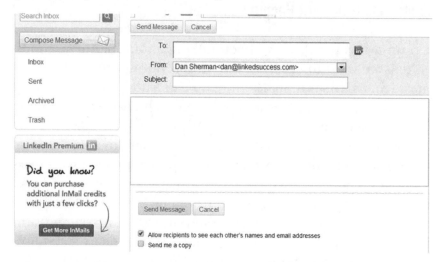

Figure 8-5. The Compose Message form allows you to send a message to up to 50 of your first-level connections. You can add contacts right from the form by clicking on the blue "in" box on the right, which will bring up all your contacts. Be sure to unclick the box below allowing recipients to see each other's information to keep the message more professional.

Tag, You're It: Grouping Contacts for Targeted Marketing

What if you want to send messages to the same group of people over and over again? There is a feature that allows this called *tags*. To create a tag, first go to a first-level connection's profile, and click on *Relationship* right under the person's picture.

Click on *Tag*, and then select a tag such as "client" or "colleague"; or you can make your own tag by clicking on the link that says *+ Add new tag* and clicking *Save*. You are able to create up to 200 of your own tags, so you can be very specific in tagging people depending on your business needs. You could have tagged groups such as "Atlanta sales managers," "Miami contacts," "business reporters," and so on.

Then, to send a message to your tagged group (50 at a time), go to *Network > Contacts*, then choose *Filter by*, and hover your mouse over the group you want to message. This will bring up all the contacts you tagged in that group. Check the box *Select All*, and then click on the *Message* link to bring up the text box where you can compose your message. Then click *Send Message*. You could also put a check next to a select few of your tagged contacts, and then click *Message* to compose your note to them (see Figure 8-6).

Figure 8-6. By clicking on the *Filter by* feature in your Contacts page, you can select the tagged group you wish to message. You can message that group 50 contacts at a time.

This tagging method will allow you to group prospects, current customers, prospects by city, friends by city, whatever you decide, and send a group message. Say you are traveling to Seattle on business. You can tag 50 Seattle prospects in a group and message them all at once saying that you are visiting and would like to set up a time to grab coffee. Or you could put your top 50 clients in a group and message them all at once with a special, an open house, a new product announcement, or something else.

Messaging More than 50 People

If you really want to send a message to more than 50 people, there is a way, but you need to have an email management program to do it. First, go to *Network > Contacts,* then select the *Settings* link by the gear icon on the right. On the next page, under *Advanced Settings* on the right, click on *Export LinkedIn Connections.* Click *Export* and save the file where you can easily find it.

LinkedIn will give you a spreadsheet with your contacts listed with their full names, email addresses, and current employers and positions. You can upload the contacts to an email management program and send out a mass email.

Finding Joint Venture Partners on LinkedIn

Now that we've discussed how to find and reach out to people, I truly hope your mind is racing with the possibilities of finding new and interesting people to do business with. Let's take a closer look at one opportunity that should have you salivating and that is, to my mind, one of the easiest success strategies to accomplish on LinkedIn: creating joint venture partnerships.

In ancient Greece, the mathematician Archimedes said, "Give me a place to stand, and with a lever I will move the whole world." Although LinkedIn was before his time, Archimedes was certain of one principle that you can always count on *and* find in abundant supply on LinkedIn, and that's *leverage.*

With over 300 million professionals using LinkedIn, you've got to assume that there are others who are serving your marketplace with noncompeting products and services. Why not employ leverage and get in touch with some of these professionals and market to their clients? By marketing to someone else's list, you've got built-in acceptance from clients on that list and an established brand whose coattails you can ride.

I mentioned at the start of the chapter the concept of "centers of influence"—that is, professionals in your area with whom you can create partnerships and who serve clients you'd like to serve, but with a noncompeting offer. To demonstrate the concept, let me describe a joint venture partnership with a center of influence that I created in one day on LinkedIn and that continues to be lucrative for both parties.

As a LinkedIn trainer, one of the niches I serve is the real estate market. Since I have worked as a Coldwell Banker real estate agent, I know the marketing options available to agents and why it's key for them to get involved with LinkedIn. So naturally, I am in a few real estate groups where my real estate agent prospects congregate and I can listen in on their concerns and offer advice when appropriate. One day I saw a post in one of these groups from a woman living nearby in Orlando, Florida, who operates a real estate training company and was looking for students for her real estate and mortgage classes.

The light bulb went off: "Hmm," I thought, "I wonder whether her students would also like to learn LinkedIn?"

I wrote her a message saying congratulations on her school, explaining what I do in the area of real estate agent LinkedIn marketing training, and inviting her to a 10-minute call to see if we might collaborate. The next day we spoke, and she was thrilled to be able to offer my training to her clients. We agreed on financial terms, and we set up an ongoing webinar program for her clients in which she introduces me and I provide my training with an offer to work personally with me. Many real estate agents take the free training. Then they sign up to work with me as their marketing coach, or they take advantage of my online course. This joint venture was created in one day thanks to LinkedIn, and it is responsible for an additional revenue stream for both of us.

Using this example, I want to point out what I feel are the elements of a successful LinkedIn message proposing a joint venture:

- **Immediacy.** I read her post in a group and obviously deduced that growing her training company was top of mind for her. Since this was what she was focused on right then, my message spoke to her immediate need.
- **Praise.** I know that running a business is hard, so I was sure to congratulate her on the school. Entrepreneurs need love too!
- **Targeted messages.** My message to her was about her and her school and how she could make more money with that school and her client list. This was not a dart thrown wildly. Targeted messages have the best chance of success on LinkedIn.

I hope I've inspired you to start reaching out to joint venture partners. Don't assume that someone you see who looks interesting won't work with you! Instead, assume that everyone is on LinkedIn to improve their lives and businesses (which is true), and that with a thoughtful, targeted message, you can establish a partnership that helps both of you achieve your goals.

Insider Tips for Contacting Reporters on LinkedIn

While I strongly encourage you to use social media platforms like LinkedIn to promote your brand, please remember to keep an ongoing outreach to "traditional media" as part of your marketing plan. Being seen in the media can have a major business-boosting effect, and sometimes it's a life-changing experience (just ask anyone who has appeared on a major television show like *Shark Tank* or *Good Morning America*).

So how do you get media coverage? The good news is you can combine your LinkedIn activities with your media outreach to journalists because there are many of them on LinkedIn. In fact, a 2011 survey by the Arketi Group, a public relations and digital marketing firm, revealed that a whopping 92 percent of all journalists have a LinkedIn account. Since journalists *are* on LinkedIn looking for sources for their stories, all you need now is the know-how for working successfully with them. For that inside information, I turned to Kelly Diedring Harris, owner of a public relations firm, who has a solid track record of getting coverage for her clients on major media outlets. The following is what Kelly said:

Here's how I recommend you approach a reporter on LinkedIn:

- **Get connected and pitch!** LinkedIn is a fantastic way to interact directly with journalists. If you're already connected to them—great! If you have specific journalists you want to pitch to, send them a LinkedIn request to connect—most journalists accept these types of requests. Once connected and before you pitch to them, do your homework! Make sure your pitch is relevant to what they specialize in and write about. Nothing irritates professional journalists more than receiving pitches that have nothing to do with them. Once you decide it's appropriate to pitch to them, keep it short but informative. Don't fill your pitch with buzzwords; be genuine. In a paragraph or less, preferably just a few to-the-point sentences, tell them how you can help them. Send a photo if you can. And finally, make sure your pitch is newsworthy and not overly promotional. Journalists are not advertising executives. They write about news, so keep it topical.
- **Think outside the box.** Journalists receive hundreds, even thousands of pitches every day via phone, email, and social media. It's really important to craft a pitch that is topical and newsy, and you'll get bonus points for being different, presenting a new perspective, or showcasing a new spin on

an old subject. Before hitting *send* on your pitch, think for a moment, "Is my pitch creative? Is it unique in some way?" Reporters that may have already written something about your topic may appreciate a different spin and may write about it again—featuring you, your company, or your product.

- **Follow up as promised.** Nothing irks reporters more than requesting additional information and having to wait for it. If journalists bite on your pitch, consider it your ultimate responsibility to provide everything they need and ask for—the same day, even within the same hour, if possible. Reporters are often working on very tight deadlines, and if you are the first to send the information they are looking for, you have a better chance of being included in their piece.

- **Ask if it's OK to pitch them again.** If reporters aren't interested in using your news at the moment, that doesn't mean they never will be. If you've established contact and they are responding to you in some way, politely ask if it's okay to send them information again, when you have something similar and exciting to pitch. You might even ask if they have any upcoming stories they are working on that you could potentially help them with. By politely asking if you can keep in touch, you may open the door for future opportunities.

- **Always be polite and professional.** With social media, we sometimes feel as if we can let our guard down and be more casual with individuals. Remember that LinkedIn is for professionals, so keep it that way. It's even better if you can compliment someone in advance; professional flattery can work wonders. Open your pitch with something like, "I read your latest column, and it was fantastic. It really got me thinking." Never respond to reporters with rude or abrupt comments.

Now, if reporters contact *you* on LinkedIn, follow these strategies:

- **Respond as soon as possible.** Congrats! If reporters contact you via LinkedIn, that means your profile is set up with the appropriate keywords to attract attention. You've already done something right! If you receive messages from reporters to whom you are not already connected, send a connection request. If you are, respond right away with the information they have requested. Never keep reporters waiting; they will move on to another source.

- **Do your homework and prepare.** Be sure to do an Internet search for these reporters, and learn all you can about what they write about. This will help you craft your responses to their inquiries. Ask questions about their stories, and make sure you send them all the information they are requesting in a timely manner. If you are doing in-person or telephone interviews, be yourself, and let your natural passion come out. Don't try to impress them with buzzwords; they've heard them all. They are most interested in the facts and the uniqueness of your story. Don't overly promote, but be sure to promote a little. Mention what you are promoting once or twice by weaving it naturally into the conversation. Also remember, there's no such thing as *off the record*. If you don't want it reported, don't say it out loud or write it. If you feel they are trying to spin a negative piece, it's okay to decline to participate.

- **Follow up.** Ask about their deadlines, and follow up afterward to make sure they have everything they need. It's also acceptable to ask when their story will run and how you can secure a copy. Once the piece runs, it's always a good idea to compliment them and thank them for including you.

- **Stay in touch.** Once you've established a positive relationship with reporters, it's a great idea to keep in touch when you have more news to share. Be respectful of their time, and always keep your correspondence short, professional, and to the point.

- **Join the reporters' groups.** Once you're connected with journalists that found you on LinkedIn, see what other groups they belong to that you don't yet belong to. Connecting and participating in groups with journalists and other professionals in the same field is a great way to get noticed again!

Kelly Diedring Harris is the CEO of KDH Communications, a full-service public relations and communications firm. KDH Communications specializes in media relations, and it has secured national and local publicity for its clients, including segments on *The View, NBC Nightly News, Daytime, Wall Street Journal*, and *Fox & Friends*. For more on Kelly, visit http://www.kdhcommunications.com.

Finding a Mentor on LinkedIn

I hope you are beginning to realize that there are a great many different types of helpful contacts you can make on LinkedIn. It's really only limited by your imagination and determination. I could go on about making valuable connections for days . . . but it's time to close this chapter. So I'll end with one more tip for making a valuable connection on LinkedIn—someone who can be your mentor.

You know the old saying, "Don't reinvent the wheel," right? Well, whatever you are working on, whatever projects or businesses you are striving to perfect, chances are good that someone out there has traveled the same road as you and can shed light on the process. Why wander around the forest without a flashlight when someone who has succeeded in your field can light a path for you?

Finding a mentor can cut your learning curve and let you achieve great results faster. And with over 300 million professionals on LinkedIn, your potential pool for a good mentor is really substantial. So, how do you identify someone to help you find your way?

I used LinkedIn to contact a true expert on mentoring, Judy Hojel of Sydney, Australia, and asked her to provide her top 10 tips for finding a mentor on LinkedIn. Judy has a master's degree in education, and she is a professional speaker, writer, and business coach who has mentored hundreds of people in both the corporate world and the small business world. She's an experienced CEO who specializes in leadership development and business growth.

Whether you are actively looking for a mentor or not, I still encourage you to read Judy's tips. What she says is excellent advice that applies to meeting anyone you want to connect with on LinkedIn to further your professional goals.

Here are Judy's top 10 tips:

A great mentor inspires you, teaches you, introduces you to new ways of thinking, pushes you out of your comfort zone, supports you in your business or career plans, and often acts as a sounding board. Finding a mentor can be a challenging and time-consuming process, although if you're on LinkedIn, you're already ahead. Here are 10 smart tips that will speed up the search for your ideal mentor on LinkedIn.

1. **Be Clear About Your Mentoring Needs**

   This may sound obvious, but you need to be very clear about what you want from a mentor. Identify your expectations and needs:

   - Is the mentor to help move your career, business, or brand forward?
   - Do you need support and advice from someone who has been there and done that?
   - Do you need strategies for meeting your sales and profit targets?
   - Are you restructuring your business for growth?
   - Do you need fresh ideas or a different perspective on your everyday challenges?

   Remember too that you can have multiple mentors using LinkedIn, people who can each help with specific situations and issues.

2. **Ask Your Own LinkedIn Network for Their Recommendations**

   Begin your search for referrals among your own LinkedIn network and contacts. Ask for the names of people they use or might recommend from their own experience and why they would do so. If the referrals sound promising, you can learn more about them by studying their LinkedIn profiles and determining your best method of approach.

3. **Grow Your LinkedIn Network**

   In general, the advice is to connect with as many people as you can. This will help enormously in your search for a mentor on LinkedIn. Connect with business contacts at all levels of an organization as well as those who own their own businesses. You benefit from having an expanded network, but you also benefit by being exposed to quality connections from your network. Don't forget to get to know the people in your LinkedIn network—you need to stand out and be memorable in their minds.

4. **Join Work-Related Groups on LinkedIn**

Join and participate in the LinkedIn groups that match your needs. There are millions of special-interest groups on LinkedIn, and current rules permit you to join up to 50. You can search for them by keywords, or you can note the groups to which your potential mentors belong. The college you attended might have an alumni groups, as might your previous companies. Both are useful hunting grounds for recommendations for mentors.

Join up, watch the activity, and determine whether the group is going to be helpful for you. If not, simply leave that group and try another.

5. **Participate in the Group Discussions**

The group discussions where members can post questions and encourage discussion are very valuable. Pay attention to those who offer good, sound advice that resonates with you. Contribute to the discussions yourself by sharing an article or blog post you found helpful. You never know where an exchange may lead in the search for your mentor.

Consider asking a couple of those difficult questions you would put to your mentor in your most appropriate group. If it's the right group, you will find many members who will willingly and generously give their time and expertise to help others. Not only do you benefit from their knowledge, but you will also have the opportunity to build more connections.

Reply personally to everyone who has contributed to your discussion, and be prepared to share a little of yourself in your email response to them. Many great email conversations begin by saying, "Thanks so much for responding," which may turn out to be the perfect starting point to trust, respect, and establish rapport—the foundations of a strong mentoring relationship.

6. **Watch the Events Your Group Managers Are Promoting**
   LinkedIn no longer offers an event listing feature. However, many
   organizers continue to promote their events through relevant
   groups by gaining permission directly from the group managers.
   Make sure at least two or three of your groups have subgroups
   based in your local city for maximum benefit.

   Should you be there? Absolutely! Attending a professional
   event, whether it is a breakfast briefing, a conference, or an after-
   work networking gathering is a great place to continue your
   search for a mentor or to determine your compatibility with a
   couple of people you may have already identified.

   Contact them through LinkedIn to say you will be attending,
   and say how much you look forward to meeting them. Having
   face-to-face contact is often the best way to tell whether you
   really connect well together. If you do, approach them about
   becoming your mentors, or arrange another time when you can
   talk more freely.

7. **Turn Good Connections on LinkedIn into Good Relationships**
   Numbers aren't everything on LinkedIn! Social networking is
   all about building relationships. Think about how you can help
   others, as much as you are wanting help yourself.

   Build a quality network, and become memorable by sharing
   articles, contributing your expertise, participating in discussions,
   liking posts, and commenting positively on information shared
   from your network. Remember, you want to be the type of person
   that others would be excited to mentor, so put effort into building
   win-win relationships.

8. **Recognize That Mentoring Comes in Different Formats**
   You may be looking for the traditional longer-term mentoring
   relationship to help you with your career development or business
   growth, but don't ignore the benefits of short-term mentors
   outside your city and even your country.

   Your network and your groups are filled with multiple
   potential mentors, ready with specific expertise or wider
   experience, to advise you right now on how to address those
   challenging issues.

Think about those people in your network or your groups whose responses help you see things with greater clarity. Whose guidance or style appeals to you? Connect with them and explain your situation. This is where the investment you have put into your LinkedIn relationships really pays off.

9. Think Creatively About Finding a Mentor on LinkedIn

There may be some people that you would love to have as a mentor, but you are worried that they might be too busy or too high ranking to mentor you. The only way to find out is to be a little creative in how you approach them.

Use the connection you have developed through LinkedIn to invite them to speak at a work event, or ask them to submit an article for the company newsletter. Most independent professionals are always glad to get paid work, and this may be a great way to get to know them on a face-to-face basis. If they say no, thank them for their time and consideration. After all, every no gets you a step closer to "Yes, I'd love to talk about mentoring with you"!

10. Keep Your LinkedIn Profile Up-to-Date

Your LinkedIn profile showcases you to potential mentors. When you start building relationships, you'll find people heading over to your profile to learn more about you, and it's important that their impression is favorable! Invest time in building your brand, and you'll find that potential mentors are more willing to invest time in you.

Next Steps

There is no reason to keep the mentoring relationship online if you find it has gone to the next level. Many people prefer a face-to-face conversation, while others remain happy with phone calls and emails. It really depends on what suits both your needs, but as with everything worthwhile, it will take some work to get it just right.

The right mentor can make all the difference to your career, your job satisfaction, and your earning capacity. With so many professionals on LinkedIn and so many ways to find the right mentor, the search process has never been easier!

Judy Hojel, MEd, is a professional speaker, writer, and business coach who has mentored hundreds of people in both the corporate world and in their own business. An experienced CEO, she specializes in leadership development and business growth. Find out more at http://au.linkedin.com/in/judyhojel.

Final Thoughts on Mentors: Work at the Relationship

Putting in place Judy's great tips is really the start of the process. I'll just add that mentoring requires a time investment on the part of the professional you want to work with and whom you need help from, so work on building a relationship first, before you ask for mentoring. If you ask people out of the blue to help you with mentoring, you may not succeed. But if you get to know them over time by conversing with them, following their activity on LinkedIn, and talking with them in person during events you both attend, you stand a much better chance.

*　*　*

Searching for people and contacting them on LinkedIn is easy. Get active on the site and start networking, and soon you will have many people you want to reach. When you direct message them, be respectful and tactful, and remember that people want to feel unique. What is it about them specifically that made you want to reach out? As long as you are honest and precise, you will find other LinkedIn users open to hearing from you.

What's another great way to expand your network of potential customers, partners, mentors, and advisors? The answer is in the herd—namely, LinkedIn groups. Judy touched on this, and now we will take a look at one of the most powerful features on the site.

Chapter 9: Power in Tribes: Joining and Creating Groups

You've heard the saying, "Birds of a feather flock together"? That old saying definitely applies to LinkedIn. The millions of professionals who have joined the site have aligned themselves into a dizzying array of combinations: there are corporation groups, alumni groups, nonprofit groups, professional groups, networking groups, city groups . . . a million of them in every language under the sun from Croatian to Slovak to Chinese to Polish. There are also groups to help you become better at LinkedIn (not so subtle plug: I own one called "Link Success with Dan Sherman").

What that means for you is an incredible opportunity for prospecting and finding exactly the right person you want to meet to achieve your goals—be it selling a product, finding a partner, hiring someone, finding a job, or something else. The people you need to find are all waiting there for you in groups. You can join up to 50 groups at a time and begin the networking that will lead you to getting to know and contacting the people you want to meet.

Groups are great for building your brand. You can answer people's questions and post articles of interest for group members to read. This establishes you as an expert, so it's a great way to be found on LinkedIn by people who may need your services and wish to hire you. Groups will also help your offline marketing: you can learn about upcoming network events that might benefit your career or business, and you can promote your events to like-minded individuals. You can search for jobs (every group has a job board) and contact fellow group members even if they are not a first-, second-, or third-level connection.

What's helpful is that as your interests and goals change over time, so can your group lineup. It's a snap to leave a group (no one is notified, and there's no shame involved) and join one that fits your current needs. And groups drastically extend your reach. Yes, you should be adding first-level contacts daily, but additionally, by joining 50 groups with 1,000 potential customers in each group, you just added 50,000 prospects you can now network with and contact in order to conduct business together.

Joining Groups

Across the top menu bar, click on *Interests* > *Groups*. Alternatively, you can also click on the drop-down menu on the left of the search box and click *Groups*.

Now, type in a keyword and look for groups you can join that match your interests. You'll be tempted to join groups of your peers, and that's a great idea. Join a few industry groups in the field in which you are involved so that you can stay up-to-date on the very latest events and trends (see Figure 9-1).

For example, I teach social media, which is a field that changes minute by minute. So I find that by being in the largest social media groups, I have access to what the thought leaders are saying and how the landscape is shifting. Look for the largest groups in your field and join the discussions.

Another benefit of joining groups in your industry is that all the groups are displayed on your profile, and everything counts toward searchability and credibility. So I have joined many social media groups and LinkedIn groups not only to

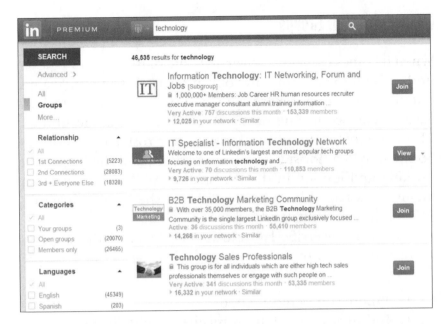

Figure 9-1. On the Group search page, you can enter keywords and find groups that match your interests. You can join them on this page by clicking on the "Join" button on the right.

learn but also to have the group titles appear on my profile. They are terms I want to be found for, and they show readers of my profile that I'm keeping current with trends in my industry. Having social media groups in my profile serves to create consistency in my brand: I teach social media and I network with other social media enthusiasts and thought leaders.

The next thing you might do is join your local groups. Type in the name of your city in the keyword search box and see what the largest groups are. I am in a half dozen groups in my town because even though online networking rocks, in-person contact is still critical to meeting referral partners and finding customers for my services and local training events. My local groups keep me informed of upcoming networking and social events right in my backyard.

Diversifying Your Groups

When it comes to groups, diversify! One of the key strategies to undertake is to join not only your industry and alumni groups, but also the groups where your customers are likely to be. I gave this advice to one of my clients who was an accountant who was looking to add a florist to her roster of customers. So she joined a florist group on LinkedIn, and she began networking and joining in the discussions. Within days, a group member messaged her and asked her if she handled payrolls. Affirmative. New client added.

As I said, diversify. Here are some ideas of the kinds of groups you can join:

- Where you went to school
- Industries you sell to or receive supplies from
- Professional interest or areas of expertise
- Products and services you offer
- Professional titles of your customers or suppliers
- Clubs and associations
- Companies you worked for in the past
- Nonprofits and hobbies you are interested in

And most of all, join groups where your clients are going to be congregating. Select *Group* on the top menu, and in the search box put the keyword or title for your best prospects. If you sell to human resources executives, then add that keyword, and click the magnifying glass on the blue button. When a list of potential groups appears, click on the title of the group you want to explore, then check out some discussions and find groups that are active, meaning that there are discussions added every day. Then make the leap: click on the yellow button that says *Join*. Remember, it's easy to switch in and out, so there's really no pressure. Some groups are auto-accept (meaning that by clicking the yellow *Join*, immediately you are in).

For other groups, the group manager will look you over a bit before agreeing to accept you. In the seven years I've been on LinkedIn, there were maybe one or two that never approved me . . . but there are so many groups to join that overlap in content that it's not an issue if one doesn't accept me. I just move on to the next group and apply.

When it comes to joining groups, size matters. Once you put in your keyword, the groups will appear ranked by number of members. It's always a good idea to join the largest groups so you have exposure to more people and can make the most connections. Join the largest groups in your region and you can network with lots of people right in your own backyard. Also, try combinations of words to see if you can locate the perfect group for your purpose. Include a region and a field, like "New York doctors," or "Phoenix social media." You don't need quotes or Boolean search terms (such as "and" or "not"); LinkedIn will search the group profiles and return groups that contain those words in the profile.

You can research a group you are interested in joining by clicking on the "i" on the far right near the *Join* button, then clicking on *Group Statistics*. That will open up a screen that will show you interesting facts, including how many members have joined, where they are located, what their job titles are, how fast the group is growing, how much activity the group is experiencing, and more.

Another strategy for selecting groups is simply this: as you join in conversations on LinkedIn and find interesting people such as prospective partners, customers, advisors, or competitors, look at their profile and see which groups they belong to by scrolling down to the end of their profile page. You may make some interesting discoveries and find groups that will benefit you, and you can join the groups right from their profile. There is a + *Join* right under the name of any name you have not joined yet. This comes in handy if you want to send messages to people who are not first-level connections; just join a group that they are in and you have that ability.

Navigating Your Groups

Once you join a group from a keyword search or you find it on someone's profile and you are accepted, you will see a toolbar across the top within the group (see Figure 9-2). The first tab is Discussions. There is where everyone is talking about the group topic. To join a discussion, just click on a headline of a post, and you will see a space to add your comment. By commenting on discussions and adding relevant, helpful information, you increase your presence in the group and reinforce your brand. When people see what you wrote, they can click on your picture, read your profile, and contact you for further discussions on how you can work together.

Figure 9-2. The tabs across the top within the groups give you access to much information, including discussions, promotions by members, jobs that are being posted by companies and group members, a list of members, and a search feature. Group owners also get a "Manage" tab.

What else can you do in the Discussion area? Underneath each discussion post, you have a list of options. You can do the following:

- You can "like it," which puts your smiling face on the discussion page, which helps to increase awareness of your brand. This also updates your status, meaning that all your first-level connections also see your action on their home pages.
- You can comment and thereby open the possibility of someone's connecting with you because of what you said.
- You can follow the discussion and get email updates on the thread.
- You can also click on *Reply privately*, which opens up a text box where you can initiate a conversation directly with the posting member—enabling you to connect with those LinkedIn members who are like-minded and who may be open to assistance from you or who may be in a position to assist you in achieving your goals.

The next tab is Promotions, where members post information about products and services they are offering to the group. The next tab is Jobs, where you will see paid job postings. Also in this section are the job postings added for free by the group members; over on the left, click on the hyperlink *Job Discussions* to reach those listings. The next tab is Members, where you will see a list of all group members. Last, there is a Search tab for finding discussions by keyword.

You can access more information by clicking on the "i" in the group header. Here you will find out who the group owner is, and you will find links to the group profile and group statistics. You can also click on *Group settings* by the gear icon in the header, and it reveals a menu where you can set up how often and what types of messages you receive from the group.

To visit the members page, where you can learn more about members of the group as well as contact any of them, click on the *Members* tab heading or on the number of people in the group in the header, which is a hyperlink (for example: *45,000 members*).

Here you will see all the members in the group sorted by the ones closest to you (first level, then second level, and so on). This will show you people whom you might want to connect with. There's even a keyword search for members. At the top of the page is a gray *Search* button that you can use to put in a title, a city, or anything else to sort the members. For example, I'm in the "Branded Entertainment" group with over 4,000 members. If I put in my city, "Tampa," in the search box, I get 17 members—these are local people interested in a topic I find fascinating, namely, product placement, whom I can connect with.

When you find a group you like, one strategy that is helpful is to send a message to the group manager and offer to connect with him (that is, to become first-level connections). If the manager has started and manages a very large group in an area of interest to you, he would be someone good to know. Within the group header, click on the "i." There you will see the group manager's name as a hyperlink to his activity in the group. On this page, look on the right for the gray button that says *Follow [name]* and a drop-down menu. Click on *View Profile* to learn more about him. Then you can send a message to him introducing yourself and offering to be a moderator or anything else you can do to help, such as helping to organize local meetings.

Messaging Group Members

Speaking of sending messages, one powerful reason for joining many groups is that you can message people directly even if you are not a first-level connection, and without spending money on an InMail. So if there is someone you want to connect with, say, a second- or third-level connection, within the group, go to the top and look for the Members tab or the number of members in the group, which is a hyperlink.

Click on *Members* or the number of members, and you will be taken to the members page. Click on the *Send message* under the name of the person you want to reach, and a box will open up for you to send your message. If you join 50 groups with 1,000 prospects each, that's 50,000 more people you can message and look for ways to do business together. Most groups have many more than 1,000 people . . . so your potential for reaching the right person is unlimited.

Leaving Groups

"Parting is such sweet sorrow," said Juliet to Romeo in Shakespeare's immortal tale of star-crossed lovers. And so it is with groups. You joined the group all hopeful it was going to be a bonanza, but it became a dud. You therefore have mixed emotions about the group. Should you stay, or should you go? If you decide to leave, no problem. You can leave at any time simply by going to the group page and in the header looking for the gray button on the right side that says *Member.* Hover your mouse over it, and it changes to *Leave.* Click on it, and you are automatically out of the group.

As a group manager, I can tell you that there is no stigma involved; no one knows but you. No one is notified. So you can shuffle around your 50 allotted groups as often as you like to suit your present needs, and no one is the wiser.

So, you can see that groups open up a whole range of possibilities for you in terms of learning new things, meeting new people, connecting with prospects, and establishing your brand. But just as they say on TV: "But wait! There's more!" You can start your own group and build a perpetual prospecting machine.

Creating Groups

You've heard about the Golden Rule? The one that says, "Those who have the gold make the rules"? Well, LinkedIn offers you the chance to have the gold and the control, be the big kahuna, and make all the rules. All you need to do is start you own group, and you can create up to 10 of them. Once you do, you are in a position to establish yourself as a thought leader. You can gain credibility and expand your networking capabilities, and you can be found for opportunities. Also, and very important, you can use group management automation features to create a system that delivers prospects and website traffic to your door around the clock so you get leads while you sleep.

To get started, come up with an idea for a group—perhaps a group for your industry, or a group that combines locale and industry, or a group for a passion of yours. You might make a group where your potential customers can congregate. Say you sell computer equipment—you'd want to start a group for IT professionals. If you sell sales training, start a group for VPs of sales. Whatever your expertise is, whatever products you sell, you can start up a group in that field and begin networking with prospective clients. One strategy is to create a local group for your customers that will allow you to meet people and then move conversations offline. So if you sell to sales managers, instead of a sales managers group, you create "Portland Sales Managers" or whatever your locale is.

To begin the process, hover your cursor over *Interests* and select *Groups* from the menu. Click on the *Create a group* button on the right. You will see a very simple form you can fill out in two minutes and begin promoting your group right away. Here is what you will need to add:

- **Logo.** This should be something clean and professional. More people will join if you have a logo rather than the default LinkedIn image. Just find a royalty-free image from the Internet.
- **Name.** This can be as long as you want, but you should use up to four words that create a concise message of what your group is about. Keep in mind when creating your name that it will be searchable in the keyword search on LinkedIn. So make sure it contains the keyword that you feel your potential group members will be typing in to find groups to join.

- **Group type.** You have several choices here, including professional, networking, corporate, and so on. Pick the one that best applies to your purpose.
- **Summary.** This should be a benefit-oriented statement: What is it that people will gain from joining your group? What's in it for them?
- **Full description.** Elaborate on the benefits of your group, and add in details about what people should talk about, whether this group will be online only or will include offline events, and how to reach you if they have questions. Include keywords that you think people will use to find the group because that's where LinkedIn looks when someone runs a search.
- **Website.** Put your company website or blog here so that you can drive traffic to your site from your group.
- **Email.** Include an email address that you check often in case someone writes to you with an opportunity.
- **Access.** There are some settings you need to select to finish the process. One is to select *Auto join* or *Request to join*. With *Auto join*, whoever applies is accepted immediately while *Request to join* means that you have to approve them. In my experience, the request-to-join option is too much work because you need to approve everybody. I now use auto join, and I let whoever wants to join my groups do so—it's easy to remove them if you need to later. However, if you are starting a group for only a very select cross section of people, say, your premium clients, or those with a certain degree or background, then use the request-to-join option to screen applicants.
- **Language.** Select the language of the group from the drop-down menu.
- **Location.** Check the box if the group is associated with a specific geographical area.
- **Open or closed group.** At the end of this form, you will be asked if you want this to be an open or closed group. If you are creating the group to be a traffic generator, definitely choose open because open discussions can

be seen by anyone on LinkedIn and searched for on Google as well. Also, in an open group, people who aren't members can still add discussions from anywhere in the LinkedIn network, encouraging more interaction.

Promoting Your Groups

Once you create your group, it will have its own unique hyperlink address. The link is pretty long and ugly; to send it to others, you can go to a free website address shortening site like https://www.Bit.ly or http://www.tinyurl.com and create a smaller link. Once you've done that, here are some ideas on how to promote your group:

- Send the website address via email to any contacts who may be interested in joining such a group.
- Add the website address to your email signature.
- Add it to your LinkedIn status update on a regular basis, inviting your first-level connections to join your group (your status update appears on all your first-level connections' home pages). I put the link to join my group "Link Success with Dan Sherman" in my status update about once a week.

To actively promote your group, go to your group, click on *Manage,* and you will have a wide array of methods for reaching potential group members (see Figure 9-3). Here you can:

- **Send invitations.** This allows you to invite your first-level contacts to join your group. Click on it, and you will see the invitation form. You will see the blue "in" logo next to the box marked "connections." Click on it, and you will see all your first-level connections. You can click on 50 people at a time and invite them to join your group. If you are creating a local group, then select connections

Figure 9-3. The Manage Group section gives you a wide variety of tools for managing your group and many communications methods for establishing your personal brand.

in that locale. If you are creating an industry group, sort by industry. Send your messages by clicking on the blue *Send Message* button.

- **Group link.** Click on *Send Invitations* to get to the invitation screen, and you will see *Group Join Link* on the lower left. This hyperlink connects right to your LinkedIn group page. Copy and paste that into your status updates and posts on other social media sites like Facebook and Twitter; put the link on your website; put it in your email signature; add it to your LinkedIn profile. This will provide a wider exposure for your group, and you'll get more members as a result.

Over time, your group will slowly build. One nice feature of LinkedIn that will help you is that when someone joins your group, it appears in that person's status updates, which also appear on all their first-level contacts' pages. When a friend of your contact sees that your contact has joined your new group, she may be inspired to join as well if she is interested in the subject.

Creating Subgroups for More Influence

When you click on *Manage* in your group, way down on the bottom of the left-hand menu is *Subgroups.* This feature extends your ability to create groups because you can have 20 subgroups for the 10 allowed groups you can create. Let's say you create a group around a passion, say start-ups, where you talk about building the next Google or Apple. You could create subgroups for different locations around the country, such as "Start-ups Denver" or "Start-ups Houston," which will enable you to create and send targeted messages to people if you're planning an event in a particular city.

Subgroups give you the ability to extend your influence and also create highly targeted groups of professionals. You can send a different message to each subgroup promoting different things or discussing different aspects of your group topic. The process for creating a subgroup is identical to that for creating a group; it's just a part of your larger group.

Subgroups give you flexibility. Let's say you want your main group to be open and automatically accept everyone. You could make the subgroups more selective so you would approve individually everyone who wanted to be in those groups.

Building Your Business with Groups

Once you have your groups established, you can use them not only to build your personal brand, but also to build your lists of prospects through automation. Here is what I do with my groups. I maintain two groups on LinkedIn. The first is "Tampa Bay Marketing Professionals," with over 5,000 members; this group is for professionals in sales, marketing, advertising, and public relations to network and share opportunities. Even though it says "Tampa Bay," I get people from all over the world joining, which is fine—it increases my exposure. This group helps my personal brand immensely as an Internet professional and social media expert.

My second group is "Link Success with Dan Sherman," which I created to provide a place for conversations around achieving professional goals by using LinkedIn. This group also gives me the opportunity to brand myself as a LinkedIn and social media expert.

So how do these groups help me create my brand and pull more opportunities to me as a LinkedIn expert? Let's look at some ways.

Manager's Choice

When you start a group, one of the areas you have total control over is the main part of the group: the discussion area. You can select what discussions appear on the site, and you can choose to not accept other discussions. To set up how you want your group discussion selection to run, go to your group, click on *Manage*, then click on *Group Settings* on the left. Under *Permissions*, you can choose to have everything submitted to you for approval, or you can set it to where everyone's discussion posts appear automatically.

In my two groups, I set up "Tampa Bay Marketing Professionals" so that all discussions submitted are automatically posted because it is a pretty diverse group in terms of membership and interests. (I still have the option to delete discussions that are not appropriate, or I can move them to other areas.) In "Link Success with Dan Sherman," I set it up such that I need to approve all discussions because this is a very niche group only about LinkedIn, and I want tighter control.

In both groups, I can make any discussion I want to be the most prominent by selecting it as *Manager's Choice,* and it appears at the top of the discussions, so it's the first thing people see when they come to the group. It's easy to make a discussion in your group a Manager's Choice; just click on the discussion headline, open it up, and click the hyperlink *Add to Manager's Choice* below the discussion.

Announcements

As group manager, every seven days I can send an announcement to my group members that gets delivered to their regular email inboxes. So I use this quite a bit with my Tampa group to announce upcoming local LinkedIn training sessions that I'm going to be running. In the message, I write a catchy subject line, and I include a link to an online invitation to come to my training. (I use https://Eventbrite.com for many of my training sessions. https://www.Eventbrite.com is an event organizing and fee collection website with a robust set of management features.) So I have a 5,000-plus, targeted email list I can mail to. I get about five people a day signing up to my group, so my email list grows organically. The larger you can make your group, the more people you can reach with your announcements.

To make an announcement, go to *Manage* in your group, and select *Send an announcement* from the left-hand menu.

Templates

I have completely automated both of my groups with marketing messages that go out to any LinkedIn professional who wants to join. What these messages do is introduce me and promote what I can do personally for them. They also provide all my websites, products, and resources, and they tell people how they can contact me to further the relationship.

These messages are fully automated and work 24/7 for me, promoting my LinkedIn training sessions and helping to build my brand with people from around the world who join my groups. Let's see what the two messages look like.

Here's what LinkedIn users get in their email box when they apply to my Tampa group. You can see that I'm branding myself and giving them my website address where they can learn more about me:

Thank you for applying to the Tampa Bay Marketing Professionals Group. I'm Dan Sherman, group manager, and I approve your application!
Dan Sherman, LinkedIn Expert, Social Media Coach, Trainer, Author, and Speaker
http://www.LinkedSuccess.com

I have this group set to auto-accept everyone. Once they are automatically accepted into the group, they get this message in their Gmail or Outlook (or Hotmail) account . . . whatever email program they are using:

Do you want to grow your business? Learn advanced LinkedIn techniques with a consultation or seminar with Dan Sherman, LinkedIn expert. Call 813 . . . or email dan@linkedsuccess.com.
Welcome to our group of professionals in all areas of marketing, sales, public relations, and advertising. As group manager, I encourage you to actively participate by asking questions, offering advice, and letting everyone know about upcoming events related to our profession.
I am an open networker, meaning that I accept all invitations to connect. Please send me an invitation to connect with you. Again, welcome, and let me know how I can assist you in achieving your business goals with LinkedIn.
Dan Sherman/LinkedIn Expert
http://www.linkedsuccess.com
dan@linkedsuccess.com

Here you can see I'm promoting my LinkedIn training, I'm branding myself as an expert, and I'm providing hyperlinks to my main site, where they can read more about me and purchase my books and trainings; I'm inviting them to connect with me so I build my sphere of influence; and I am giving them my email address and phone number so they can contact me.

These templates are a snap to set up. You just go to your group, click *Manage* from the top toolbar, select *Templates* from the left-hand menu, and then notice the *Manage Message Templates* screen, where you create your automated messages to go out to people who apply to join and who are accepted. You have the option to also send yourself a test message from this screen so you can see how your message looks in your inbox. If you include hyperlinks, be sure to add the "http://" so that they come out as hyperlinks.

Imagine what you can do with this ability:

- You can create a free offer.
- You can drive new members to a place to sign up for your newsletter.
- You can drive people to a website where you can capture their email address in exchange for a free report.
- You can sell a course or promote an event.
- You can provide a way for them to reach you or connect with you on other social media sites.

The possibilities are endless, and they are automated so you can grow your email list and make sales while you sleep.

A Wise Name and Logo Choice

Here's another creative way I use groups to strengthen my personal brand and create more visibility for myself. It's by the use of my name and a very clever logo for my group "Link Success with Dan Sherman." You can see that I'm branding myself with the name of the group by associating my name (my brand) with "Link Success" (due to copyright restrictions, LinkedIn does not allow anyone to use its full company name in a group title).

Also, the logo is my brand, too. Log onto LinkedIn, go to *Interests > Groups,* and search for my group "Link Success with Dan Sherman." Then join! Trust me, you'll like the group. Now the group is going to show up in your list of groups on your profile. If you look at the logo for the group, you'll discover my smiling face. Yes, I am the logo for "Link Success."

What this means is that I'm branding myself with my face on YOUR profile and the profile of every other person who joins the group. And my face (which is part of my brand as a speaker) shows up next to the words "Link Success with Dan Sherman," which anyone can interpret as success with Linked-In. Now anyone scanning your profile or the profile of any other group member gets a brand reinforcement of me as the LinkedIn expert. So the more people who join the group, the larger my brand grows on LinkedIn.

This is an example of how you can get very creative with groups to establish yourself as a thought leader in your field and have others seek you out.

Getting Group Members Engaged

When you start a group, you need to assume leadership and proactively start conversations, post timely news, and quickly react to the discussions and questions of others. This includes moderating discussions and removing distracting posts that are just total self-promotions and contribute nothing to your group. As your membership grows, discussions become self-generating, but it's important to check the engagement in your group and generate discussions regularly.

One tactic you may want to try is sharing worthy posts you see in other groups that your members would enjoy. It's easy to do because every group post contains a *Share* feature with which you can select other groups where you can display the post. Just click on *Share* under a post when you want to put that post from one group into yours. Clicking on the link brings up the Share box, which allows you to post the discussion in your update, post it to groups, send it to other connections on LinkedIn, or post it to other social media sites (see Figure 9-4).

Figure 9-4. The Share feature can be found under every post in LinkedIn groups, so you can share your post, or the post of another group member, throughout social media. There is also a URL of the post that you can copy and use to send the post to others via email.

Another strategy is to read industry blogs, and when you see a post that would interest your group members, share it with your group. For example, I like sharing interesting articles I read about LinkedIn and social media with my two groups. So I regularly read three well-known blogs: *Business Insider*, *Mashable*, and *Tech Crunch*. When I read articles I feel my group members would enjoy, I use the sharing features in the blogs and add those articles to my group discussions.

A Superstar Group Owner Shares His Secrets of Success

Managing a LinkedIn group brings with it tremendous benefits as well as tremendous responsibility and effort. No LinkedIn user can set up a group, sit back and cross his fingers, and hope that hordes of people will sign up and contribute thought-provoking posts. Creating a LinkedIn group requires setting the rules, creating the tone, and then monitoring the discussions (or in the case of larger groups, naming other members as moderators to help with this task).

One group of which I am a member, the "Sales/Marketing Executives Group," fits the description of a well-run, tightly focused community where the group rules are followed. I belong to this group because one of my target markets is sales executives. In the group, I enjoy listening like the proverbial fly on the wall to my prospects talking about their challenges, which is great market research for me, and I contribute my knowledge where I can.

Leading the group is Eric Blumthal. He has set the rules of the group as a peer-to-peer forum, where sales leaders can ask advice of each other. On a recent day, some of the posts in the group were:

Suggestions Wanted for Powerful Sales Titles
How to overcome the price issue?
Can anyone recommend a lead generation company for the
    pharma/biotech industry?
How effective is online training for sales teams?

You get the picture . . . this is crowdsourcing in action. Members of the group realize they don't have to reinvent the wheel when starting a new initiative; they can tap into the wisdom of the other sales leaders in the group. I caught up with Eric and asked him how he managed to create such a successful community that is clearly a benefit and time-saver for all the members.

Q. Eric, tell us a little about yourself.

A. I live in Sarasota, Florida, with my wife and two sons. I've been a technology sales executive since graduating from Georgia Tech in 1989 (Go Jackets!). In 2005, I cofounded a software company called count5 that uses proprietary technology to double the impact of important employee training, communications, and coaching.

Q. How did you come to be the owner of the "Sales/Marketing Executives Group"?

A. It wasn't my group originally. I actually started as a participant. I joined when the group had 5,000 members. I really enjoyed reading and participating in the B2B sales discussions, but I got frustrated because there were many members who were not seeking advice or asking for it, but rather posting purely promotional messages.

I asked permission from the group owner to let me moderate the group, and I did that for two years. The group owner wasn't very active, so I then asked if he would transfer ownership to me. The rest is history. Currently, the "Sales/Marketing Executives Group" has over 162,000 members, and we're adding over 1,000 new members each week.

Q. How did you get the idea to create a forum where *asking for advice only* is the driving guideline?

A. I modeled the group on what I liked about https://www.Quora.com, which uses a Q&A format to drive discussions. Since I spend most of my social media time on LinkedIn, I decided it would be easier to create a community of B2B sales and marketing executives on LinkedIn rather than Quora.

Q. You have the largest sales executive group on LinkedIn. What is the reason for your success?

A. The primary reason is that we are different from many other groups in that we focus on peer-to-peer advice. Some groups' discussion areas resemble a Twitter-like feed of random articles, blogs, and promotions. While I am a huge fan of promoting and sharing relevant content, sales executives have hundreds of groups and other social media channels in which to read or to distribute content, but very few places to go to ask like-minded peers for advice. So I guess we carved out a niche.

Q. What benefits do your members get from participating in the group?

A. There are three categories of participants that benefit from the group:

1. **Question askers.** Members asking questions in the group gain valuable insights, ideas, and best practices from other experienced members.

2. **Question responders.** Some members respond just because they want to help someone else. Others want to help, but they also want more exposure to the group by sharing their thought leadership and experience with solving similar problems. This improves the credibility and trust of their personal brand, it helps them make new connections, and it potentially creates new business opportunities.

3. **The silent majority.** I think too many people overlook this group. While we have 162,000 members, only a small subset actually participate regularly in discussions. The silent majority just monitors discussions they find interesting. They may visit the group and scan for interesting discussions, or they click on a discussion link on the weekly email summaries LinkedIn sends automatically each week. I get several LinkedIn messages each month from members of the silent majority thanking me for having a group with such valuable discussions.

I don't think many people trying to generate business on LinkedIn realize the value of consistent participation in group discussions. If you are starting, facilitating, or participating in interesting discussions in our group, your discussions are being emailed to over 162,000 people every week! That's a lot of exposure for using a social media system that's free with the basic account. It's quite powerful.

Q. What benefits do you get as the group owner?

A. One benefit is that people remember me. For example, you wouldn't have asked to interview me for your book if we hadn't met in this group.

Also, I get a lot of personal satisfaction from helping others, so that's one itch that gets scratched by owning this group. When I network at live functions, I always focus on helping others, making valuable connections for them, and so on. If I do that enough times, my relationships with people deepen, our mutual trust strengthens, and eventually it comes around full circle and someone helps me. I treat LinkedIn groups the exact same way.

Group ownership (and active group participation) is a key part of my content marketing strategy. I've created a magnet that attracts sales executives, and I do everything possible to make the group valuable to them so that they stay. It's a way for me to strengthen my brand, credibility, and trust, and it's a way to expand my connections and to help other people. I do this without ever promoting my company's capabilities in the group. I let my profile headline that appears below my name every time I post in the group do my selling. If people are interested in what I do, they reach out to me. And I guess the best metric of all is that I attribute over 50 percent of my company's recurring revenue to relationships made in the "Sales/Marketing Executives Group."

Q. If you were to advise someone just starting a LinkedIn group, what are the things they need to do to lay the groundwork for a successful endeavor?

A. Because I took over the "Sales/Marketing Executives Group," I'll have to draw my advice from the one group I started from scratch called "Sales Training Best Practices," which currently has about 10,000 members.

1. **Get active in a group first.** You don't have to own a group to get benefits from participating (I still participate actively in other sales groups). But if you want to start a group, first learn how to participate in and facilitate valuable discussions; learn what makes some groups engaging and interesting and what makes others noisy and spammy. You are developing a skill set and best practices around knowing what works and what does not work.

   Do a LinkedIn search for groups where you think your target audience is likely to spend their time. Join those groups, and participate in discussions. Start interesting discussions, and ask people sincerely for their opinions or help with something—and do *not* make it about what you sell. If you sell customer relationship management (CRM) systems with a Red Widget feature, nothing will shatter your credibility more than posting, "Does anyone know of a CRM with a Red Widget feature?" And be willing to make mistakes: it's the only way you learn.

2. **Define your objectives and strategy.** Don't form a group before you understand what you are trying to accomplish. Then, consider these factors:

   a. **Group name.** The name matters because the name of your group needs to attract your audience. It is also the primary text used by LinkedIn when users are searching for groups—so make sure it has the right keywords. Type in some search terms to locate similar groups. LinkedIn ranks groups by keyword match and by group size, so if there are 800 groups with 10,000+ members using your keywords, you may want to use different words in your group name.

   My official group name on LinkedIn is "Sales/Marketing Executives (CSO/CMO)" because I wanted to be found if someone typed in "CMO" instead of "marketing executive." Unless you are a huge industry player like http://www.salesforce.com or IBM, don't name your group after your company because no one will join. Trust me, I tried it.

b. **Why will people join?** What does the group need to have to make people want to spend time there? Ask some people if you don't know.

c. **Lonely groups stay lonely.** If you build it, they won't come if there is nothing happening in the group. When I started "Sales Training Best Practices," I invited everyone I knew to join the group (I had about 400 contacts actually join)—and more important, I made sure a couple of training consultants and friends I knew were willing to join the group prelaunch and start some interesting discussions.

3. **Launch and learn.** Be willing to make mistakes, and make sure to learn from them.

4. **Be patient.** This is a long-term commitment. It requires discipline and lots of patience. I used to schedule time in my calendar every day for group tasks. I'm on autopilot now, but it took a while to develop a habit. Realize that you have many other high-priority things that make you successful that have nothing at all to do with LinkedIn. Make sure you are prioritized and disciplined with your time and not 100 percent infatuated with social media.

5. **Be yourself.** Seriously, this is social networking. Be yourself; don't try to be someone you're not. People are on LinkedIn because they want to connect with real people.

6. **Have fun.**

Eric's firm, count5, sells a *knowledge retention application* called Q MINDshare that uses its Cut-Thru Technology to double the impact of important employee training, communications, and coaching. count5's customers include Georgia Power, Verizon, and American Express, which have large populations of customer-facing sales or service employees who need to keep up with important changes in products, messaging, strategies, and policies. You can visit Eric's site at http://www.count5.com.

Building Website Traffic with Groups

As we leave our discussion on groups, I want to share with you one more strategy that you can use to turn your group memberships into solid traffic for your blog. It's simple and easy to do.

Let's say you have a blog, and you want more readers to visit it and get to know about your expertise and your products. Basically, every time you create a new blog post, add it as a discussion in a group where the members would enjoy the subject and where the subject is relevant. Go to the group where you want to publicize your blog post, and go to *Start a discussion or share something with the group.* Describe what the post is about in the first box. Next, in the *Add more details* area, provide more reasons why people should be interested. Include the hyperlink to the blog page in your post. Select *General, Job,* or *Promotion,* and click *Share.*

Then, once the discussion has been posted, click on *Share* under the discussion post. This will bring up a *Share* box. Select LinkedIn by clicking on the blue "in." That will open up a box where you will see *Groups.* Enter group names that are relevant to your blog post, and add them. Fill in *Subject* and *Detail,* and then press the blue *Share* button. Your blog post will now appear simultaneously in the appropriate groups with a link to your blog. Group members can click on it and read your post on your blog's site, and if they are intrigued, they can stick around, read more posts, learn more about you, and perhaps sign up for a newsletter. This will enable thousands of group members to visit your blog and learn more about what you have to offer.

However, I would caution you in two ways. One, don't overuse this. Apply this strategy once or twice a month so you don't inundate your groups. And two, make sure the blog post is relevant to the subject matter of the group *and* that it's in keeping with the rules of the group. Some groups discourage blog posts while others accept them, so you want to know this in advance. If the rules do not prohibit blog posts, and you've seen others do it, then you are okay to post. To make doubly sure, write a note to the group owner and tell her your plans and ask if it is okay. You want to err on the side of caution because if a group manager deletes your post and marks it as spam, you may face restrictions on what you can post in *all* groups, not just the one in which your post was deleted.

* * *

So begin joining groups, and use your groups to interact with others and to contact the people whom you want to do business with. Then start your own groups to help you achieve your personal branding and professional goals. You will be amazed at the possibilities.

Did you know that in addition to your personal profile, you can also have a profile for your company? And if you have multiple companies, you can have a profile for each one? Read on and learn about the Company feature on LinkedIn, which gives you the chance to gather more prospects and customers for your business.

Chapter 10: Good Company: Create Your Company Page and Follow Other Companies

When you register for LinkedIn, you do it as an individual, and most of your activities will be in branding You, Inc. as the leading expert in your field. That's because whether you work for yourself or for a company, you need to build your network and establish yourself as a thought leader every day. This will bring you business if you work for yourself, and it also prepares you to receive new opportunities if your job goes the way of the pay-phonebooth manufacturers (just where *does* Clark Kent change into Superman these days?).

But that doesn't mean there isn't a place for company profiles on LinkedIn because there is, and it's a very important area to get to know. In the Companies section, you can promote your own company or the company you work for and provide an entertaining, multimedia display of information. You can also use the Companies area as one of the most powerful prospecting and information tools you will ever use to seek out new business, find new opportunities, stay up to speed on your industry, and—if you're job hunting—locate the perfect position.

Creating an Engaging Company Page

Let's talk first about the benefits of creating a company page for your enterprise. To get your company profile started, go to the Companies page by clicking on *Interests > Companies* on the top toolbar. This will take you to the Companies home page, where you can begin the process by clicking on the *Add a company* link on the far right (see Figure 10-1). You'll be taken to a page where you enter your company name and company email address. Note that you cannot use an email web service address like Gmail or Outlook (Hotmail); it has to be a company address such as Hulk@TheClobberingCompany.com.

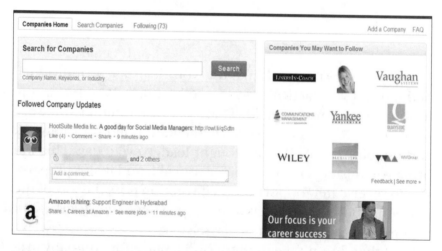

Figure 10-1. On the Companies home page, you will see a text box for searching for company pages, and over on the far right a blue hyperlink that says "Add a Company," which will take you to the "Add a Company" form.

What if you haven't registered with LinkedIn using your company email address? It's simple enough to add. Remember, you can associate as many email addresses as you like with your personal LinkedIn account. To add your company email address to your profile, simply click on your picture in the upper right of any screen and select *Review* next to Privacy & Settings in the drop-down menu. Click on the *Change/Add* hyperlink next to Primary Email in the upper left. This will bring up the *Add & change email addresses* box, where you can add your company email address; then click the blue *Close* button.

Now, back to setting up your company page. Once you are finished adding your company to the site, you will get a message from LinkedIn to check your company email inbox to confirm your identity. Then once you click on the link LinkedIn sends you, you're approved, and you can start to fill in your company profile. These are some of things you will want to add:

- **Company type.** Here you will state whether it's a public company, a partnership, a privately held company, or something else.
- **Company size.** Select from "myself only" to "10,001+."
- **Company website address.** Add your company's website here, and don't forget the http://.
- **Main company industry.** Select your industry from the drop-down menu.
- **Company operating status.** List your company's status. The options are: Operating, Operating subsidiary, Reorganizing, Acquired, or Out of Business.
- **Year founded.** When did your company begin operating? List it here.
- **Company locations.** Here you can list five different locations.
- **Image.** Add a picture that represents your company using a PNG, JPEG, or GIF file up to 2 megabytes.
- **Logo.** Add a standard logo (100 by 60 pixels) and a square logo (50 by 50 pixels) for use in network status updates.
- **Company description.** Tell the world in general terms what it is your company can do and how you can help them.
- **Company specialties.** Here you can zero in on specific things your company does.

When you've completed this page, click the blue *Publish* button in the upper right. Don't refresh the page or leave the page before clicking *Publish* or you will lose all your hard work!

Adding Details About Your Company

When you are done filling in the information, click *Publish*, and your company page is live. When you look at your company's page, you will see four tabs across the top: Home, Products & Services, Insights, and Analytics (see Figure 10-2). The Home page will show you all the information you added, a text box for adding a company status update, a list of your recent company updates, and two buttons: *Follow* and *Edit*. When people land on your page and click *Follow*, they will be able to keep up-to-date with changes happening at your company. When you click on *Edit*, LinkedIn provides a drop-down menu with options to edit the page, add a product or service, view analytics about your page followers and page views, or add job listings. Note that you can add job listings to your company page only if you have bought an optional company subscription that adds a Careers tab to your page (see Figure 10-2).

On the Products & Services tab, you can add your company products by clicking on the *Edit* button and choosing *Add product or service*. On this page, you choose whether it's a product or service, and then you can add the following:

- The category of product or service
- The product or service name
- An image
- A description
- A list of key features
- A disclaimer
- The website for the product or service
- Company employees on LinkedIn who can answer questions
- A special promotion
- A YouTube video

Figure 10-2. The company page you create will have four tabs across the top. There is also a text box for creating a company status update, a button that allows others to follow your company, and a button leading to your page administration tools. An optional *Careers* tab is available with a paid subscription.

This section is a great way to drive traffic to your site or sites. You will want to add the hyperlinks where you want people to go when they click images. You can add up to three images (640 by 220 pixels) and hyperlinks, and LinkedIn will create a rotating spotlight module (or carousel) to display on your company page. When you are done adding a product or service, click *Publish* to save your work.

To check and see how it looks, go back to your Products & Services tab and review your work. You now have the opportunity to request recommendations from your connections for each product or service you listed. Under each listing, you will see a hyperlink that says *Request recommendations.*

Just as you should seek out as many personal recommendations as you can, you should also ask for recommendations for the products and services you offer. When you click on the link, you will get a text box you can use to ask for recommendations from your LinkedIn contacts. The more social proof you have for your company, the better, and these recommendations will be seen by anyone considering purchasing products and services from your company.

A note on the recommendation box: as always, LinkedIn gives you a prewritten subject line and request, but I suggest you customize everything you do on this site. So erase what they give you, and write something personal to the people you are approaching. Remember, you are asking them to take time out from their busy day to help you; the least you can do is personalize your request.

Going back to our toolbar, you will next see Insights. On this page, you will find former employees you may know, similar companies that other visitors to your page have viewed, and the most recommended employee profiles.

Finally, on the Analytics tab, you will find statistics including how many followers you have and their demographics, how many people saw your company status updates, and how your company compares to others.

Create your company page, and you will have one more corner of the web in which to promote your business and educate your prospective clients. Just like a website, it can be a multimedia extravaganza; but it's better than a website because you can add social proof in the form of recommendations from your connections, and readers can click through and see who is recommending you. Anyone can make up quotes for a website (not YOU, of course). Company page recommendations are from real people whose profiles can be accessed, making it very powerful.

Creating a Company Status Update

According to LinkedIn, there are over 3 million company pages, and half of all members are following companies. So how can you create engagement with customers, prospects, and potential employees? LinkedIn allows you to create company status updates for this purpose so that company pages have the same functionality as Facebook business pages.

Company status updates are posts you can make to share anything from company news to product releases to promotions to relevant industry articles. Company posts can be seen on your company's Home tab by any LinkedIn member. Anyone who follows your company will see the posts directly on their home page.

All LinkedIn members have the ability to view posts, click on embedded links, or view videos. They can also comment, like, or share a post. Company status updates will enable you or anyone you have assigned as administrator of your company page to post updates up to 500 characters in length to the Home tab of their pages.

To create a company status update, the first thing you need to do is correctly affiliate yourself with the company. In order to do that, after you have created a company page on LinkedIn, you must update your LinkedIn personal profile to reflect that you are currently working at the company.

The way you do that is to click on *Profile > Edit Profile,* go to your Experience section, and click on *Edit* above the position that correlates to the company page you just created. On the Edit Position page, click on *Change Company* next to your company's name. Then begin typing the company name in the correct text box. LinkedIn will display all the companies that have pages as you type, so select your company from the options they provide. Click on the *Update* button to save your changes. In doing so, your profile will be synched to your company page.

When you are correctly affiliated, you will see a little note card icon that looks like a sticky note next to your company name on your LinkedIn profile in the Experience section. When you hover your mouse over it, your company information will appear in a dialogue box.

Once you start creating status updates, you will be able to see impressions and engagement on each update on the Analytics tab of your company page (*impressions* gives you the number of views, while *engagement* counts likes, clicks, and shares). Of course, the more company followers you have, the better because it means you are getting more exposure.

So, make sure to work on getting followers by publicizing the page regularly in your LinkedIn profile status updates, in your email newsletters, in your email signature, and in any other client communications. Cross-promote your page by linking it to your LinkedIn groups, Facebook page, Twitter feed, and your company website.

Company Page Success Story: Getting a Massive Number of Leads

One of the strategies you can follow is to turn your LinkedIn company page into a traffic-generating machine, the way that HubSpot has done. The inbound marketing software company has loaded its Products tab with valuable resources for visitors. When you click on a free product that you would like, you are prompted to enter your email address, and then you receive your free goodies. HubSpot features a wide variety of free content for LinkedIn users, which helps HubSpot by filling its sales pipeline with quality leads.

I caught up with Kipp Bodnar, HubSpot's VP of marketing, and I asked him to share his strategy with you to help you build your own lead-generating company page.

Q. Kip, what was your strategy as you built your LinkedIn company page?

A. Inbound marketing's bottom line is to get found online through great content, and we keep that principle top of mind across all of HubSpot's marketing efforts. We built our LinkedIn company page to help generate new leads to HubSpot with the same approach we use to attract new visitors across all our platforms: through valuable content.

LinkedIn is a perfect avenue for a B2B company like HubSpot to syndicate content because these leads are generally business oriented and marketing savvy, making them more qualified than audiences on other social platforms. For this reason, we also share more advanced content on LinkedIn. If you visit HubSpot's LinkedIn company page, you'll find our Home tab full of blog posts, e-books, templates, webinars, and SlideShares updated every few hours to keep our 63,000+ followers engaged and to direct new page visitors to http://www.HubSpot.com.

We've set up Hubspot's Products tab to capture leads with 16 different HubSpot offers, including free trials of our software, e-books, and a free inbound marketing assessment. These offers feature detailed descriptions, LinkedIn user reviews, and a link to a HubSpot form where the user can provide his or her email address to get free content. The Products tab delivers high-quality leads into our sales funnel because we feature offers here that appeal to leads familiar with and already somewhat interested in HubSpot.

Q. How do you handle fulfillment and follow-up with the LinkedIn professionals who enter your sales pipeline from the page?

A. At HubSpot, we believe every touch point that a visitor, lead, prospect, or customer has with a company should be personalized and valuable. Once qualified leads from LinkedIn fill out a form on a HubSpot landing page to download an offer, they are entered into a nurturing campaign that matches their interests. The nurturing content these leads receive is personalized based on the offer they converted on and the fact that they are active on LinkedIn. For example, if leads from LinkedIn download an e-book on mastering Facebook marketing, they'll be entered into a workflow to receive intermediate to advanced social media content because they expressed a preference for that type of content. Knowing that leads came from LinkedIn gives us more context to offer them more relevant and valuable information that they can actually use.

Q. How would you compare the leads from your LinkedIn company page to other sources?

A. In HubSpot's *2013 State of Inbound Marketing* report, we found that 43 percent of marketers had acquired a customer through LinkedIn. Why is this percentage higher for LinkedIn than for other social platforms? LinkedIn audiences are generally more qualified leads because the platform is business oriented, so it attracts B2B audiences who are already familiar with your industry and maybe even your company.

LinkedIn may not provide as large a volume of visitors as Twitter or Facebook, but quality trumps quantity here, as the majority of engaged LinkedIn followers are further down the sales cycle. LinkedIn leads are more inbound marketing savvy and have a better grasp on how HubSpot can be a business solution before even talking to a sales rep, making their journey through our sales cycle easier.

Q. What kind of results are you seeing from your page?

A. We're excited about the LinkedIn community's response to HubSpot's content and offerings on LinkedIn. Our company page has 63,000+ followers, and we see new visitors engaging every single day. We're always analyzing which type of content performs best and how to make our page a useful resource for followers and new visitors to keep growing opportunities.

Q. What advice would you give to other companies who are developing a new company page or seeking to improve their existing page?

A. Here are a few tips that helped us build HubSpot's LinkedIn page into an engaging, lead-generating machine:

- **Show your content, then explain.** I'm surprised at how many companies I see not taking advantage of images on their LinkedIn page. It's easy to add thumbnail images of your offerings to make your feed more visual and enticing. Our team at HubSpot designs each tab's cover photo to stay on-brand across http://www .HubSpot.com, our blog, and our other social platforms. A company should communicate a consistent look and feel across channels, and using images on LinkedIn is a great way to really own your LinkedIn presence.
- **Don't use LinkedIn just for human resources.** LinkedIn is a professional social media network, so it's not a surprise that a lot of companies will focus their efforts on this platform on recruiting and networking. It's helpful

to remember that LinkedIn can be a lead-generating vehicle as well as an HR tool, so sharing helpful content should be a key component in your LinkedIn strategy. Take advantage of the Products tab to feature some of your top performing content.

- **Keep them coming back.** LinkedIn isn't a once-and-done deal. You have to give your followers a reason to visit your page frequently. We post new content to HubSpot's LinkedIn feed every few hours to keep our audience engaged. Come up with a schedule that works for your business to share fresh content with your followers.

Making Your Company Page Exciting

Once you start promoting your company page, you are going to want to make it an inviting place for your customers, prospects, potential partners, and employees to visit. That means continually updating it with great information. Here are some ideas to get you going:

- **Build out your tabs.** Fully develop your Home and Products & Services tabs, and optimize each one with keywords. This will improve your page's ranking in Google and LinkedIn search results, which will increase the reach of your company profile.
- **Promote your products.** On the Products & Services tab, add descriptions and videos for each of your products. The shining example for creating a rich user experience on its company page is Hewlett-Packard (HP), the giant technology company. HP has over 1.4 million followers on its page, and if you look at its Products & Services tab, you will see how visually inviting it is. This was the first company to cross over the 1 million followers mark, so it's worth learning from HP. Visit the company's page to see all that is possible to do to leverage this free advertising medium.

- **Get social on your company page.** Allow users to make recommendations on your Products & Services tab in order to provide social proof and make it interesting to read. Again, look at all the products HP has listed along with the recommendations.
- **Add video testimonials.** For every product you add, you can add a link to a YouTube video. On the Products & Services tab, click on *Edit.* This is a great place to add a video of a client talking about why he or she recommends the product.

Take time to create a LinkedIn company page and turn it into another form of communications with your prospects and clients. Use it as a traffic-generating machine, and expand the reach and presence of your company. It's an amazing free resource that you could be using right now to augment all your other marketing efforts.

Prospecting for Business Using the Companies Section

Let's turn from promoting your own company to using this feature to rapidly fill your sales pipeline full of qualified buyers. Basically, if you sell to companies, then the Companies section is your new best friend. As anyone who has ever picked up a phone and made a cold call knows, it's an appropriate name. Often the reception you get on the other end is "frosty," and I don't mean the famous jolly snowman.

What if you had an introduction to the person you want to meet? What if you could get to know people in the department you want to sell into who could turn you on to the person you really need to talk to? Enter LinkedIn Companies.

Select *Interests > Companies* from the top toolbar, and you'll be on the Companies home page. Type the name of the company you are targeting in the Search for Companies box, and you will be directed to that company's page. Let's say I search for Apple. I get taken to the Apple company page, and I see the company description, but what I'm really interested in is on the right-hand side, where I see that there are 61,863 Apple employees in my network.

That breaks down to 9 first-level connections and 6,678 second-level connections; the rest are fellow group members and third-level connections. So overall, I can reach out to any of the 61,000 employees in my network through InMail (which costs money unless you have a premium account); I can send them a direct message if they are first-level connections or members of groups I'm in; or I can reach them through introductions if they are second- or third-level connections.

Contacting People at Your Target Company

The first thing I might do is see which first-level contacts I can reach for free. I would read their profiles and get to know them a little bit better. Then I could send them a direct message introducing myself and asking them if they could steer me to the right person I need to talk to at Apple (or whichever company I'm targeting).

The next thing I can do is look to see who are my second- and third-level connections. If I want to reach one of them without spending an InMail, I can click on a person's profile and look on the bottom for the groups that we share. If we share a group, you will see a check mark and *Member* under the group name. I can click on the group's name, which is a hyperlink, and then when I arrive at the group, I can click on the number of people in the group in the header (*20,000*, for example). That takes me to the members page, where I can search for that employee by typing her name into the search box. When I see the person I want, I click on *Send Message* beneath her name, and I'm ready to reach out to her.

I might begin the message by introducing myself, explaining that we share a group, and asking for some information about her, her department, or her company. Always ask for information first . . . never sell first on the first contact. You are fact-finding at this point, so work on building a relationship.

If the person you want to reach has a premium account and is a member of OpenLink, then you can message him for free. And you could also use the InMail system if you buy InMails or have a premium account.

Using Introductions for Prospecting

What if you are trying to sell into a department and you have no first-level connections in that department? Then you move on to second-level connections. At Apple, I have 6,678 second-level connections. That's a lot, and you might come up with a smaller number for the company you are targeting. Either way, I can look through all my second-level connections and find either just the person I'm looking for or at least one who works in the right department.

Let's say I want to reach John Smith, a second-level connection. First I'll see if we share a group so I can message him directly. But let's say we don't share any groups. Then I need to use the introduction feature, and here's how.

Under John's name there is a hyperlink that says *20 shared connections* (or whatever the number is). This is how we are connected—we have first-level connections in common, so I have a lot to choose from. I click on the link to look at all the first-level connections we have in common. I scan the list and pick the person I'm familiar with. Then I go to the information box on John's profile and click on the drop-down menu on the gray button that says *Send John an InMail.* I will see the *Get Introduced* link, click on it to reveal the Introduction Request form, pick a connection, and begin the process outlined in Chapter 8.

This way I'm getting a warm introduction to John Smith. It's not guaranteed that your introduction will go through. But if the first-level connection is someone you know and your request is sincere, chances are good that the person will forward your introduction.

So, first-level connections, second levels, and group members can all be approached . . . it's just a question of creating a strategy of identifying the people you want to meet. Third-level connections can also be approached, but it's harder to do, since the introduction has to go through two people. There are also InMails and OpenLink messages to use as part of the process of prospecting. Try everything, and remember to ask for information and establish a connection before promoting anything.

Leveraging Company Information

In addition to providing connections to a target company and finding the right person to talk to, the Companies section gives you valuable product and company knowledge that you can use when researching them prior to contacting a staffer there (see Figure 10-3).

Figure 10-3. The Company page offers a rich source of information for anyone prospecting for new clients, doing research on a potential employer, or keeping tabs on a competitor.

Using HP as an example, if I'm on the HP LinkedIn company page, on the Home tab I can view the Recent Updates section and discover up-to-the-minute happenings at the company. Anytime something happens at a company, it can reveal new needs and new pains you can address. That's why you want to read up on what's happening with your target company so you can make a well-informed first approach. This type of selling, known as *consultative selling*, works better than just using a canned sales pitch for every company you approach. Knowing what's happening at a target company *right now* sets you apart from other salespeople and improves your chances for success.

The next thing I recommend you do is review the products and services of the company. So, if I'm on HP's page, I will go to its *Products & Services* tab and read up on the 19 areas in which it offers products and services for sale, and watch the accompanying videos. No company today will appreciate an ill-informed sales representative or job candidate. If you walk into a meeting today where you are selling something and you say, "Tell me a little bit about your company," at best you will turn them off . . . and you might just be shown the door. Before you visit or call a company, research its products and services on its company page to see where your products, services, or expertise might be able to assist it.

Follow That Company

If you have identified a company you wish to sell to, join as an employee, or simply keep updated on (that is, it is a big industry player or competitor), LinkedIn gives you an option to follow that company and keep up with any news or changes happening there.

On the right side of every company page is a yellow button that says *Follow*. Click on it, and you've updated your personal profile status automatically. This will show up on the home page of all your first-level connections.

Once you do this, the button turns gray and indicates *Following*. Now anytime that company creates a status update, it will show up in the feed on your home page. This is a great way to stay up-to-date with happenings at that company, including events it is sponsoring, new product launches, job opportunities, and management changes.

Another option for looking at the status updates of companies you are following is to go to the top toolbar and click on *Interests > Companies*, which will take you to the Companies home page. On this page, you will see *Followed Company Updates,* which displays updates from the companies you are following as they come in live. You are allowed to follow up to 1,000 companies, so if you are following a lot, as I do, you will see quite a mix of updates here—everything from a video tour of company offices, to a free e-book download, to a company's open positions around the country.

Along the top of the Companies home page, you will see a tab that says Following( ) with the number of companies you are following in parentheses. Click on this to bring up the complete list of companies you are following. This very handy page keeps all the companies you are following in one neat place for you, so you can scan them all at once and add or delete ones according to your needs. From this list, you can click on an individual company you are following and go right to its page to read all its updates.

In addition, LinkedIn provides a suggestion tool on the right side called *Companies You May Want To Follow,* which offers companies for you to follow that are similar to your current selections. Click on any of the company logos to go right to their company pages.

Using Company Pages to Create Opportunities

The Companies section is a data-rich area where you can create tremendous opportunities. There is an unlimited number of ways to use this area to enrich your professional goals. For example, you can do any of the following:

- Find, get to know, and target company employees you wish to connect with.
- Follow companies you want to sell to.
- Follow companies you may be thinking of acquiring, merging with, or partnering with.
- Identify windows of opportunity by reading the latest news about companies.
- Find ways to approach a company when it hires or promotes people.

- Use the section as a job-hunting tool by following potential employers in your area—or where you want to relocate to.
- Research competitors in your industry, and get a leg up by seeing everything that is going on there.
- Follow previous employers to keep up-to-date on your colleagues.
- Stay current in your field by following the leading companies in your industry.
- Follow vendors that supply you with products, and learn what is new and exciting that you may wish to get involved with.
- Follow your customers to make sure you know what they are up to, so you will be aware of their signals that indicate it might be a good time for you to penetrate their business with more offerings or that indicate they are searching for a new supplier.
- Look for updates you can use as talking points and relationship builders to reach out to your connections at companies.
- Follow companies that are influencing current events so you stay ahead of the curve.
- Follow start-ups and learn from their successes and challenges.

*　*　*

It's a great idea to create a robust company page, update it often, and use it as a powerful way to connect with your customers and prospects. If you market to companies, follow the companies you want to sell to and use their company pages to gain insights and connections that would not be possible any other way. The information and contacts you discover will put you light-years ahead of your competition.

Now let's look at one of the most powerful uses of LinkedIn, which many on the "outside" (not a LinkedIn insider like you!) still believe is the only function of the site—namely, finding the perfect career. You will find that LinkedIn is the indispensable tool for landing your next job.

Chapter 11: Off to Work We Go: Finding Your Perfect Job

When it comes to the job-hunting game, I've sat on both sides of the table as a job seeker and as a hiring manager in corporate America. So I know that job hunting is never going to be fun or glamorous, nor will it be something we will undertake if we have a better option, like winning the lottery or discovering we are related to Rockefeller or Gates.

Still, it's a part of life that will always be with us and that we must master. Navigating the twists and turns, the ups and downs, the straightaways, and the dead ends—that's what it's all about. Riding a roller coaster is about the best metaphor I can conjure up for job hunting—it's scary and exciting, and you are relieved at the end.

If you are currently looking for work, or you if you are working and want to keep your finger on the pulse of the job market to see what else is out there, you simply must be using Linked-In. A survey released by recruitment software firm Jobvite in 2012 revealed that out of 1,000 human resources professionals polled, 93 percent were using LinkedIn to source top talent. It far outdistanced other social sites mentioned in the survey as a talent source (Facebook was used by 66 percent, and Twitter by 54 percent).

LinkedIn is counting on that recruiter business, and it has created many resources for headhunters to ensure that LinkedIn is doing everything it can to be the number one job source. LinkedIn offers special recruiter membership levels and the ability to place paid job listings. It sells a service, LinkedIn Recruiter, that enables hiring managers and HR pros to find, track, and stay in touch with potential hires and candidates. Recruiters are key to the LinkedIn business model. In 2013 professional recruitment solutions made up 56 percent of LinkedIn's revenue, with advertising and subscriptions making up the rest.

Whether recruiters use the services LinkedIn markets to them, whether they post paid listings, or whether they just monitor discussions in the LinkedIn groups to meet candidates—it's the place they go first. Logically, it makes sense for recruiters and hiring managers to turn to LinkedIn first to check out the profiles and search through the groups for experts. With over 300 million profiles to select from, recruiters can attract the job hunters searching for a position as well as the coveted satisfied employees they'd love to attract away to a new opportunity.

So, yes, recruiters are as thick on LinkedIn as flies on honey. They are there looking for you, and you can reach out to them. You can be proactive and search for recruiters using the Advanced People Search. Select *People* from the drop-down menu in the center, and click on *Advanced* to the right of the magnifying glass. Typing *recruiter* into the *Title* search box and using the *Keywords* box to enter your area of expertise will enable you to find recruiters specializing in your field whom you can approach about potential opportunities. You can also find them geographically by filling in the Postal Code box.

When you write to recruiters on LinkedIn, don't be shy. Remember, they are there to meet you. Carefully read their profile to ensure that they really do recruit talent in your industry, and then write a polite note, something like this: "Hi, I see you are a recruiter in my field. I have extensive experience in my industry, and I'd like to get on the phone with you for a few minutes to talk about some of your searches to see if there might be a match with what I am looking for."

Remember that recruiters are essentially sales professionals, so don't be discouraged if the ones you contact don't all respond. It just might be that they don't have any jobs right now on their desk that match your qualifications—and without the proper financial incentive, they won't be reaching out to you. But what if you use a tried-and-true approach that works so well elsewhere on LinkedIn, namely, offering help? Turn the tables by not asking them to help you, but rather by offering to be a valuable resource to them in filling the jobs they are working hard to source.

You could write: "Hi, I see that you are a recruiter in my industry. I have a very deep network in my field, and I may be able to help you with one of your searches. Would you like to get on the phone for 10 minutes and see if there is anyone I know who would be great for one of your searches?" In this way, you present yourself as someone who can help make them more money (always a powerful motivator to get someone on the phone!). When you speak to the recruiter, you are creating the start of a relationship that may at some point help you in your job search.

Reaching out to and building relationships with the plethora of recruiters on LinkedIn is certainly one way to go. But before you even do that, the first step is to ensure that your profile is 100 percent complete and optimized using the tips in earlier chapters. Next, make sure you've invited all your previous managers to be first-level connections. That way you can request recommendations for your profile and also seek them out easily for leads and help with your job search. That includes past colleagues as well; make sure you invite as many of them as you can to be first-level connections so you have a solid network to call upon for help and posting recommendations to your profile.

Why LinkedIn Crushes Job Boards

If you are like most job hunters—and I know this from personal experience when I was job hunting—you spend hours a day searching the job boards. And while job boards should be part of your strategy, there are so many reasons to shift your focus to making LinkedIn your primary job search site. Here are just a few of the reasons why LinkedIn is superior:

- **You can build your brand.** On LinkedIn, you can build your brand as the go-to person in your field by constantly updating your profile and adding documents and presentations to it, getting recommendations, and participating in groups. Branding is so key to your job search that I will dive into the whole subject of "self-branding" in just a little while.

- **You can update your status often.** You can let your entire network know that you are job hunting simply by updating your status on your home page. With one post, you can let your network of millions of people know that you are looking by talking about a job fair you went to or a great informational interview you just had.

- **You can network easily with people in your field.** Statistically, 60 percent of job hunters find their job through networking. LinkedIn lets you find a job using networking because it takes networking to a much more in-depth level. Through the People Search and in the groups and companies features, you can identify and connect with those who can help you find a job. As they say, "It's not what you know, but who you know." Use all your connections—first level, second level, third level, and fellow group members—to reach the person who is hiring.

- **You can gain credibility.** More than just a résumé posted on a job board, your LinkedIn profile lives side-by-side with all the activities that support the expertise you say you have—for example, your participation in discussions throughout LinkedIn.

- **Recruiters can find you by your abilities.** When you apply for a job, chances are good that the recruiter will Google you, just as you would a potential employer.

Search engines favor information from social media and LinkedIn in particular, so if you have an optimized profile, it will be found on the first page of Google results when your name is searched on, giving you an advantage over non-LinkedIn users.

- **You can socialize with other people.** Looking for a job can be lonely, especially if you just pore over job boards every day. LinkedIn is a living, breathing community of business professionals where you can make connections for career advancement, read business advice from your peers, and share your insights with others. This makes LinkedIn a community of like-minded people . . . a place where job hunting is not a boring solitary task.

- **You can get immediate answers.** With a job board, you submit your résumé and wait. And wait. And wait. On LinkedIn, you can find worthwhile connections—people in your target company or people who might refer you to hiring managers—and message them and often get a response right back.

- **You can get your foot in the door.** With LinkedIn, you can request and arrange informational interviews by contacting people in your network who work at your target company. If the meeting goes well, they are likely to keep you in mind when a job opens or steer you toward an opportunity they know about. Remember that most positions are never posted anywhere: in fact, a *CNN Money* article states that 80 percent of all jobs are not posted. That means the majority of jobs are filled by referrals. So the more people you can meet and interact with, the better a position you will be in when a job comes up matching your talents. That's why it makes sense to try to set up calls or short meetings with hiring managers at your target companies on LinkedIn whether they currently have an opening or not.

- **You have global access to jobs.** Many job boards focus on an industry or a region. LinkedIn is worldwide.

The reason why LinkedIn is superior to job boards was explained by personal branding author Dan Schawbel in an essay he contributed to *Dancing with Digital Natives* by Michelle Manafy and Heidi Gautschi (CyberAge Books, 2011), a book about the generation that grew up using the Internet:

> The web has broken down hierarchies and connected everyone in disperse networks, so that you can reach individual employees directly at companies you want to work for, without applying through job boards. . . . The best method for companies, candidates, and recruiters to connect remains networking, according to ExecuNet, which found that just 10 percent of open executive-level positions are publicly posted online (*ExecuNet's 2010 Executive Job Market Intelligence Report,* April 2010). That number will probably drop to zero in five years. If you are looking for a job at any level today, it's time to follow the digital native's lead and start using those social networking sites you thought you were too old to join.

Cracking the Hidden Job Market

It's important to expand your thinking about what kind of job opportunities are out there for you. I like to think that there are three different kinds of opportunities: (1) jobs that are not posted but exist in the hidden job market I mentioned above (which is fully 80 percent of the available jobs); (2) jobs that don't exist yet and must be suggested or "pointed out" to a target company; and (3) traditional job postings such as those you see on job boards. Let's tackle the first category: those hidden jobs.

Now, just why is there such an enormous hidden job market? Why doesn't every company post every job and make it that much easier for you? In order to find the answer, you need to put yourself in the shoes of the employers. Walk a mile in their moccasins, so to speak. As an example, I'll use my own experience as a hiring manager in Silicon Valley.

If it becomes clear that my marketing department needs a fantastic new graphic designer, for example, I do not immediately pick up the red Hotline phone on my desk that goes to a recruiter or to a salesperson at a job board. Instead, I'll do something that will benefit my company (because I like my job and want to keep it): I'll reduce risk and save money by looking for a referral.

First, I'll ask everyone inside and outside the company if they know a great designer. I may even institute an employee referral program that pays out cold, hard cash to the employee that brings in the new talent. This will reduce the risk of a bad hire because the new employee will be a proven quantity . . . not just someone off the street. And I'll save thousands by not hiring a recruiter or posting an expensive ad. By making a qualified hire who hits the ground running and does amazing work, while saving cash in the process, I'll look like a real star.

I'll go with this referral method for a few months. If for some reason my internal and external networks come up dry, I might bite the bullet and start paying LinkedIn, Monster, CareerBuilder, or some other job board to post the job. I may reach out and send a job order to my friendly neighborhood recruiter. If I do so, note that it has been *months* since I first got the idea to hire someone for my department, and thus this job has been hidden from the world.

Now, throw in the rather challenging economic times we've been going through lately, when it's more important than ever for companies to conserve funds, and multiply this little fable by millions of hiring managers, supervisors, directors—and you get the hidden job market. The corporate world simply wants to save money and reduce risk when it hires (and save the time and hassle involved in making an error by bringing onboard—then ditching—someone who looked like a super-hero on paper but turned out be the evil twin of Doctor Octopus). The hidden job market is real, and so you need to adjust the way you look for work.

Turning Your Job Search into a Marketing Campaign

With this new reality, job seekers are being called on to transition from being simply readers of job ads to self-marketers. In order to be a self-marketer, you need to first undertake self-branding and (gulp!) *sell yourself!* If selling yourself is strange and unfamiliar to you as a job seeker, believe me, you are not alone. I have coached thousands of job seekers who thought that just being an expert in whatever field they were in should be good enough to land a great job. "What about all the education I have? The degrees? The years of experience?" they say to me. "*Now* I have to learn *sales?*"

I know. It's not fair. I worked with one gentleman recently, teaching him how to use LinkedIn to market himself, and this man was literally a rocket scientist. He built the rockets that took our brave astronauts into space on the space shuttles, but as you know, our space program is on the wane and he was forced out of his NASA job. As I explained the importance of self-branding and self-marketing to him, I could almost hear his poor brain screaming in revolt: "But I built the rockets that went into space, for goodness sake!"

So you're not alone if you violently recoil at the thought of self-marketing. Fortunately, you have an amazing tool—LinkedIn—to use in this process, and you are going to market yourself just as one would market a product on LinkedIn. So let's get started, shall we? First, before we log onto LinkedIn, let's understand branding. You know about Coke, Apple, and Nike; they are all brands that create some kind of feeling, some kind of association in your mind when you hear or read the names. Thanks to the miracle of million-dollar ad budgets and word of mouth, you know that when you pick up a Coke, you are going to open happiness; that when you walk into an Apple Store and pick up a mini iPad, you will feel cool and hip; and when you tie on your Nike sneakers, you will feel like a rugged, champion athlete waking at the crack of dawn to punish your body.

In much the same way, you need to create a brand for yourself that you can then market on LinkedIn. The process, called *self-branding,* is described beautifully and in great detail by Catherine Kaputa in her book, *You Are a Brand* (Nicholas Brealey Publishing, 2012):

> Creating positive impressions in the minds of other people is the work of self-branding. It used to be about "Can you do the job?" Now, many people can do what you do. So it has to be about something more. Above all, branding is a strategic process. The goal is to provide that something more that will help you succeed in a highly competitive business environment (and to be authentic and even to enjoy yourself in the process).

So how do you stand out? How do you create a brand for yourself that makes marketing yourself on LinkedIn a snap? One that differentiates you from others and makes you the one, the only, the indisputable candidate for the position? Basically, it means thinking about yourself in ways that you never have in the past; it means looking at yourself as a product that will fulfill a company's needs (by "needs," I mean skills like building market share, reducing expenses, raising profits, inventing cool new stuff, and so on). It starts with self-exploration and answering these questions:

- **What's your brand idea?** This is what are you all about, your *unique selling proposition* (USP) that sets you apart from others. Another way to say it is: What's your different idea?
- **What's your brand promise?** This is the value that you bring to a business and to your customers (that is, your "customers" as your managers, clients, coworkers, and others).
- **What are your strengths?** These are the abilities you have that you can capitalize on. This is your authentic self.

- **What do you stand for?** You need to define yourself, or you risk someone else doing it for you.
- **What have you achieved?** Now is not the time to be bashful. Looking at your accomplishments and having them ready at the tip of your tongue will make marketing yourself easier.
- **What's your story?** You can't influence people to hire you or help you with your job search if you bore them. Now is the time to gather up your stories to add emotion and drama to your brand promise: how you came back against the odds, how you turned the corner on a difficult project, how you succeeded when others turned back. Sell yourself with a story worthy of a Hollywood treatment.
- **How are you memorable?** Your goal is to be top of mind (TOM) with hiring managers and staffers at places you want to work. Just as Coke wants to grab mind share, you also want to be so memorable to your connections that they dream about you.
- **How are you packaging your brand?** What's your self-presentation? You need to effectively convey your value online through a superb LinkedIn profile and offline through a professional appearance and demeanor.

Take some time and record your answers. You are going to need this information to market yourself on LinkedIn. With so much competition for great jobs, it's a war out there, and these answers are your ammunition. Also, when you are devouring the news on your iPad or TV, tune your antennae to the world of branding and self-promotion, and watch how celebrities have this act down cold. Music stars and movie celebs know how to get attention and be memorable. I realize you won't want to swing on a wrecking ball sans clothing in a music video à la Miley Cyrus or wear a meat dress à la Ms. Gaga, but the *principle* is the same: stand for something!

Acing the Informational Interview

With 80 percent of jobs being filled by referrals and networking, the work of the active job seeker is to become a marketer, meaning you must *get the word out about yourself!* With over 300 million professionals on LinkedIn, many of whom are hiring managers or who are working at your dream company, there are a great many people you can approach to start the conversation about your job search. And if you've done your self-branding exercises above, you've got a fairly good idea about the product you are selling. You know your worth and your brand promise.

Now comes the time to network on LinkedIn and set up informational interviews with those who are in a position to hire you or who know where the good jobs are. You can use the Advanced People Search, you can meet people in the LinkedIn groups, and you can use the search capabilities on the group member pages to find two excellent sources for your interviews: (1) hiring managers and (2) what I call *internal advocates.* These are people working at companies where you'd give up a year's worth of Ring Dings and *Dancing with the Stars* just to hang your hat.

Here is the strategy for nailing down an informational interview on LinkedIn. I want to stress that this interview is really a conversation. It's a chance for you to find out more about the company, to see if it's the right place for you, and ideally, to make a friend on the inside.

Step 1. Read Her Profile!

Never, never, never (is that clear enough?) write to someone on LinkedIn requesting a conversation without first digesting at least some of her profile. First, you can't write a targeted message without knowing the person you are writing to; and second, why bypass all that rich information? Many people have put a lot of work into their profiles, and that's where you can find out ideas for establishing rapport with your potential conversation mate. Where did she go to school? What jobs has she held in the past? Where did she work? Look for things in common, or at least ways to start off your targeted message.

Step 2. Write Your Targeted Message

It's great to start off with something you have in common, such as a LinkedIn group you both belong to or a charity you both support. Then, you may want to mention something you saw in her profile. This assures your potential target that you did indeed read about her, and it tells her why you picked her out of millions of people to write to.

Your goal is to move the intended target from LinkedIn to a phone call, and be sure to ask for only 10 minutes because we are all busy. This 10-minute call should be about *her*. You are only fact-finding here, not presenting your credentials. Here are some sample scripts.

With **hiring managers**, you can ask for information or advice, or you can offer help. This is an example of asking for *information*:

> Hi, Mr. Smith, I see you work at XYZ. I have always been interested in your company, and I am particularly interested in what you are doing now. Do you have 10 minutes to get on the phone with me so I can ask you a few questions about XYZ?

For *advice*:

> Hi, Ms. Jones, I read your profile, and I think you are doing amazing things at ABC Company. I am very interested in what you do there, and I wonder if you have 10 minutes to get on the phone with me and give me some advice about the kinds of skills and abilities that ABC looks for when hiring people?

To *offer help*:

> Hi, Mr. Blue, I read your profile, and I see that you are
> currently working on a new challenge. I faced such a
> challenge in my last job, and I had great success using a
> certain solution. Can you get on the phone with me for
> 10 minutes so I can tell you about what we did [or: so I can
> tell you about a resource, white paper, or something else]?

With **internal advocates**, that is, people working at the companies you'd like to work for, the best idea is to do some fact-finding. Ask for *information*:

> Hi, Ms. White, I see you work at Acme. I am very interested
> in what Acme is doing in the area of X now. Would you mind
> getting on the phone with me for 10 minutes, so I can ask you
> a few questions?

Step 3. End the Call with Next Steps

Depending on how the call went, you can end it any number of ways that further your job search. If the conversation finds its way to the other person's asking, "So what do you do?" make sure you are prepared with your brand promise that can be said in 30 seconds or less. Then you can ask, "Whom else should I be talking to?" This will lead to more phone calls, conversations, and the all-important networking. For hiring manager calls, you could ask, "Would there be anything open for me?" if the conversation is going really well.

If you make enough of these calls, you will begin to learn more and more about your targeted industry and companies. You'll meet more and more people and find out about places where you can meet IRL (in real life). You'll become an educated job seeker, with contacts and friends on the inside. And most important, you'll find out about jobs that are not posted anywhere.

Remember that everything you do on LinkedIn serves to support your brand and the brand promise you are making during the calls. So make sure your written messages are professional and free of typographical errors; that your profile supports all your claims and accomplishments; and that your updates and group postings demonstrate your industry leadership. Then use the power of LinkedIn to network your way to an exciting new career.

Creating a Job That Does Not Exist

When I was working at Charles Schwab, there was an unwritten rule about getting a promotion that went like this: if you wanted a better job, you had to do it first before you actually had it. You had to prove to the powers that be that you were capable of the new job and that you were excited enough . . . and had enough initiative . . . to do what it took to make it happen.

Let's just say, I got the memo. When I started within Schwab Institutional, the fast-growing department that served financial advisors, I was primarily in a support role. I was in charge of the database of our financial advisor clients. I managed all our mailings, and I wrote and produced the monthly newsletter that went out to our clients. It was decent enough work, but I coveted a marketing manager position.

So I followed the unspoken rule, and I began doing the job while I was holding down my other duties. I came up with several marketing programs designed to increase our business, had my manager sign off on them, and then rolled them out. These included a discount buying program for our clients to enable them to get office equipment cheaply, and a referral program that paid financial advisors to recommend us to others in the money management game. Within a few months, a marketing manager position opened up in a department, and I got the job immediately. I had shown them that I could do the work and that it was what I really wanted.

This unwritten rule about doing the job first also applies to those outside corporate walls. There is no rule that says that all jobs have to have a written job description, and that's a good thing.

You might have a combination of talents and skills that a company does not even know it needs, and you may have the drive, guts, and hustle to make sure the company knows about you.

LinkedIn can be your research database for looking up the kind of information you need to create your own job. Here are some of the ways you might use LinkedIn in combination with the research you are already doing on your target industry through other media and social media websites (you *are* doing research daily on your target industry, right?):

- On LinkedIn, you can easily find the hiring manager in any company you want and present her with your ideas for a new position.
- You can read a hiring manager's profile and ascertain what keeps that hiring manager up at night. What's his biggest problem? Then present yourself as the solution.
- You can scour a target company's LinkedIn page for updates on new ventures you want to be a part of, or new facilities being opened where you can contribute.
- You can do competitive research on companies working in the same field and come up with some new ideas for your target company.

What you need is your dream job and your dream company. Use the self-branding exercises to figure out what you're great at, what you love doing, and where you want to do it, and match up those qualities with companies you find on LinkedIn. Or look for a glaring need that is not being handled—for example, a company needs better PR, a better website, or more presence in a certain type of market. If you can solve a manager's biggest problem, you can get your foot in the door.

The story of Tristan Walker really demonstrates this strategy. A business school graduate in 2009, he was lusting after a job with a hot new start-up in Silicon Valley called Foursquare. He did what we all would do: he applied on the website. But he never heard back. Then he found the CEO's email address on the company's website and sent him a note. He got no response, but he would not give up. He emailed him eight more times. Still, no response.

So what did he do? He began to work for the company as a salesperson. He called up other companies, he told them he was a student, and he asked if they would be interested in advertising on Foursquare. Since it was a new company, he had to explain what Foursquare did. A few of the companies he reached out to agreed to advertise.

Then Walker emailed the CEO a ninth time and told him that he had some advertisers lined up. This time the CEO responded, and they met the next day. And that is how Walker went on to run business development at Foursquare.

As you can see, there are no rules when it comes to job searching. You can make them up as you go along, and you can write your own success story.

Getting the Low-Hanging Fruit

Now that we have looked at job opportunities in the hidden job market, as well as the strategy for creating your own position, let's turn to the familiar standby: the job posting. While it's true that connecting, networking, and sharing are critical to your success on LinkedIn, this does not mean there aren't job listings like the ones on the boards you've come to know and love, because there are. As soon as you log into LinkedIn, the jobs are not far away. In fact, when you go to your LinkedIn home page by clicking on *Home* on the top toolbar, you will see *Jobs You May be Interested in* along the right-hand side. These are jobs that LinkedIn has displayed based on keywords in your profile. Click on the title of the job, and you will be taken to a page with the following information (see Figure 11-1):

- The full job description and write-up about the company
- The name and title of the person posting it, along with a button for sending an InMail to her

- Hyperlinks to the profiles of LinkedIn members you may know who work at the company
- Estimated salary range
- Links to similar jobs
- And a blue button that says *Apply Now* or *Apply on company website*

When you click on the *Apply on company website* button, you are taken to the company's own website where you can fill in your information. If the job has an *Apply Now* button, clicking on it brings up an online application, to which you can add a cover letter and résumé. When you hit *Submit,* all your information, including your LinkedIn profile, is forwarded to the hiring manager in an instant. That's another reason why you need to make sure your profile is fully complete and truly represents your brand and brand promise—it will help you make a great first impression (and you never get a second chance to make a great first impression!).

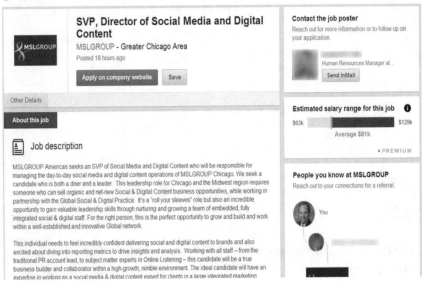

Figure 11-1. A company-paid job listing on LinkedIn provides you with the full description of the job, a button to send an InMail to the recruiter, and a list of your connections who can introduce you to the person posting the job.

Searching Paid Job Listings

After you look at the jobs LinkedIn has served you on a silver platter, you can then click on *Jobs* on the top menu bar and be taken to the Jobs home page. That's where you can type in a keyword just as you would on other job boards and pull up jobs in your field of expertise and in the location you desire.

If you want to refine your search, click on the *Advanced Search* hyperlink under the search box. There you can select criteria including industry, department type, and location. Premium members can also sort by salary ranges. Fill in your criteria, click on the blue button marked *Search*, and you will see your matches. To get even more criteria, click on the hyperlink *More options* to the right of the *Search* button (see Figure 11-2).

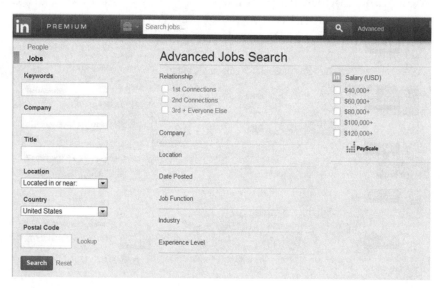

Figure 11-2. The Advanced Jobs Search functions like a job board, allowing you to search through all the paid job listings on the site.

In that sense, LinkedIn can function the way a job board does. But the great thing is the feature I mentioned earlier with which you can see all the people in your network who can connect you to the person posting the job. For example, if I type in "social media" in the keyword section and pick my location, which is Tampa, I get lots of jobs to choose from. So I pick out "senior marketing manager" at a local tech company and click on it. I see the job description, and in this case, 25 people in my network who know the person posting the job. So I can click through and see who might be able to make an introduction for me, thus turning a cold call or a random résumé into a warm call.

I can reach out to any of my connections and ask for an introduction. Also on the job listing page are the names of people in my network who work at the company. I can reach out to them, tell them I saw a job announced at their company, and try to get information on the job that I can use to better position myself to get the interview.

You can gain valuable information by cross-referencing the job with the firm's Company page on LinkedIn. When see you a job that appeals to you on LinkedIn (or another board, for that matter), search for that company by going to *Interests > Companies* in the top toolbar. On the Companies home page, type in the name of the company in the keyword search box. Then when the Company page is displayed, you will see all your connections who work there. Find one who might be able to share with you the "secret" job requirements. Get the inside story on why the job is open and what the company is really looking for in terms of skills. You can also view the profiles of people who work at the company to get a sense of what kind of skills and background the company values.

So, you can do your job searches on the Jobs home page and find connections at that company on the Company page. You can save 10 job searches in the Jobs section. Go back and look at your saved searches every day because you never know when something new will appear.

When you see a job that you want to apply for, click on the *Apply* button, and you'll be taken to a form where you can enter a cover letter and attach your résumé. In some cases, you will be directed to the company's applicant tracking system. Just follow the instructions and apply.

Searching for Jobs in the Companies Section

The company pages will be a great boon to your job search. If you are targeting a certain company, a great strategy is to view its page. Go to the top toolbar, and click on *Interests > Companies* to get to the Companies home page. Type in your target company in the search box and visit its page. There you will get all the updates on the company, including news about the company you can use to your advantage in interviews. You can see who in your network works at the company—valuable information for requesting an informational interview.

There are also job postings. If you click on the *Careers* tab on a company page (most have them, but some won't), you will see all its paid job listings. Using Starbucks as my example, when I click on *Careers* on its company page, I see 71 job listings (see Figure 11-3). If I click on any job headline, I will see a full

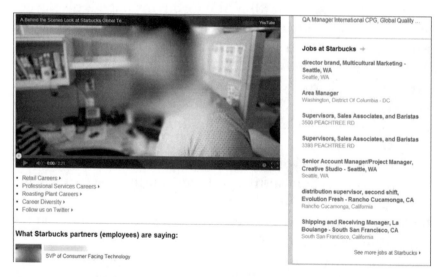

Figure 11-3. Clicking on the Careers tab on a Company page will bring up a list of all its job postings on LinkedIn.

job description and a button I can click on to apply for a job. On the job description page, it also shows me my first-level connections at the company.

Looking for Jobs in Groups

Another place to look for job postings is within LinkedIn Groups. Most groups have a Jobs tab where every member can post a job, and I strongly urge you to take a look at that. Up until this point, you've been looking at paid listings. As a group manager, I know that not every organization wants to shell out the cash for a paid job listing, so they save money by posting in the groups. In my "Tampa Bay Marketing Professionals" group, I get lots of these postings every day. So they are there . . . under the radar. Which may be good for you as a job seeker because fewer people see them than see the paid job listings.

Go to any group you've joined in a field you are interested in, click on the *Jobs* tab, and LinkedIn will take you to the group's jobs page. LinkedIn heavily promotes the paid job listings, so it downplays the free postings, and you will initially see only the paid listings. But the free ones posted by group members are there to the left of the paid listings under *Job discussions*. Click on that hyperlink, and you will see many open jobs. For example, in my Tampa group now, there are 11 posts, including one from a recruiter I know who has listed a multitude of jobs he has open. So, don't overlook this feature; you might even make it a point to join groups in your field so you can get access to their two job boards. Join 50 groups in your field and that gives you 100 targeted job boards to explore.

The difference in finding a job in the groups job area is that you don't have the lists of people in your network displayed who work at that company the way you do when you click on a paid listing. But it's so easy to do research on LinkedIn with company pages and the Advanced People Search that it should not be a problem for you to find connections at any company. There is one advantage to looking at jobs in this section: next to each job is a hyperlink to the profile of the person posting the job. So you can research who the poster is and send him a direct message through the group about your interest in the position.

Turning Your Profile into a Job-Hunting Machine

Let's talk about your profile and go over some job-hunting strategies. Now, put yourself into the shoes of recruiters. They have deadlines and pressure, and the heat is on them to fill the stacks of job requisitions on their desks. They do the easiest thing first: they do a People Search, and they type in the keyword of the skill they need: *HTML coding*, or *Adobe Photoshop*, or *chemical engineer*. The profiles that come up on top are most likely going to get looked at first, and those people will be called first.

That's why it's so important to have a position-ready, optimized profile. First, make sure your profile is complete—your chances of being found will go way up. Next, make sure you have optimized it with the job skills you want to be found for. Be specific—two to three words at most, and make sure that the keywords are in the four crucial places I mentioned in Chapter 6 on optimizing your profile.

Here's a tip: be that recruiter and search for someone to fill a job that you are looking for by going to the Advanced People Search. Click on *People* in the center drop-down menu, then click on *Advanced* on the right. On the next screen, type in your keyword phrase and location and see who comes up. There's your competition for that job. Now look closely at the profiles, and see where the highlighted keywords in yellow appear. At this point, your task is clear: add those keywords in a higher quantity in the exact same places, and guess who will come up number one in that search next time? Yes, you. Try it today and you will see instant results.

Advanced Profile Tips for Job Seekers

If you really want your profile to be a job-hunting machine, here are more ideas. Turn your headline into an ad for your job hunting. Go to *Profile > Edit Profile,* click on the pencil icon by the line under your name, and in the section that's labeled "Your professional headline," announce to the world that you are seeking opportunities.

Write: "Actively Seeking an Opportunity to Bring My Extensive Sales Leadership Experience to Increase Profits." Or: "Seeking a Role in Advertising Copywriting Where I Can Create Compelling Groundbreaking Ads." Or: "Pursuing an Engineering Opportunity to Write Code for the Next Big Internet Success Story." In your headline, say what you are looking for, but say it in a way that demonstrates how you will add value to any company that hires you. This is the perfect place to put your brand promise—that is, to state what you bring to the table. Let's face it: recruiters and hiring mangers care *only* about what you can do for them, so broadcast it in your headline.

What this does is that every time you make a post anywhere on LinkedIn—such as in the groups, for example—people see your name and headline. If you make a great impression on people and they need someone like you, or they know someone who does, you may be on track for an interview or possibly a new position.

Next, handle the Current Position section in your profile with care. If you list your last job there, you will only confuse people as to whether you need a job or not. And it's slightly unethical to say that you work somewhere when you don't. Remember, everything on LinkedIn brands you. Instead, I recommend putting "consultant" in for your current job; you could elaborate and say, "Consulting and looking for a full-time position." If you don't have a company yet, you can start one by adding your last name to "consulting," as in "Sherman Consulting." Another idea: if you manage a LinkedIn group, you might want to use that title, since it brands you as an expert, it shows that you are staying busy, and it tells readers that it is not a full-time gig. If you have a leadership role in a volunteer organization, you can put that as your current job.

Continuing, use the Summary section (go to *Profile* > *Edit Profile* and click on *Edit* next to Summary) to create an ad for yourself as a job hunter. Talk about what the perfect position would look like for you, why you want it, and what about your experience makes you the perfect person for it. Create an ad for yourself using the branding exercises we have covered, always keeping in mind making it value oriented to the reader—that is, say what's in it for them if they hire you. A clearly spelled out Summary section should allow the reader to know right away if you are perfect for the job.

I recommend creating your job-hunting summary in an outline. Write it in MS Word first, and copy and paste it into LinkedIn; that way you can spell check it and use the cool bullets that Word offers. Here are my suggested headlines for your Summary outline:

- **About Jane Jobhunter.** In this section, give a three- to four-sentence overview about your skills and talents and what you can offer a company.
- **How I Can Add Value to Your Organization.** Here is where you would put a bulleted list of the different ways you can help a company.
- **Highlights of My Experience.** Here in a bulleted list is where you can add very specific, quantifiable results that you have provided to other companies. Use numbers where possible.
- **What I'm Looking For.** Here is where you put what kind of position you want, the type of organization you want to join, and where it is located.
- **How You Can Reach Me.** Under this heading, put every single contact method you can think of so that recruiters and hiring managers can easily get in touch with you.

These are just suggested headlines for your Summary outline. Modify them for your particular job search.

The next step is to make sure you add all the skills you possess and want to showcase to your future manager. In *Edit Profile* mode, go to *Skills & Expertise* and click *Edit.* Type a skill into the search box, and then click *Save* so the skill shows up on your profile. Add as many as you can find that represent your skill set up to 50 skills. And remember, with the Endorsement feature, you can have your first-level connections endorse your skills. When a connection endorses your skill, his picture with a hyperlink to his profile appears near the skill he endorses. The more people endorsing a skill, the more smiling faces appear by that skill.

Next, make sure you have recommendations for each of your profile jobs. Social proof is key. Aggressively seek out recommendations from everyone you worked with in your past jobs. Recruiters will give more weight to managers you reported to and customers you satisfied. Recommendations from coworkers can be shrugged off by recruiters because it's too easy for people to trade recommendations with friends.

Focus on Accomplishments

It goes without saying that you should complete all the sections in your profile because recruiters and hiring managers will check you out on LinkedIn. In the Experience section, where you list past jobs, focus on your accomplishments, not just your responsibilities. If you increased sales by 25 percent, say so; if you cut costs by 15 percent, say it. Be specific. Hiring managers want to know the results of what you did at work.

Don't forget that you can also include any part-time work, consulting assignments, and volunteer positions if it helps bolster your reputation and credibility for the type of job you are looking for. Add your accomplishments there as well in very specific terms. Everything on your profile adds to your brand, so add jobs that support your positioning in the marketplace.

Use the Media Box to Provide Your Résumé

Say a recruiter is looking at two LinkedIn profiles, and he needs to fill a job in a hurry. He needs to see a résumé fast. If your résumé is already on your profile, you have the advantage. The recruiter does not need to take time to call or email you for your résumé.

You can have your résumé available to recruiters by uploading it to your Summary or Experience section. In *Edit Profile* mode, look for the media box, a box with a plus sign (+), on the top of your Summary and Experience sections. Click on it, and you will then be able to upload your résumé as an MS Word document or PDF after you have removed any confidential information. If you want to upload it as a PDF file, you will need a PDF creator such as Adobe. If you don't have that, you can go to a FedEx Office location where a copy center associate can make the conversion from MS Word to Adobe and put it on a removable USB thumb drive for you.

Go Multimedia and Stand Out

Make your profile even more of a job-hunting machine by using that media box feature to upload your portfolio or a PowerPoint presentation that explains your unique experiences and qualifications.

You might want to consider making a video résumé. Put on your best outfit, and have a friend video you in a well-lit room with no clutter in the background. Make it as professional as you can by filming in an upscale setting such as a conference room or an office you can borrow from a friend. Talk about yourself and your experiences, and let the video convey who you are and what can you bring to any organization. It's more powerful than a résumé or profile full of text, and it gives a dynamic, well-rounded view of your abilities.

To upload your presentation or video to your profile, go into the *Edit Profile* mode, and click on the media box symbol

+ by your Summary or Experience section; then click *Add Link* or *Upload File.*

Be Available and Show It

If you're looking for work, be sure to click the box next to *Career opportunities* in your contact settings. To do this, go to your picture in the upper right of any screen, click on it to get the drop-down menu, click on *Privacy & Settings,* and then select *Communications.* Put a check next to *Career opportunities* from the choices, and press the *Save changes* button. The reason for doing this is that your contact preferences must be consistent with the rest of your "job-hunting machine" profile or recruiters might dismiss you.

Leveraging Your Alma Mater

Take advantage of your alumni status by connecting with people who went to your school and who may be in a position to give you an informational interview at a target company or even refer you to a hiring manager:

- Search the Group Directory for your alumni group, join it, and network with graduates of your school. You might also send a message through LinkedIn to the group manager introducing yourself and describing why you have joined the group. She might be able to provide valuable insights and advice.
- Run an Advanced People Search with your school name as a keyword, and use different variations of the school name, including acronyms (search both "University of California Los Angeles" and "UCLA").
- Use the alumni search function by clicking on the *Network > Find Alumni* from the top menu. This will take you to a screen where you can type in your years of college attendance, and LinkedIn will show you all your former classmates who are in your network.

When you find a fellow alumnus you want to network with, ask for information first, then a referral. This way you can get to know them, and you can form a relationship that could be the basis for their helping you out.

Participating in Groups

Groups can be one of the most powerful tools in your job-hunting arsenals. You can join 50, so I encourage you to maximize this feature and join up to the limit. Consider joining groups that are made up of professionals you'd like to work for and with—and then get active! Don't sit on the sidelines. Respond to interesting posts with your own thoughtful input. Every time you do, it gives you one more chance to be noticed by people who can potentially help you. Additionally, recruiters often hang out in industry-specific groups looking for experts they can approach.

When you participate in groups, you want to be genuine and helpful. Connect with as many people as you possibly can who participate in the groups because you never know who can help you find a job. As a group member, you are allowed to send direct messages to other members, so don't be shy, and be sure to reach out to people who write interesting posts or who work for companies you would like to know more about.

In addition to joining groups in your field, consider joining some of the thousands of groups devoted to job hunting. Some of these groups are massive! For example, in the top center search box, select *Groups* from the drop-down menu, type in *jobs,* and press the magnifying glass. In the results you will see general-interest groups like "Jobs: Job Openings, Job Leads, and Job Connections!" with over 600,000 members. You will also find niche job groups, such as "Oil and Gas Jobs and Recruitment Network" with 198,000 members.

These groups are filled with job seekers like you, but also with hiring managers and recruiters who are posting jobs. You'll see that in addition to the many job posts, there will be helpful and free advice on résumés, interviewing, and job search strategies posted by career coaches. Join some of these jobs groups, and take advantage of the postings and advice to accelerate your search.

Searching Your Specialty to Uncover Jobs

Say you have a specific specialty, such as a programming language like JavaScript, XHTML, or Ruby on Rails. You could use the Advanced People Search to find companies in your area who hire people like you.

Select *People* in the top center search box, and click on the *Advanced* hyperlink by the magnifying glass to get to the Advanced People Search page. Type in your specialty in the keyword box, and select your location. You will then be presented with lots of profiles of people who have your skill. Scan them and see what companies they work for. Then, find out how you can approach specific companies to see if they have any openings. At least try to get an informational interview so you have someone you can keep in touch with and stay top of mind with when a spot does open up.

Upgrading to a Premium Job Seeker Account

LinkedIn offers so much with its free accounts to assist you in your job search that it might just do the trick. But if you want to add to your capabilities, consider upgrading to a *job seeker premium account.*

When you get this account, LinkedIn puts a small briefcase "premium account" icon near your name on your profile, notifying recruiters and hiring managers that you are looking. You also get more benefits such as these:

- Positioning at the top of candidate lists as a "Featured Applicant" when you apply for a job

- More job searching features
- InMails to contact people outside your first-level connections
- A complete list of everyone who has read your profile

Look through the job seeker premium account options, and see if they appeal to you for the price. Click on the *Upgrade* link at the top right of any screen, select *For Job Seekers,* and see if it's right for you.

Doing Research for Your Interview

When you do get an interview, look for the organization in Companies on LinkedIn to read up on it so you will be well informed. You will really shoot yourself in the foot if you walk into any interview these days and say something to the effect of, "So, tell me a little bit about your company." The interviewer will most likely look at you as if you were from Mars and be thinking to herself, "Has this candidate, who is now wasting my time, ever heard of a little invention called the Internet?" Check out the company's LinkedIn page, read the updates, learn about its products and services, and click through to its website to get an even deeper background for your meeting.

Also check out the profile of the person who is going to interview you. Print it out, and bring it with you. If you don't know who is interviewing you, call and ask the company up front who the interviewer is. If it is a team interview, try to get everyone's name and look at all their profiles.

This is all about first impressions; you want to shine when you walk in the door. By researching the interviewer's profile, you can look for areas of common interest that can break the ice. By reading his profile as well as recommendations he wrote for others, you get to know his likes and dislikes so you are prepared to do well in the interview. You might see that he once worked at a company you know well or have admired, or you might notice that he volunteers for a cause you also support. Mentioning these things in the interview will impress him because you cared enough to research him and didn't just walk in cold. It also shows that you are social media savvy, which is important to every business on the planet today. Take advantage of LinkedIn as your research database to make you look every bit as smart as you know you are.

A LinkedIn Job Search Success Story

I have instructed thousands of job seekers on how to use LinkedIn as a job seeking tool, and as a result, I have received many fine testimonials from those who have landed plum jobs. This is especially true of those who follow to the letter my job seeking program. One such job seeker was Ron, a senior-level executive who was not much of a social media fan before we worked together, but who nonetheless followed my advice to a T and wound up quickly assuming a leadership role at another company.

Ron did everything I asked him to do:

- He uploaded a professional photo that showed he meant business.
- He worked hard at building his network with people he knew, and he also became an open networker and added thousands more he had yet to meet.
- He networked in groups, and he spent a lot of time contacting potential new coworkers and managers.
- He posted a status update regularly about what he was working on.
- When people started finding him because of all his LinkedIn activity, he was ready with a job seeker–optimized profile that included a benefit-oriented professional headline and an easy-to-read, benefit-oriented Summary section (see Figures 11-4 and 11-5).

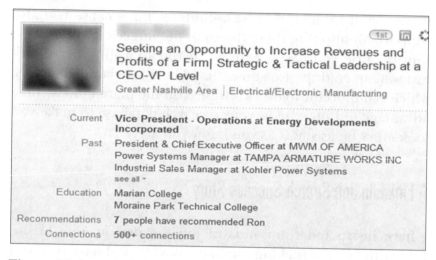

Figure 11-4. A benefit-oriented professional headline projects your brand promise, i.e., what you can offer in your next position.

Summary

ABOUT

I am an expert in growing companies with senior executive experience. I have been in the power business for 20+ years involved in executive leadership, sales, sales management, field engineering, and technical training. I was in such diverse markets as Manufacturing, Distribution, Industrial, Consumer markets. I'm very passionate about reaching team objectives.

HOW I CAN ADD VALUE TO YOUR COMPANY:

I understand what it takes to run a business, and as the next executive team member of your company I can help you grow by:
• Increasing sales
• Strict cost control
• Managing Vendor/Partner relations
• Increasing operations efficiency

MY ACCOMPLISHMENTS INCLUDE:

As CEO of a large engine/generator manufacturer, I increased revenue by 188% in just 3 years, and grew the bottom line by 183%. I did that by;
• Increasing sales,
• Targeting high profile customers
• Strategically focusing sales efforts

As the VP of Operations for an energy provider I:
• Decreased operating expense by 10% the first year, increased reliability and availability
• Created a new health and safety program at all facilities and a new safety conscious culture resulting in a 74% decrease in injuries year

While the Division manager for a large generator distributor I:
• Increased revenue over 75% in 3 years

Figure 11-5. Using an outline format in your profile summary makes it easy for readers to scan and quickly see what kind of value you can provide to their organization.

A few weeks after Ron began my program, he told me the following:

> I got a call from a California company, who asked if I would be interested in running a division of theirs, and it happens to be in Hawaii. He had read my profile and thought it matched a senior position they were looking for. I had my fifth phone interview today, and I'm heading to California to meet with the COO, and from there, on to Honolulu.
>
> Next, I got a call yesterday from a company that I used to compete fiercely with in the past. People that I knew there were getting notices from my updates and different things I was doing on LinkedIn, and they had gone in to check it out. They have two senior-level positions open that are not posted anywhere, one of which is a new venture for them that they talked to me about.

Ron is now a senior executive and satisfied LinkedIn user. It takes some effort to achieve this kind of result, but I firmly believe that LinkedIn is the key to a new career and brighter future for anyone who is looking for their next job.

Social Media Job-Hunting Advice from a Career Coach

As we end this chapter, I thought it would be a great idea to call on a career coach for a few closing tips. Lee Silverstein specializes in helping job seekers find work quickly by using social media to be discovered by recruiters and hiring managers. Lee has 30 years of experience in leadership and organizational development, training, interviewing, and hiring.

> Here are the top 10 social media job-hunting strategies that I share with job seekers:
>
> 1. Do not cut and paste your résumé into your LinkedIn profile! When you interact with hiring managers and/or recruiters, one of two things will happen: they will find you on LinkedIn and then

ask for your résumé, or they will get your résumé and then check out your LinkedIn profile. In either scenario, do you really want them to say, "Yeah, I already know that"? LinkedIn provides you an opportunity to share additional information about yourself and to do so in a different voice. Take advantage of it.

2. The past is the past; target everything else for the future. If your previous job was in accounting, but you want to get into financial planning, then be sure your headline, summary, specialties, and skills (more on this one later) are all targeting financial planning.

3. Personalize your LinkedIn profile summary, and write it in the first person. Writing in the first person shows you as "human." Your summary should include keywords focused on the position (not the job) you are interested in. It should also answer the following questions:
   - What do you do?
   - How do you do it?
   - Whom do you want to do it for?

4. Always remember that when you are searching for a new career, you are selling. The product is "you." Your goal is for the buyer (the hiring manager or recruiter) to want to buy what you're selling (you). Anthony Parinello in his book *Selling to VITO (the Very Important Top Officer)* (Adams Media, 2010) states that successful salespeople prove that their product can help a company in at least one of the following four areas:
   - Increasing revenues
   - Improving efficiencies
   - Reducing costs and/or expenses
   - Meeting legal or regulatory compliance mandates

   In your LinkedIn profile and résumé, you must site specific examples of instances in which you have done at least one of these four things in each job you've held.

5. Treat your connections like your garden: grow and nurture them. Use the steps Dan mentions in Chapter 7 to build your connections. Nurture them by writing recommendations, joining and participating in their groups, and introducing them to others.

6. Be sure to highlight all your skills in the Skills & Expertise section. Prioritize your list based on what you believe your target employers are looking for, then "drag and drop" the items on your list to reflect that order.

7. You get what you give. Be generous (yet sincere) with your LinkedIn recommendations, leave positive comments on blogs, and retweet other people's articles.

8. Build your professional online reputation. When you search Google for "you," what do you find? If your answer is "nothing" or just your LinkedIn profile, you have work to do. Companies want to see that you have a reputation as an expert in your field. A quality LinkedIn profile is a great first step. You should also set up professional profiles on Google (https://profiles.google.com/), and set them up also on the free, personal profile sites About.me and Flavors.me.

9. Read blogs, especially those related to your field. Bloggers are a great source of information and make great connections. Leave positive comments where appropriate, and share the posts that you particularly like on LinkedIn, Google+, Facebook, and Twitter.

10. Spend time in the "virtual hangouts" of people you want to connect with. Interested in working at Dell? Did you know that Michael Dell is very active on Google+?

11. I know Dan asked for 10 tips, but I always believe in giving a bit extra! Get to know your connections IRL (in real life). You won't land your next career sitting in front of your computer all day. Pick up the phone, call your connections, and find out more about them. If they're local, arrange to meet over coffee. And don't forget that post-meeting thank-you note.

To learn about Lee, visit his LinkedIn profile at http://www.linkedin.com/in/leesilverstein.

Whether you are on the roller coaster of a job hunt or checking the waters to see what's out there, I am convinced that making LinkedIn a big part of your day will only help to further your career. Since people hire people—and there are over 300 million of them on LinkedIn—you want to expand your opportunities by interacting with the other professionals on the site as much as you can. Let me end this section with these closing tips:

- **Get the word out.** Make sure as many people in your network as possible know you are looking for work.
- **Be active.** Add to the group discussions and share interesting articles you have found with your network. The more value you can provide, the better and more visible you will be on LinkedIn.
- **Be proactive, and meet with people by picking up the phone.** Yes, that electronic device in your pocket does more than send disappearing selfies.
- **Spend time researching your contacts at your target companies for potential hiring managers or future work colleagues.** Then contact them directly.
- **Build two-way relationships.** LinkedIn is about helping others first, and that good will may come around to you.
- **Expand your job-hunting research beyond LinkedIn to Google.** Using Big Brother Google (just kidding, guys), you can actually set up automatic notifications of any topic written about on the web, and Google will send them right to your email inbox. It's called Google Alerts, and it's a free service. You can tell Google to notify you when your target company is mentioned anywhere on the web; same goes for a hiring manager you are targeting, or a certain position you are going after, or any happenings in your field. Go to http://www.google.com/alerts to set up as many notifications as you like.

* * *

You may be familiar with this saying: "Nothing happens until somebody sells something." In other words, until Joe Consumer plunks down his gold MasterCard for a shiny new game console, until Sally Purchasing Agent signs for a new shipment of cashmere sweaters for her company's e-commerce site, until Fred the Builder loads his Ford pickup with slabs of sheetrock at Home Depot—until people buy *something*, the gears of industry won't turn, and everyone in companies far and wide will be staring at empty to-do lists, and no one will have a new job.

So selling has been and always will be the main driver of our economy, but the *way* things are sold these days has changed radically because of social media sites like LinkedIn. In the old days, you could get by like Willy Loman in Arthur Miller's *Death of a Salesman*: "Riding on a smile and a shoeshine." But selling has changed drastically, and if you don't master new tools like LinkedIn, you may go the way of the dinosaur.

Read on to learn how to harness the power of the world's largest database of professionals to sell your products and services, and discover how to use a resource that will make your selling successful in this brave new world.

Chapter 12: Successful Selling on LinkedIn: How to Do It Right

If you want to know how the advent of new technologies is improving our lives in so many ways (and you *do* because you're reading this book!), then you ought to meet Marc Ostrofsky. Marc is a bestselling author, futurist, serial entrepreneur, and domain-name investor best known for his world-record sale of the domain name Business.com for $7.5 million. Marc's book, *Word of Mouse* (Simon & Schuster, 2013), is a must-read overview of how changes in technology have forever altered the way we work and play, opening up a world of opportunity for those who adapt.

Marc also has a sense of humor about the digital divide that appears so often today between us baby boomers and the millennials. Marc writes:

> Our oldest daughter is out of college. When a storm was heading up the East Coast last year, we called her on her cell phone and said, "If you can't use your cell phone to let us know you are okay, be sure to find a landline and call." Her response was priceless: "What's a landline?"

Yes, ch-ch-ch-changes are happening fast in our world (a tip of the hat to David Bowie), and you need to get onboard. Nowhere are changes more evident than in the new ways we need to market and sell our products and services. That's because social media has changed the selling game completely. The playing field is now level. No longer do marketers and advertisers stand high up on Mount Olympus shouting down their pitches and laying out their agenda as to what we will buy and how we will buy it.

Two major shifts have occurred with the advent of social media that have created a paradigm shift:

1. **Selling is now social.** Buyers, be they consumers or businesses, are looking not simply for transactions, but rather for conversations. They want to get to know you in order to trust the things you are saying and trust the promises you are making. Engagement is now the rule of the day: you must engage your prospective clients in meaningful ways long before you present your offering.

2. **Selling is wildly influenced by recommendations.** The conversation buyers are looking for is not a two-way conversation between buyers and sellers. Today, buyers are wading chest-deep in an avalanche of information in the form of reviews and recommendations from their peers to sift through to make their own choices. They are having more conversations with each other about *you*. So, keep this in mind: recommendations are the new advertising.

Because of this paradigm shift in selling, the power has swung to the consumers. A survey done in April 2012 by Nielsen, a global provider of consumer research, stated that online consumer reviews are the second most trusted source of information, after word-of-mouth recommendations by friends and family, with a whopping 70 percent of global consumers surveyed saying that they trust this source. In contrast, the survey went on to say that only 47 percent of consumers surveyed trust paid advertising. Said Randall Beard, global head of Advertiser Solutions at Nielsen:

> Although television advertising will remain a primary way marketers connect with audiences due to its unmatched reach compared to other media, consumers around the world continue to see recommendations from friends and online consumer opinions as by far the most credible.

Social Selling Means Creating Value

So where does that leave the marketer today? By that I mean, where does it leave *anyone* who attempts to persuade another person to buy something, including entrepreneurs, small business owners, retailers, service providers, and big corporations? You see, everyone is in the same boat: we all have to adopt a new way of social selling, and the formula is as follows.

First, identify your target audience: Who are your ideal clients? Second, identify the needs of your potential clients by learning their hopes, dreams, and fears. Third, engage with them by listening first and interacting. Create the conversation buyers are seeking. Fourth, help them with their needs by providing lots of free, valuable resources up front. And finally, fifth, offer your products or services once they are in your sphere of influence.

In the new way of marketing, the actual sales offer comes way at the end, after you've created a relationship with the prospects and they've come to know, like, and trust you. By building a relationship first and delivering lots of value in the form of free education or information, the buyers see you as the preferred provider. Yes, they will still check with their peers for reviews or recommendations, but you're now on their short list or at the top of their list when it comes time to buy. In fact, you may have done such a great job of engagement and building trust that the buyers would not even consider going with anyone else.

I like the way my friend and fellow speaker David T. Fagan describes it when he says we need to completely flip the old model of getting customers first and turning them into fans. In these times, we need to make fans first:

> The process of finding new clients and making them raving fans is fading away. . . . Now we have to make people FANS FIRST and BUYERS SECOND! Crazy, I know, but in this new digital age of social media and overall interaction, that's exactly what we have to do.

In his very informative book *Likeable Social Media* (McGraw-Hill, 2011), Dave Kerpen agrees with that sentiment:

> By consistently providing great content over time, you won't need to advertise how wonderful you are—your community will already know based on what you've shared. And when they're ready to buy your product or service, they won't need to respond to ads telling them whom to turn to. They won't even need to search Google to find what they're looking for. They'll already feel like they know you—they trust and like you—so they'll turn to you to solve their problem.

Well, how do you make fans first in this new social media–driven model? How do we master social selling and create that all-important relationship with prospects? One way is by giving to people, adding value to people's lives, and serving them. We can then earn the right to interact with them. People like to work with givers, not takers.

Create Value First, *Then* Sell

When it comes to social media sites like LinkedIn, too many marketers are skipping the first few steps outlined above. They think it's another broadcast medium like radio or TV that just happens to be free. But what you need to do is put yourself in your prospects' shoes. In a general sense, you'd probably agree that people are interested in themselves. There is something they need to achieve, some goal they need to accomplish. What is that goal? What is that need? Focus first on helping them achieve it, and you are on solid ground in the new way of selling.

So how do you do that? Well, take an inventory of what you've got that could perhaps fulfill your prospects' needs. What information products have you assembled in the form of e-books, videos, articles, blogs, interviews, white papers, webinars, or teleseminars? Make sure they are valuable, that they speak to your prospects' immediate needs, and that you give the information without expectation of a purchase.

If you help people for free, then how do you eventually sell to them? What you can do is give them this valuable, problem-solving content in exchange for their opting into your lead capture system. Make use of the various email management programs, and set up an opt-in box on your website where prospects exchange their email address for content. Then you can continue to educate, enlighten, and inform them over the weeks and months ahead, building a solid relationship of trust while you add in a soft-sell of what you'd like them to purchase.

Create Something Amazing and Give It Away

If this sounds like a long, complex process, I'm afraid it is, and you'll just have to get used to it. You can't just barge onto LinkedIn or any other social media website and start selling. For example, I have a friend who runs a well-known national marketing company. He was unhappy because he was not getting any new clients from his sales efforts on LinkedIn. When I asked what he was doing, he said he was targeting certain types of small business owners, like dentists and chiropractors, and sending them direct unsolicited messages through the LinkedIn system offering his marketing assistance.

That would seem like the logical thing to do, but it does *not* work. I get four or five direct messages a day on LinkedIn offering some kind of service, and I ignore them. You simply can't skip the engagement process. On LinkedIn, you can pull up someone's profile, get to know what she is like, try to ascertain her needs, then offer her some free content rather than just coming right out of the gate and trying to sell to her.

For example, here's how my friend might have handled his messages on LinkedIn for greater results:

> Hi, Dr. Smith, I read your profile here on LinkedIn, and I see you have a family dental practice in Smallville. I have helped hundreds of dentists just like you triple their client base in a very short time by leveraging social media. I'd like to send you my free report *The Top 10 Social Media Strategies for Building Your Dental Practice.* There's nothing to buy and no strings attached. Please let me know if I can send it to you. Thanks for your time.

This type of message will get a lot more responses. Then my friend could send a report, and in the back of the report, he could include a soft-sell to the next step in the sales process. This is what's known as "getting them into the funnel." You start with something that's free or low cost, creating a minimal barrier to entry. You get them involved and then move them slowly and surely through the funnel, going from free or low-cost items to a larger sale.

For the next step, he could offer a free 20-minute phone call to assess where the dentist is in terms of using social media and how social media could be used to help him immediately. Remember that today's buyers want a conversation, not a transaction. A phone call is the most obvious way to be a "social seller." If the dentist accepts and engages in the call, now he's pulled into my friend's sphere of influence, and he could potentially be moved along the sales funnel to a lucrative consulting assignment for my friend.

Of course, this particular strategy is dependent on your having a free giveaway. If you don't have any valuable content, either information or entertainment oriented, that you can give away, then that's a project for you. Begin to build up valuable resources you can give away for free by listening to the needs of your prospects, and then creating tools and resources to help them achieve their goals.

Don't forget the magic word: *repurpose!* You might have created some content already, but it's in another form. You can turn almost anything you've created into free gifts. The speech you gave and recorded can be transcribed and turned into an e-book. You can pull the soundtrack from one of your videos and give away the MP3. An example of this is when I took many LinkedIn articles I had written over a long span of time and turned them into an instructional e-book that I now give away on my site as a free bonus for signing up for my newsletter.

One thing to consider is that you don't have to build content all by yourself. There are multitudes of professional artists and writers available to help you at affordable rates, and you can find them all on outsourcing sites like http://www.Guru.com and https://www.Elance.com. I particularly like https://www.Elance.com, and I hire artists from the site all the time to create the professional packaging and polish I need for the online content I create. I recently started using another outsourcing site called http://www.Fiverr.com, where you can contract with people from all over the world to help you with your marketing tasks at $5 a project.

Be creative as you come up with something to give away that provides value for your prospects. It doesn't even have to be something physical. It could be a service you offer that requires only your time—something like starting and managing a popular LinkedIn group! Remember tech company founder Eric Blumthal whom we met in Chapter 9? He manages and moderates the "Sales/Marketing Executives Group," a forum where over 162,000 sales leaders congregate to share selling tips and strategies. As you recall, Eric gets 50 percent of his company's business from this group. So what kind of group could *you* start? What kind of service do *your* clients and prospects need?

Find out what people need, and provide it for free, and slowly you will create the all-important relationships that afford you trust and credibility and cut through the noise. By doing that, by being a giver, you will build a following of people who will become loyal fans, and you will have potential paying clients in your sales funnel.

Get Ready for Successful Social Selling

Up until this point, I've covered why it's crucial to your success to embrace social selling with an emphasis on conversation over transaction. It's crucial that you get onboard now (you do remember what happened to the dinosaurs, right?). I've also disclosed one of my favorite social selling strategies: to create value first for your prospective clients in order to get them to know, like, and trust you—and eventually buy from you.

Now, let's get into the specifics, the nuts and bolts, of transforming your LinkedIn account into a powerful social selling profit generator. You have three initial tasks that will put you on solid ground for your social selling efforts: (1) create a customer-centric profile, (2) grow your network strategically, and (3) post helpful and relevant status updates.

Create a Customer-Centric Profile

Like all great social sellers, I'm sure you visit a prospect's LinkedIn profile before you pick up the phone. So it comes as no surprise that your prospect is visiting your profile as well. If it's bare bones and simply a recital of your work history, your prospect is not going to be impressed, nor will he be jazzed to work with you.

So what can you do make a solid first impression and turn your profile into an extension of your selling efforts? Let me count the ways:

- **A professional headshot.** They say a picture is worth a thousand words. When it comes to social selling, a pleasant, professional photo of you smiling in your best clothes may well mean a thousand sales. Look at your competitors' photos if you want some inspiration, and by all means don't overlook this one simple tactic. I tell my clients that what they earn is in direct proportion to how well they are dressed on LinkedIn.

- **A memorable professional headline.** By default, LinkedIn lists your current job title as your headline. That does not exactly light up your prospects. It's the first thing that they see after they gaze at your smiling face. So you want to have a headline that positions you as a valuable resource and also speaks to your credibility. No wonder, then, that I recommend what I call the *benefit-credibility headline*. Examples:
    - I Deliver Superior Networking Products to Speed Up Your IT Resources and Increase Productivity | 20+ Years of Experience
    - I Help You Make Superior Decisions Involving Real Estate Transactions | Thousands of Satisfied Clients
    - My Unique Graphic Designs Create Raving Fans and Eager Buyers | 10+ Years of Experience

  Make sure what you put in your headline turns them on, and *never* turns them off (don't say, "I'm a Never-Say-Die Sales Hunter").

- **An engaging profile summary.** Writing in the first person, use this space to build an ad for yourself that speaks directly to the needs of your clients and to your credibility. You could pull in readers with a question, such as, "Do you wish you knew more about social media marketing to gain new business?" or "Do you wish you could save money on your telecommunications expenses?" Add statistics that back up on the promise you are making: "I have helped over 100 clients achieve a positive ROI of 25 percent on their technology purchases." Make your profile work for you by being concise and easy to scan.

- **Go multimedia, and let your profile provide value.** With the media box available to you in *Edit Profile* mode (you will see a box with a + on the top of your Summary and over every position listed in Experience), you can upload information that creates value for your prospects. Think about how you can best present your company, and then upload case studies, e-books you've written, PowerPoint presentations, video testimonials, articles written about your company, and anything else that is relevant to your prospects' goals.

- **Recommendations from past and current clients.** Social proof goes a long way to reassuring your prospects that you are, as they say, the Real Deal. Once you've got all your clients into your network as first-level connections, reach out to them and ask them to send you a recommendation for your profile; you can ask them nicely to mention certain outcomes you have achieved.

Grow Your Network Strategically

Make it a point to add your past and current clients to your LinkedIn network. This makes it easy for you to request a recommendation, as mentioned before, and it provides many other benefits:

- You'll keep up-to-date on what is happening with them through their updates; you'll know if they change jobs or get promoted. This is valuable intel: a change in jobs might mean they take you along as a vendor to a new company, while a promotion might afford an opportunity to upsell.
- You'll be a second-level connection to everyone they have as first-level connections. This could mean colleagues at their firm and in other companies you may wish to approach. You are three times more likely to get a sales call returned if you can mention a mutual acquaintance.

Once you've added all your clients, be sure to reach out to current and past colleagues, former classmates, and others you meet in the community at networking events. The larger your network, the greater your influence.

Post LinkedIn Updates Regularly

One way in which a large network benefits you is if you are posting LinkedIn status updates on a regular basis. Doing so means that everyone you are connected to can see them on their home page.

With LinkedIn updates, you want to demonstrate that you're a credible resource and you're someone who is worth getting to know. Some guidelines for LinkedIn updates include the following:

- **Share helpful information.** Always be on the lookout for content that you can share—that is, a link to an article, a case study on your website, or an upcoming event— that will help the people in your network.
- **Stir people's curiosity.** Your update might be some-thing that gets people interested to learn more, such as: "Read this case study to see how one company increased client loyalty by 20 percent," and link the case study to your site.
- **Announce business events.** Use updates to alert others about large sales your company just made or upcoming events where you will have a booth presence.

Search and Research: Build a Highly Targeted Prospect List

If I wanted a list of targeted prospects back when I was a cor-porate marketer, my first step would have been to contact my trusty list broker. He'd be so happy to hear from me, and he'd have his palm out in eager anticipation of that juicy corporate check. If you had told me that someday, instead of paying for prospects, I would have a free, comprehensive database accessi-ble over the Internet that not only told me about my prospect's job title and company but also gave me a complete rundown on her work history, college attended, charities supported, personal interests, testimonials she'd received and given out, groups and organizations she belonged to . . . well, I would have fallen off my Triceratops (that's a dinosaur, naturally, and even if it wasn't *that* long ago, it sure feels like it!).

Without question, LinkedIn is the most important advancement in the history of sales and marketing. Plunk yourself down at your computer, press a few keys, and you have a targeted prospect database that's not only rich in data but also contains important connections to other professionals who can help you open the door. In this regard, the two key functions that you should master are searching for prospects and then researching them. Let's cover searching first, and you'll discover how LinkedIn can be used to generate up-to-the-minute prospect lists while you are contentedly counting sheep.

Search for Your Best Prospects

To start off, go to the Advanced People Search, which will give you access to everyone in your network including group members. On the top toolbar, select *People* from the drop-down menu, then click on *Advanced* on the right. On this page you can select from any number of filters to find your prospects. So if I were selling to a VP of sales in the technology field in my hometown, I would type in those criteria to get my target prospect list (see Figure 12-1).

Next, and this is the really cool part, I can click on *Save search* in the upper right on the page with my results, and then I get a screen in which I can customize the name of the search and tell LinkedIn to send me updates on a daily, weekly, or monthly basis, whenever any new prospective clients appear in this search. Essentially, I can have LinkedIn as my 24/7 prospecting partner, working tirelessly to bring me an unending stream of potential clients.

Another search tactic that's extremely powerful is to run a People Search in any of the 50 groups you have joined. The benefit here is that you are starting with a targeted list, that is, everyone in a geographical area, or with a common interest or job title. To run a group search, start by going to one of your groups. Click on *Members* on the group toolbar or on the

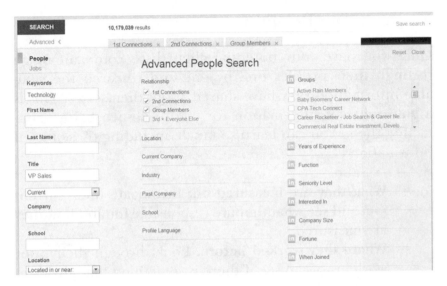

Figure 12-1. The Advanced People Search allows you to develop targeted prospecting lists. By clicking on the *Save search* link in the upper right, you can create a 24/7 prospecting database, with LinkedIn sending you the names of new members who meet your search criteria.

number of people in the group located in the upper right of the group page to get to the members page. Type a job title or any other keyword you want into the text box, and press *Search*. Up will come your targeted list of prospects in the group. You can now click on *Send message* underneath any user's name to send a direct message to his or her LinkedIn inbox.

A third search strategy is to run a company search. Select *Companies* from the center drop-down menu, then click on the blue magnifying glass. This will bring you to the Companies home page. There are filters all along the left side of the page where you can indicate company size, location, industry, or other characteristics to narrow your search. When you run a search, you can then select a Company page to visit, and on every Company page, you will see in the upper right, "How You're Connected." There you will see all your first- and second-level connections at that firm, and you can use this list to begin conversations with your network in order to find the right person at the company to approach.

Research Your Prospects

Once you have your potential client lists, you want to go through their profiles one by one and research the valuable information they have shared about themselves. This is a gold mine of information for you to absorb before contacting them. You can learn so much, including these bits of information:

- **What they are measured on.** Investigate their current job, and see what they are responsible for and how they are measured.
- **Where they worked before.** Look through their prior work history to see if there is something that gives you a personal connection, such as a personal referral you can call on.
- **What you have in common.** Check out their organizations, charities, community involvement, and groups. Find something you can use to develop rapport.
- **What's on their mind.** Look at their status updates, and find topics you can talk to them about or learn what they are working on right now.

All of this information allows you to decide if he's a great prospect for you and the best way to approach him.

Join Groups to Sell More

Imagine this: all of the decision makers you want to reach have assembled from far and wide in a hotel ballroom in your town, and they've invited you to join their gathering in order to have a meaningful discussion about their industry and their current needs. Would you go?

Any marketer or sales professional would say, "Heck, yeah!" And that's the beauty of LinkedIn Groups. Your best customers have self-selected and organized themselves into millions of special-interest groups that you can join. There's a group for every industry, and you have the opportunity to learn from and engage with your best clients, demonstrate what a valuable resource you are by posting interesting information, and send a message to anyone in the group, even if you are not first-level connections.

It's an opportunity to be a fly on the wall and listen in as your best prospects describe what's happening with them right now, and it lets you discover the problems you can solve.

If you're not salivating at the idea of joining 50 groups where your best prospects are, you should be! So let's get started: Go to the search box at the top center of any LinkedIn page. Select *Groups* from the drop-down menu, and click on the magnifying glass to get to the Groups search page (see Figure 12-2).

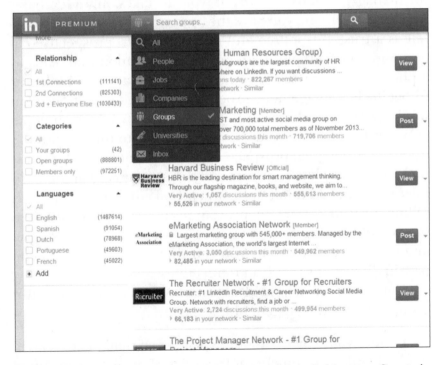

Figure 12-2. Go to the Groups search page by clicking on *Groups* in the drop-down menu on top. There you will find 2 million groups of every description where you can learn from and interact with your best prospects.

There you will find close to 2 million groups to join, where you can learn more about your potential clients and their wants and needs, build awareness of your company, and engage people in meaningful online conversations. Click on a group name, and you'll be taken right to that group's page, where you can check out the discussions. Try to find groups with lots of active discussions. You can tell if the discussions are new by simply looking at the bottom of each post; it will say when it was posted.

If the group looks promising, click the yellow *Join* button in the upper right, and your request to join has been submitted. Some groups are of the auto-acceptance kind, where as soon as you click on *Join*, you are in; others take a little longer to get into because the group manager will look at your profile first to see if you are a good match for the group. In cases in which the manager reviews you first, it typically takes only a few days.

Once you are in, you have the opportunity to establish yourself as a trusted resource and to reach out to prospective clients and engage them in an online conversation that leads to a phone call. Groups are one of the best places on LinkedIn to begin the engagement process. However, be cautious. You would not in a million years go to a chamber of commerce event and hurl 100 of your business cards into the air with the hope of hitting great prospects on the head, nor would you just walk up to complete strangers and thrust your card at them. In the same way, you don't waltz into a LinkedIn group and start selling. Instead, listen to conversations for a few days, and then slowly wade in with some great ideas of your own. As your reputation in the group grows, you can then engage group members in discussions that lead to meetings.

Here are more helpful ideas to assist you in turning LinkedIn groups into solid lead-generating vehicles:

- **Add your voice without expecting an immediate return.** Think engagement, not salesmanship. Get the group to see you as a valuable resource.
- **Check out profiles.** When you see people in a particular group you want to meet, click on their profile and

review all their information to help you create the best approach.

- **Go where your prospects are.** You have 50 groups allotted to you. Make them count! And if a group does not work out for you, don't hesitate to change your group lineup. Once you are in a group, there will be a gray *Member* button on the top right. To leave, hover your mouse over it, and it changes to *Leave.* Click it to leave the group and join another one. No one is notified, and there's no shame involved.

- **Share interesting resources.** Give away a white paper or a free e-book. Share a link to a great article. Give out free advice. Then follow the discussion, and look for ways to interact further with those who post.

- **Ask a question.** Start a discussion by posting an interesting question, but make sure it's not a thinly disguised pitch. Group participants and the group manager can smell a pitch a mile away, and you face backlash and even expulsion, depending on the group.

- **Divide and conquer.** If you have a partner, join different groups in an industry to increase your presence.

Get started, max out your 50, and begin the process of engaging your clients. Groups are one of the best ways for you to begin to fill your sales pipeline.

Start a Group to Create a Ready Market of Targeted Prospects

When I started my LinkedIn group "Tampa Bay Marketing Professionals," it was for the purpose of creating a community where my fellow marketers (including advertising, public relations, and sales professionals) could discuss current trends in our industry and how we could best achieve our career goals. Now that the group is well over 5,000 members, it has also become a ready-made prospect list for me. Whenever I conduct an online or offline marketing training course, I invite my group members to join the event, and because it's a targeted list of professionals interested in the topic, I always get a great response.

As you learned in Chapter 9, you can start a group in just a few minutes. Then it becomes a matter of your devotion to growing and nurturing your group until it becomes a profitable lead source for your business. So how long does that take, and how does it compare to other lead-generating activities? I asked fellow business coach and LinkedIn enthusiast Nile Nickel if he had any hard numbers comparing the time and money it took to grow a LinkedIn group for lead generation versus pursuing traditional marketing avenues. Nile said that he encourages all his clients to establish LinkedIn groups to build prospect lists, and he said he recently took a client through the process. Here's what Nile told me:

> My client Larry was working on a direct-mail campaign to offer accounting professionals a free book with information on how to better market their services to clients. The book was offered purely to get these professionals on his mailing list in an attempt to sell them on the value of his coaching programs and seminars. To do this, Larry had to find and buy the right list and then have a direct-mailing partner mail his information packet and free book offer out to clients. Larry's goal was to get 100 clients within six months.
>
> Larry had just completed his first 10,000-piece mailing. Through this process, Larry had 31 people sign up for one of his programs. Larry had spent just over $10,000 for this campaign, so his cost per client acquisition was $312.91. Larry found this cost per acquisition to not be a problem because the typical client would spend in excess of $2,000 per year with Larry.
>
> So what was Larry's problem? The client cycle took about six weeks, and finding the right list for his target market was extremely difficult. Larry was thinking his next campaign wouldn't be any bigger than about 3,600 people. Based on the same metrics, then, the campaign would be expected to generate only about 11 new leads and take another six weeks.
>
> Larry had three challenges: (1) it was taking too long to get new clients; (2) the properly targeted lists were too hard to find; and

(3) while the acquisition costs were acceptable, it was costing more than Larry expected.

So my recommendation was to set up a LinkedIn group, and by using proper LinkedIn group growth strategies, I thought we could attract more clients faster and cheaper. Despite being unconvinced it would work, Larry agreed to implement my recommendations. He and I worked on setting up a group and seeding the group with his current clients, as well as putting in place strategies to target and invite new members. Now to be fair, this took some of Larry's time. But Larry agreed that it was about the same amount of time as managing the other process, so we did not consider it as a cost because it was not included in his direct-mail campaign either.

What were the results? In three weeks' time, Larry had acquired just over 200 new group members, and 71 of those group members had signed up for one of Larry's programs. The best part was the cost: free.

So with the traditional campaign, in six weeks, Larry gained 31 clients at a cost of just over $10,000. Using LinkedIn Groups, in three weeks Larry gained over 71 clients at a total cost of zero. And in just over 14 months, Larry's group of targeted potential clients had almost 1,000 members Larry can communicate with and build relationships with, and he can offer them access to his resources.

Larry is now a LinkedIn Groups believer, and I encourage you to try this proven lead generation method as well.

You can view Nile's LinkedIn profile at http://www.linkedin .com/in/nilenickel.

Leverage Your Prospects' Trigger Events

Recently a company contacted me to engage my services for some sales coaching using LinkedIn. They are a well-known communications cabling company that provides all the voice and data cabling in a firm's building. As I interviewed their sales reps prior to the training, one theme kept emerging: their sales were suffering because they were often late to the party. They would learn that a new building had gone up only after the fact. They were not alerted to the project at the design and building stages, and they never got their bids in on time.

Fortunately for them, LinkedIn has a fix for that problem, and I spent a good deal of the training going over recognizing trigger events that they could locate on LinkedIn that would tip them off to when a sales opportunity was arising. For this cabling company, it meant each of the reps' getting active on LinkedIn and looking at the status updates of purchasing managers or business owners (in the case of smaller companies), as well as the status updates of the companies. In particular, the reps needed to look for this type of information in status updates:

- Expansion and growth of the business
- Opening up new territories
- Office relocations
- Mergers requiring the reconfiguring of facilities
- Real estate and construction activity
- New products and services that might indicate facility expansion
- Venture capital (VC) funding that might mean new construction

When I pointed out to the cabling company reps that there are a great many ways to get ahead of a sale using LinkedIn, they were thrilled because they had never realized how much using LinkedIn for research like this could mean to their bottom line.

Just as I demonstrated to the cabling company the importance of looking for trigger events on LinkedIn, so too should you begin to acquire a trigger event mindset. This means you need to be constantly scouring LinkedIn for organizational changes indicating that there is a high probability that a company needs your products or services right now. You'll never be late to the party if you adopt this proactive approach to sales.

So where do you find these trigger event notifications? Just look where people are posting. It could be an update you notice on your LinkedIn home page from one of your first-level connections; it could be an update on their company page; or it could be a post in one of your industry groups. Make a list of all the possible trigger events that indicate an opening for your products and services, particularly ones that necessitate an urgent need to take action now. To get you started, here are some possible trigger events for you:

- **New management or a change in ownership.** Every new manager likes to bring in her own vendors.
- **Company name change or new positioning.** The company could need marketing and PR help.
- **New clients acquired.** The company may need to beef up customer support services.
- **Expansion into new market segments.** The company might need your expertise, such as translation services.
- **Lots of new job openings.** These would indicate expansion and growth, and the company could use a host of new services.

Those are just a few ideas to get you thinking. Go ahead and make up your trigger event list today. You might want to go over your recent client acquisitions and think about what brought you the new business.

When you see a trigger event posted on LinkedIn, think about how your products or services can help the individuals involved achieve their business objectives. Craft your approach by first thinking about what impact your offering has had on your existing clients who have had similar trigger events. Then you can initiate contact with your prospective clients by mentioning the trigger event, your understanding of what they are facing, how you've helped companies or individuals in similar circumstances, and how you can make a difference for them.

Finding trigger events on LinkedIn will shorten your sales cycle because these prospects have an immediate need for what you are selling. You also eliminate your competitiors, who are sitting idly by waiting for an invitation to sell something while you are already engaging the potential clients. And one more thing: the prospects will actually be glad to hear from you because you are arriving on the scene Lone Ranger–style to help them solve problems and achieve their goals. You'll get a hero's welcome! Isn't that how we all want to sell?

Surround Your Target and Capitalize on Team Buying

Many businesses these days are shrugging off the old command-and-control structure where managers had the final say on everything happening within their fiefdoms. The trend these days is toward team buying, or decision by committee, where there are lots of decision makers involved in the process. If you ignore the other decision makers in your sales approach, one of them might suddenly appear out of the night like an iceberg and sink your *Titanic.* You don't want this. The water of rejection is mighty cold.

What you want to do is employ social selling to get to know everyone who is possibly in on the decision. LinkedIn makes this extremely easy for you, by giving you a way to identify and engage other influencers who may be on the buying team. This is also an opportunity to find someone who may be more open to engaging with you due to something in common or a personality match.

When you are looking at the main decision maker's profile, scan the right side of the page for the section headed "People Also Viewed." You will likely see the decision maker's colleagues. Click on their profiles, and learn about their positions and responsibilities. If you identify them as influencers connected to the decision to buy your offering, see what groups they are in and what things you may have in common. Now you have several options of people to approach in addition to the main decision maker, and you can make yourself and your offering known to the whole team.

Another strategy is to use the Advanced People Search. Type in the company name where your decision maker works. Then in the keyword box, type in job functions or job titles to pull up all of the other possible decision makers. Look through the profiles and find people to approach. You are now more prepared to succeed when selling to a company that uses the team buying approach.

The Surefire LinkedIn Sales Message

When marketers and sales professionals first encounter Linked-In and realize they can engage with millions of potential buyers from the comfort of their office, their first thought is, "Wow! This is great! I can sell to millions of people without walking out the door." Then, as their fingertips graze their keyboards, their mind goes blank, and they face what we in the writing game call "the tyranny of the blank page." Suddenly they are thinking, "Well, what the heck do I say?"

So, as someone who has used LinkedIn for seven years and who has seen what works and what does not, I want to give you some brief guidelines on how to structure the Ultimate LinkedIn Sales Message:

- **Establish rapport.** All relationships begin with rapport, and fortunately LinkedIn profiles can be a gold mine if you take the time to examine them. Look for commonalities in, for example, work history, schooling, hobbies, and charities. Find something personal you can use, even geography (you can commiserate over cold weather you've both experienced, or mention the fall leaves you both knew).
- **Search for goals.** By reading profiles carefully, you can discover what is important to that person, both personally and professionally. A message that carefully aligns with someone's goals is going to be a welcome message and not an intrusion.

When crafting your message:

1. Start with a rapport builder (where you both went to school or your mutual friends or acquaintances).
2. Mention something about their profile you found interesting, such as a recent accomplishment.
3. Mention what you do in terms of the problems you solve. If you've detected a trigger event, mention it here by noting that you understand what they are going through.
4. Talk about other companies you've helped in similar situations, so they know you are a good fit for their needs.
5. Close by asking if you can reach out by phone for 10 minutes to see if there is a basis for working together. Ask for only 10 minutes because people are busy.

This is the format that I and my clients use, and it works because, above all, it is *targeted*. LinkedIn is not a mass medium, and social selling is all about using a high-quality, low-volume trusted advisor approach. Be a valuable resource to one person at a time, and that will drive your sales results.

Close Your LinkedIn Sales: A Sandler® Sales Trainer Reveals How

If you've followed the strategies presented so far, thanks to LinkedIn, your proverbial sales pipeline is full to the bursting point with targeted prospects for your business. And while I believe LinkedIn is the greatest gift ever bestowed on marketers and salespeople, I've got to tell you something now that LinkedIn *can't* do: it can't sell for you.

That's right. At some point you've got to sell IRL (in real life), which means talking in person or on the phone with your prospects. LinkedIn does many things, but it does not talk!

But let me say this: my purpose in writing this book is to give you a complete and total guide to successfully branding and selling yourself—and your company if you represent one. Now that we are so tantalizingly close to the goal line, I refuse to leave you stranded. That's why I've brought in someone who can take you over that last and perhaps longest yard in the sales process and explain how to convert all the prospects you've met on LinkedIn into paying clients. Clint Babcock is a Sandler Training® franchisee who knows more about closing deals than anyone I've met. I asked him to share with you how to take your LinkedIn leads and turn them into customers. Here's what he told me:

> Dan's been sharing with you strategies for leveraging the power of LinkedIn to grow your business. Soon, either you'll find yourself with an inquiry about your products or services, or you'll find a person you wish to connect with who may need your products or services. So now what? What if that person calls you? What if you send that individual a personalized message or request to connect, and you ask to have a brief phone conversation with him or her? This is where the difference between prospecting and selling, which are two totally different skills, comes into play.
>
> LinkedIn is an essential prospecting tool for anyone in business. However, this tool cannot sell anything to anyone. Your ability to engage your prospect through email, phone, and face-to-face conversations is going to be the difference between your prospect choosing you or your competition.
>
> As a Sandler Training franchisee, I work with companies of all sizes, as well as individual salespeople who have the ambition and drive to be the best consultative salespeople they can be. Sandler Training is an international sales and management training company with over 250 locations worldwide. Our belief is that sales is both an art and a science. The art can be summed up by your individual style, your charisma, your personality, and your ethics and morals. The science comes through understanding a sales system that you follow to ensure that you have a repeatable, reinforced sales process. Over the past 35 years, Sandler Training has evolved this sales process into a seven-step system.

Step 1. Bonding and Rapport

Sandler Rule: (a) Selling is a Broadway play performed by a psychiatrist. (b) People buy from people they like. People buy from people like them. People buy from people that like them.

This means your ability to build rapport with anybody in the first few minutes, and maintain that rapport throughout the sales cycle, is essential. Most salespeople feel they have this part down because they are very social and like to talk. However, what if your prospect is quiet and doesn't engage with you about the football game? What now? Becoming a master at building rapport first starts with understanding yourself, how you communicate, and what your body language and tonality are relaying to the prospect. Then, your ability to read people and adjust to their communication style will allow you to connect with anyone, even if he is not like you.

Step 2. Up-Front Contracts

Sandler Rule: There is no mutual mystification.

Prospects are used to typical sales pitches. "Tell me who you are, what you have, and how it would benefit me," says the prospect. Salespeople are used to telling the prospect what they have and how it would benefit her. An *up-front contract* is a process by which at the beginning of a meeting, you are setting the expectations of what is going to occur during the time you're going to be together and you are establishing *equal business stature* (EBS).

Let me explain. Before you begin your pitch or start asking probing questions, take a few minutes to share with her that you plan to ask her a lot of questions, and then ask her what she hopes to accomplish from the meeting. Finally, outline what the potential outcomes of the meeting might be. Starting strong with a good set of expectations will set the stage for the rest of your meeting.

Step 3. Pain
Sandler Rule: The problem the prospect brings you is never the real problem.

Most salespeople know they have to ask questions in order to find the needs of the prospect. However, once they find the slightest interest or first issue, the traditional salesperson jumps into sales mode and shares with the prospect how his products or services can solve the problem.

Sometimes you have to slow down the sales process in order to speed it up. Having patience during this portion of your sales cycle will help you to inquire deeper. In order to find true pain, you must first uncover how a prospect's initial issues, or as we call them *surface pains*, are impacting his business and how much the surface pains are costing him in money, efficiency, and time. Ultimately, by asking the right questions, you find out how much this pain is costing the prospect personally and emotionally. When someone is personally invested in a pain, his urgency to take action is increased tremendously.

Step 4. Budget
Sandler Rule: People buy emotionally, but they make decisions intellectually.

No matter what you've ever decided to buy, even though you may never have purchased it before, you had some idea about how much it would cost or how much you were willing to spend. At this point in the sales process, having an open dialogue about how much the prospect is willing to invest in money, time, and possibly resources to solve her pain is essential to qualifying the prospect and shaping your solution. My advice: don't wait until the proposal or last minute to discuss money.

Step 5. Decision
Sandler Rule: People don't make decisions at the same time, all the time.

If you've ever found yourself not able to determine when you're going to find out if you've earned the sale or not, then you may have missed this very important step. My personal belief is that the Decision Step is the most skipped step in salespeople's processes. This step is not about the prospect's making a decision. Rather, it is at this time that you need to determine the *who, what, when, where,* and *how* that either the prospect or his company goes through to make a decision. You may find there are multiple decision makers; you may uncover the time frame to make the decision is unclear; or you may end up in the procurement department negotiating the deal with a professional buyer. By asking these questions, you'll gain clarity into the prospect's decision-making process, and you'll be better able to adjust and forecast your opportunities.

Step 6. Fulfillment
Sandler Rule: If you wait until the presentation to close the sale, you put too much pressure on the prospect and yourself.

Now that you've explored the prospect's pains, you've discussed budgets, and you know her decision processes, you can present to the prospect your solution to solve the prospect's pains, within the budgets you've discussed, and to the right people who will be making the decisions. This step, in most instances, should be fairly anticlimactic because, during the sales process, the prospect gained a certain amount of trust that you can deliver on her issues by the questions that you've asked. Key thought: ensure you present only to how you're going to solve her pains, and be cautious not to *overpresent,* which can cause confusion.

Step 7. Post-Sell
Sandler rule: On your way to the bank, keep one eye over your shoulder.

Congratulations, your prospect is now a client! However, if you've ever personally experienced buyer's remorse, then you know that at any time your prospect may back out. Addressing this as soon as possible will help you to ensure the sale is solid and you won't lose the sale to an incumbent because it dropped its price to hold onto the client. Also, during the Post-Sell Step, you need to be setting clear expectations as to what is going to happen next in order to deliver on the solution the new client purchased. Finally, once the client is happy with your solution, having a brief conversation about future referrals will keep your pipeline full.

Clint Babcock's overview should provide you with helpful guidelines for successfully selling to prospects you meet on LinkedIn and elsewhere. Naturally, there's a lot more to applying this process in the real world and getting comfortable with the skills and techniques necessary. For more information and to find one of the 250 Sandler Training centers, please visit www.sandler.com.

Combine Your Online and Offline Networking for Greater Success

Throughout this chapter, you've learned how rewarding it can be to connect with other professionals on LinkedIn and promote your products and services where appropriate. There are times, however, when face-to-face meetings are even more valuable because they help you form stronger connections and relationships than digital meetings ever could. I refer you to the excellent book *Never Eat Alone* by Keith Ferrazzi (Doubleday, 2005) in which he says this:

> After two decades of successfully applying the power of relationships in my own life and career, I've come to believe that connecting is one of the most important business—and life—skill sets you'll ever learn. Why? Because, flat out, people do business with people they know and like. Careers—in every imaginable field—work the same way. Even our overall well-being and sense of happiness, as a library's worth of research has shown, is dictated in large part by the support and guidance and love we get from the community we build for ourselves.

Fortunately for you, meetings where you can forge bonds of friendship and camaraderie are happening all the time. My first suggestion for finding a great meeting is to leverage LinkedIn. Join several local LinkedIn groups, and you will see notices of networking events in your area posted by group members. To find local groups, go to the top search box, select *Groups* from the drop-down menu, and type in your location. The great thing about using LinkedIn groups for this task is that you can increase your visibility and boost your brand by replying to an event post and saying you are attending. You can then check out the profiles of other people who are attending and make plans for a one-on-one meeting. You can also check out the profile of the organizer and send her a message to develop a friendship and arrange some time together at the event.

My next suggestion is http://www.Meetup.com, a website that's part meeting organizer and part social network. Here you will find networking events potentially in the thousands happening around you. Sign up for a free account, post a short bio about yourself, and then search through the upcoming meetings to select a few to try. By putting yourself out there and attending the business networking events on http://www.Meetup.com, you greatly increase your chances for new business.

Networking That Leads to Business: How to Do It Right

If you are like me, you want to maximize every minute you spend at networking events. You need a plan to achieve this, and so I asked Chris Krimitsos to provide his best networking tips. As the founder of a business networking organization here in my area of Tampa, Chris knows more about networking for success than anyone I know. In fact, I have benefited greatly from attending his Meetups, and I can count several successful business deals with people I have met at his Meetup groups. Networking does work! This is what Chris advises:

> Here are a few networking tips that can help maximize your time when you are meeting people face-to-face at a business event.

Arrive Early and Stay Late

First, let's cover when the best times are to make meaningful long-term connections at most events. Usually these connections happen really early, when you can connect with the handful of other early arrivals, or when the meeting is over and there is a handful of stragglers.

There is a very simple reason for this: when an event is at its peak, there are too many people in groups to allow for really meaningful connections to happen. Arriving early gives you the freedom to strike up a conversation with anyone in the room because there is usually only a handful of people there. Staying late gives you the chance to connect with the presenter and those who stayed to talk to her.

Strike Up a Conversation

Starting a conversation is as easy as saying, "Nice to meet you. What brings you out to this event?" Then the person will answer and more than likely reciprocate by asking you the same question. You can reply, "I am always looking to learn from others [mention the speaker if there is one] and form powerful strategic relationships with other businesspeople in the community."

At this point you can then ask, "So what field of work are you in?" or wait for the other person to ask you that question. As that question is asked, request the other person's business card and say, "Let's meet up for coffee and explore ways we can work together."

Create a One-on-One Follow-up Meeting

The goal of networking at events is to schedule a one-on-one meeting. Face-to-face meetings are always the best at a neutral location like a local business club or a restaurant. The purpose of a one-on-one meeting is to explore what strategic alliances you might be able to create. You also want to inform the person of what you offer and how that product or service can help others in the marketplace.

The only time I personally go into sales mode at a get-to-know-you, one-on-one meeting is when the person expresses interest right there and then about purchasing my services. Otherwise, I ask him for an e-introduction to people that he believes could use what I have to offer. This, of course, happens only after I feel I have built up enough rapport and credibility with him.

An e-introduction is a virtual connection that takes place via e-mail. Here is an example of an e-introduction:

To: Suzy@gmail.com
From: [your name]
Cc: Sam@gmail.com
Subject line: An Introduction for You

Suzy, I'd like to introduce you to Sam Cook of [Sam's firm]. I believe that Sam would be a great person to meet because [how Sam can help].

Sam, Suzy Smith owns [Suzy's firm]. Suzy is currently looking to [what she needs]. Based on that information, I really think it would be ideal for the two of you to meet and get to know one another.
Suzy, meet Sam. Sam, meet Suzy.

You can also add a personal message such as, "Wishing you both a great weekend," or, "I am really excited about connecting two amazing individuals."

Create Your Networking Goals

Try to set a goal to attend two networking meetings a week, and at each one meet two people and schedule one-on-one meetings. That way, you will have four meetings that potentially can create 8 to 10 e-introductions. With that many introductions, you will have a pipeline full of qualified people who want and need your products or services.

In return, make sure you become a valuable connector for the people you are meeting and create e-introductions for them. It is with this simple technique that I have been able to fill up my calendar with quality meetings up to four weeks out.

Chris Krimitsos is a networking expert. He has developed and managed multiple networking groups in the Tampa Bay area, and he has facilitated well over 1,000 events. To learn more about Chris, visit http://www.ChrisKrimitsos.com. John Patrick is a master networker and connector of people who helped craft the e-introduction format and assisted Chris on these strategies. To learn more about John and his firm, go to http://abusinessstrategy.com.

* * *

Now, let's turn to what is arguably the hottest trend, mobile computing, and see how LinkedIn fits into the picture and how it's possible to stay connected every minute to your valued connections.

Chapter 13: Going Mobile: The Power of LinkedIn on the Go

You *Can* Take It with You

You don't have to walk far anywhere in this country (or in many others, for that matter) to see almost everyone strolling with their head down, eyes fixed on their mobile phone with their thumbs twitching out messages or buying products. It seems like the mobile phone revolution has completely engulfed us, and some statistics I found in a post by Local Vox, an online marketing agency, back that up:

- As of 2014, 4.8 billion people owned mobile phones, and by 2016 the number of mobile phones is expected to surpass the world's population.
- As of 2013, mobile device web browsing accounted for 30 percent of all web traffic, and that number is expected to grow to 50 percent by 2014.
- Most consumers, indeed 60 percent of them, search for businesses on their smartphones.
- By 2015, more than 50 percent of mobile device users will be participating in mobile banking.
- Retail sales conducted via mobile devices are expected to reach $12 billion by 2014.

- Business-to-business mobile device marketing is expected to grow from $26 million in 2009 to $106 million in 2014.

Those are just some of the stats indicating that we truly are becoming a mobile device–based world. For everything you can imagine doing on a PC, "there's an app for that" on your mobile device. Fortunately, LinkedIn is part of the mobile device revolution, and it provides a free application, or app, for that, and I heartily endorse it.

This app is cleverly designed to provide a great deal of the functionality of the site. On the LinkedIn mobile app, I can do the following:

- Check my inbox and see if anything needs immediate attention
- Peruse updates from my network and make comments
- Review my groups and read posts and comment
- Check out profiles of people in my network whom I may wish to do business with
- Read news brought to me by LinkedIn
- Check out possible connections suggested by LinkedIn
- Research companies on their LinkedIn company pages

Sales professionals, business owners, job hunters, and nearly anyone marketing a product will find the app invaluable. You can research a contact you just made or look up someone you are about to give a presentation to or meet in an interview. I find it very handy, and if you have an iPhone or Android, you may enjoy it too. If you don't have a smartphone that handles apps, then perhaps it's time for an upgrade?

LinkedIn Is for Tablets Too

Is the computer dead? Will we all be computing soon on tablets only, the desktop and laptop computers of our youth just a distant memory?

The debate rages on, and all I can say is that my tablet computer is just great. Now, I'm not ready to ditch my laptop just yet because typing fast on a tablet is a skill I have not yet mastered. But for important tasks like playing backgammon against players from around the world, streaming my Vangelis channel on Pandora, and extending my workday into the evening hours as I sit on the couch watching *Sports Center* on ESPN and answering emails, it's a real joy.

My tablet is an iPad; it's an amazing device and my first Apple product. I was a diehard PC user my whole life until Apple opened up one of its insanely profitable Apple stores near my home with its insanely great products out on full display. After a few weeks of hanging out in the store and playing with an iPad, I just had to have one. No wonder those stores are so profitable! (According to an article in the tech blog *Mashable*, Apple stores make more money per square foot than any other U.S. retailer.)

I quickly became an iPad user and a client of the Apple app store, where I downloaded the free LinkedIn iPad app. The app is also available for Android tablet owners through the Google Play store. When you open up the app, you'll be able to use all of the website's features. You can check your mail, read the group discussions, read the status updates from your network, research company pages, and so on.

The LinkedIn tablet app is another great way to stay in touch with your network on the site and also have access to trending topics through the news stories and updates. It's just one more way that information to help your business and career is readily available at your fingertips.

* * *

Throughout the book, you've learned about the many ways in which LinkedIn can help you create and nurture the relationships that will take your career or business to the next level. But it goes without saying that you don't just log in, set up a profile, and wait for the money to fall from heaven. You have to work at it on a regular basis. It's not a "set and forget" proposition. I mean, your cell phone is a spectacular device, but it doesn't make sales calls for you, right?

If you are in business of any kind, LinkedIn is something that should become part of your daily routine – as much as grabbing a cup of joe at Starbucks or checking your email. In the next chapter, I will talk about what kinds of activities you should consider as making up your everyday routine on LinkedIn.

Chapter 14: The Daily Approach to Success on LinkedIn

As you know by now, I'm an advertising guy, and I love good ad slogans. This one from the Navy recruitment ads from years past best sums up this chapter: "It's not just a job. It's an adventure."

That's the way I look at LinkedIn. Every day I log on and I'm not sure whom I am going to meet, who's going to contact me with an opportunity, who is going to teach me something I need to learn, or who is going to lead me to a new resource that helps boost my business. It's an adventure because I constantly meet people from around the world while sitting at my computer, and many of these people I will learn from. I may end up partnering with some of them or providing them with solutions to help their businesses.

But just as any adventure requires a little effort, so does LinkedIn. You get out of it what you put in. So it's a good idea to create a ritual for what you're going to do on LinkedIn every day, and the first place to start is with your status update.

Making the Most of Status Updates

When you wipe the sleep from your eyes and log into LinkedIn in the morning, it's a great idea to update your status box. Go to *Home,* and you will see your picture next to an empty text box that says *Share an update. . .* (see Figure 14-1). Every

Figure 14-1. The status update allows you to share interesting content with your network and engage and remain top of mind with millions of people on a daily basis.

time you create an update and click the blue *Share* button, your update appears on the home page of all your first-level connections.

You will see a paperclip icon on the right side of the text box. Hover your mouse over that, and the *Add a File* message comes up. Click on it, and you will be able to add anything you want from your hard drive, such as a report or white paper. By adding valuable content to your network feed every day, you help brand yourself in your field as someone who is knowledgeable and helpful. If you want to add a web address to the message to share an interesting site or promote a webinar or teleseminar, type the website address into the text box with your update.

Beneath the status update box is a feature that allows you to choose who can view your update. Select *Public + Twitter*, which will send it out to all of LinkedIn and your Twitter followers; choose *Public* to reach all of LinkedIn; or choose *Connections* so that it goes just to your network. So in my case, with one update I can alert 28,000 people: my 20,000 LinkedIn connections and my 8,000 Twitter followers.

The update is an excellent way to share great content or promote anything you are working on and remain top of mind with your network. With your status updates you can accomplish the following:

- Promote networking events you are organizing or attending

- Promote your seminars and webinars
- Send people to your latest blog post
- Promote others' content, such as blog posts, videos, and podcasts
- Ask a question that could help you solve a problem and engage your network
- Promote a valued partner by mentioning him and the great products or services he provides (remember that giving first is a key success factor on LinkedIn)
- Tell your network what jobs you have available if you're hiring
- Talk about job fairs you went to if you're job hunting and interviews you had, to keep your network informed that you are looking for your next big opportunity

What you hope to have happen is that someone will like or comment on your update. This will share the update with their network, spreading your message and branding even further. You can help out the people in your network by liking and commenting on updates you find helpful so the writer gets exposure to your network.

LinkedIn Etiquette Regarding Updates

Here are a few pointers to keep in mind to ensure that updates are a valuable part of your LinkedIn activity:

- Limit your updates to a couple a day. This is not Twitter, where multiple posts throughout the day are the norm.
- Restrict your posts to business topics, and save personal updates such as where you had lunch and what sitcom you watched for other social networks. Everything you do and say on LinkedIn is branding you. Make sure your status updates reflect the professional brand you want to create.

Clever Ways to Show Up in Network Updates

By updating your status a few times a day, you keep branding yourself. But you don't always have to write a specific status update because you can appear on the home pages of your connections just by being active on LinkedIn as follows:

- **Update your profile.** Every time you make a change anywhere on your profile, that change will show up in your status updates in your first-level connections pages.
- **Make connections.** Every time you connect with someone, it shows up in the network updates of your connections' home pages. So that's another great reason to build your network.
- **Get active in groups.** Every time you like or comment on a group post, it shows up in your connections' updates.
- **Follow companies.** Go to the top toolbar, click on *Interests > Companies,* and follow some companies. Your doing that will show up in the updates of your connections.

Creating a LinkedIn Goal Statement

Your daily activities should all serve your purpose for being on LinkedIn. Have you defined what your goals are for being on the site? For example, here is my LinkedIn goal statement:

> I want to be the leading LinkedIn expert, create interest and sales for my social media courses and online training, demonstrate my social media expertise, build a worldwide brand, and add value to everyone I meet on LinkedIn.

Create your own goal statement, and then get busy doing those things that will help you achieve your outcomes. The next section gives a list of activities you can do every day that will help you.

The big question is time. How much time can you devote to LinkedIn? I suggest you put in at least an hour a day if you can. That's the minimum. Now, if you are a commissioned salesperson selling for a company, I would spend four hours each morning networking on LinkedIn and getting to know prospects and then four hours in the afternoon having coffee or phone calls with the people you met. If you are job hunting, I would spend four hours each morning getting to know prospective hiring managers and four hours in the afternoon on calls and informational interviews.

But that's just me, since I love LinkedIn! It's up to you how much time you spend on the site, but remember, the more time you spend, the more results you will get. Again, what you put in you will get out.

Powerful Daily Success Activities

Here are suggestions for activities that will take you to your goals, once you have them set:

- Click on the flag icon on the top toolbar to display your notifications. You'll see who has recently connected with you, who has viewed your profile, and so on.
- Reply to all personalized messages in your inbox, and accept all connection requests.
- Stay in touch with your contacts every day when something important happens to them. Click on *Network > Contacts* to find a wide array of first-level connections who have recorded a new job on their profile; you can send your congratulations right from this screen. Select *See more people to contact,* and you will find those having birthdays in your network; again, you can wish them happy birthday right from this screen.
- See what influential people are saying and sharing each day by going to *Interests > Pulse.* On this screen you can follow thought leaders like Jack Welch, Tony Robbins,

Richard Branson, and Gary Vaynerchuk. You can also set up your own personalized news channels to be inspired and stay informed about topics of interest to you.

- Start discussions in your groups—perhaps start a debate on a hot topic that will get lots of input, or ask a question on something that will help you in your work.
- Respond thoughtfully to group posts with applicable content and not a pitch. The goal is to engage people and not to sell outright.
- Create and distribute content, such as a white paper, a video, or a report, to your groups and in your status updates. Include a link to your website if appropriate. Create videos of you and others in your organization to post on YouTube, then attach the hyperlink to that video when you create a post.
- Review the list of groups you belong to. Join new groups that will help you achieve your goals, and leave other groups that are not helpful.
- If you have a group, send out invitations every day to your network to get people to join it. Also, send a note to people in your group asking how you can help them.
- Reach out to people who look interesting, and get them to join you in an introductory phone call to find areas where you can help each other.
- Request a recommendation from someone you have worked with.
- Write an unsolicited recommendation for someone who is deserving. There are probably a lot more people in this category than you can recall. Here's a way to jog your memory: go through all your connections in your local area regularly to see whom you've worked with but not yet recommended. The more recommendations you write that are accepted, the more often your name and a hyperlink to your profile will appear on other people's profiles.
- Endorse a skill on a first-level connection's profile in her Skills & Expertise section. Your picture with a hyperlink to your profile will now appear on her profile,

so that she gets an endorsement of her abilities and you get branding. Write to some trusted friends on LinkedIn, and ask for endorsements for some of your skills.

- Check for new potential connections. With more and more people joining every day, it's a good idea to go to *Network > Add Connections* regularly. There you will be able to search your email databases for people who are new to LinkedIn and invite them to your network.

- Conduct your own LinkedIn search for yourself using the People Search in the top center toolbar by typing in the keyword you want to be found for. See where your profile comes up. If you want to be number one, update your profile with keywords and phrases that bring you to number one. This will ensure that opportunities continue to come your way.

- Offer help. When you make new connections, ask them, "Is there anything I can do to help you?" This might lead to a new opportunity for you.

- Forward introduction requests as soon as you get them because this is how you would like your requests handled. Also, make unsolicited introductions between connections if you feel they can benefit each other.

- Provide feedback in LinkedIn Groups that helps people. It's not necessary to sell anything when you post a comment because people can always click through to your profile and see what you offer if they have been helped by your comment.

- Thank people who have helped you out with a timely response to your question or your introduction request or who wrote a recommendation for your profile.

- Contact industry leaders, and ask if they will be attending an upcoming trade show or conference, and if they have a few minutes to meet with you.

- Invite people to connect with you that you've met at networking events. It's a great way to follow up with people and begin relationships.

- Check your saved searches for companies you are targeting, or start a new search.
- Check out the Advanced People Search to see if there is anyone new matching your target market, and check your saved people searches.
- Check out competitors' personal profiles and company profiles to keep up to date on strategies, products, and services that you may wish to emulate.

Turbocharged LinkedIn Success Activities

As time goes on, your needs with LinkedIn will change. It's a good idea to take a look at all your different options and make sure the site is set up just the way you want it:

- Explore the benefits of paid accounts. As you get more active with LinkedIn, you may want to get more capabilities in terms of searches and messaging. For example, with a basic account, you can see the full profiles of only your first- and second-level connections. Click on your picture in the upper right, then click on *Privacy & Settings > Compare account types* to see if you would be interested in an upgrade. You will see options for premium accounts for power users, recruiters, job seekers, and sales professionals. Personally, I made do with the basic account for my first few years on LinkedIn, but now I have the executive account. I enjoy having InMails to contact people outside my network, and I enjoy the extra searching capabilities.
- Check how you are doing in terms of visibility. If you have been optimizing your profile with keywords and engaging lots of people in groups, you should be showing up in more and more searches. You can check out how many times you've shown up in searches by clicking on *Home*. Then look on the right-hand side, and click on *Who's Viewed Your Profile*. If you are appearing in more

and more searches, you're doing well. There really is no number of times you show up in searches that's the best. Just make sure your number keeps going up every day.

- Check your email settings. You can associate as many email addresses as you want with your LinkedIn account. This is helpful because some people have had only their work email address associated with LinkedIn, and when they lost their job, they found it impossible to get into their LinkedIn account. If you work for someone else, make sure to associate a personal email address so that you always can get to your account.

  Go to your picture in the upper right of any screen, and click on it; then click on *Privacy & Settings*, and then click on *Change/Add* next to where it says "Primary Email" under your name. That's where you can adjust what email addresses you have associated with your LinkedIn account and which is the primary one LinkedIn uses to send you information. When you are done, click on *Close*.

  That settings box you have opened has a lot of different options for protecting your privacy on the site. Try clicking around, and see how you want to customize your LinkedIn experience.

- Consider creating a quick response (QR) code that directs people to your LinkedIn profile, and add it to your business cards, résumé, stationery, and email signature. To do this, you can use a free tool that you can find easily on the web. Nowadays many people have QR code readers on their smartphones, so the QR is one more way to direct others to your profile.

Creating a Leadership Reputation Every Day on LinkedIn

Every day you have an opportunity to build a reputation as a leader on LinkedIn: through the thoughtful posts you make in groups, through content you share in your updates, through the assistance and advice you offer to those in your network. Or you can remain in the shadows and do nothing! The choice is yours. To borrow a familiar quote from noted British author Thomas Paine: "Either lead, follow, or get out of the way."

I really hope you choose to lead and take advantage of all the ways that LinkedIn can help you build your reputation. To provide guidance on your path to greatness and close the chapter on an inspiring note, I asked leadership expert Joe Yazbeck to explain the best ways to maximize LinkedIn to build your leadership reputation. Here's what he told me:

> Leadership is the taking of a specific action that results in self-determined followers accepting and acting on your lead. So what does it take to be a leader on LinkedIn? Well, through my many years of coaching work in leadership development and public speaking, I have isolated the essential ingredient that must be learned and applied well to being a leader and bringing about any type of positive change. That ingredient is effective communication.
>
> Leaders who communicate well have a strong and commanding influence on the people around them. Whether you are a business owner or executive, community leader or public servant, you can use communication to inspire or influence others to:
>
> 1. Agree to what you say
> 2. Emulate what you do
> 3. Believe in the credibility you have established
> 4. Be inspired by the example you set forth
> 5. Take positive action based on your call to action

Leverage LinkedIn to Demonstrate Leadership

> This formula is very transferrable to the LinkedIn culture. LinkedIn allows you to demonstrate the above essential five elements and demonstrate your own leadership strengths genuinely. You can use LinkedIn to communicate the following:
>
> 1. Who you are

2. What you have accomplished

3. Why you care

4. What others say and feel about what you have accomplished

5. Where you are going from here

6. Where you are leading your followers and what's in it for them

Your LinkedIn presence must establish you not only as a leader, but also as a respected and recognized leader in your industry. There are numerous ways to take advantage of the tools on LinkedIn to achieve this and generate the respect and recognition you are seeking.

Be an Authentic, Not a Synthetic, Communicator

One of the best ways to be a leader on LinkedIn and gain respect and recognition is to be authentic in all your communications. In my book, *No Fear Speaking* (Paradies Publishing Company, 2014), I explain the differences between an authentic and a synthetic communicator.

Authentic communicators are expressive, natural, and interested, while synthetic communicators are trying to *impress* rather than *express*. Their statements breed artificiality, not natural ease. Synthetic communicators convey *being interesting* and draw attention to themselves, rather than *being interested* by drawing attention to the people they serve.

You cannot fool others. I recognize it when I am being offered a dose of artificiality, and so do most people. Be an authentic communicator on LinkedIn. Stay true to your intended audience, and they, in turn, will stay true to you. In fact, they will follow you and follow your ideas. They will want to contact you and engage you in conversation and then perhaps create alliances in some fashion.

Your LinkedIn profile helps to establish you as a leader. Ensure that you have a current biography, a mission statement or purpose, an ever-accumulating list of recommendations, and videos of others talking about your work or accomplishments. But above all, continue to communicate where you are going with your messages, articles, and comments. Stay focused on your intended call to action.

Lead by Serving

Lead people by serving them. Provide them with valuable tools based on workable successful actions that improve their lives and careers. You will not only have a consistent audience but you will also be mounting a working basis to truly be a thought leader on LinkedIn, regardless of your industry.

By effectively communicating and continuing to convey messages that are authentic and valuable to your groups, not only will you have a following but you will also become the recognized and respected authority in your field or industry.

Isn't that real leadership? And it can be accomplished on LinkedIn.

Joe Yazbeck is the founder and CEO of Prestige Leadership Advisors and the author of *No Fear Speaking*. For over 30 years Joe has successfully helped thousands of individuals and businesses in numerous industries throughout the United States and abroad with his unique system for public speaking, effective presentations, media communications, and leadership development. His websites are http://www.prestigeleader.com and http://www.nofearspeaking.com.

* * *

LinkedIn will reward you with many opportunities to establish your reputation as a leader in your field, and it will help you gain clients and partners from around the world *if* you put in the time. It's such a great resource that I strongly urge you to spend at least an hour a day on the activities outlined in this chapter and create the success you are seeking.

And now—*drum roll!!*—I will go to the big finish, pull everything together, and inspire you one last time to get active on this amazing website.

Conclusion: Opportunity Is Knocking at Your Door

Your opportunities on LinkedIn are endless. As a professional resource, LinkedIn is growing daily in popularity, which means there are more and more people joining the site who can help you achieve your goals. While it surpasses all other sites in terms of helping you find a job, it's much more than a job search site. LinkedIn is a worldwide database that offers you a wide variety of different opportunities to enhance your business and career depending on your objectives.

To get a read on the diversity of the ways LinkedIn helps people, I took a poll of the people in my network to find out how LinkedIn was assisting them in propelling their businesses and careers. I know you will find the answers inspiring and informative in terms of the diversity of responses:

A project I was recently on ended earlier than expected, and I turned to my network to let them know I was open to consulting opportunities again. I posted a notice that I was available. A few days later a contact from about 15 years ago wrote and said, "Talk about serendipity! I've been looking to outsource online marketing for my clients." We are now collaborating on "white labeling" my services to his clients.

—**Maria, Digital Marketing Manager**

I was writing a news release, and I needed to find a professor at the University of Michigan to get a quote. He was retired and not listed in any directories. By asking for help from members of my U of M Alumni Group, I found the connection I needed in just a few hours!

—**Gloria, Media Specialist**

I would say the greatest success would be linking up with the other coauthors of *Improv to Improve your Business*—a book that was born directly from LinkedIn and is now out in the market. I knew none of the other coauthors previously, and for me that's where the real magic happens on LinkedIn—the unexpected opportunities that come from broadening your circles.

—**Rob, Author**

LinkedIn is an amazing "poll pool" that features some of the greatest thinkers of our time. I can post a question and in minutes I can get a feel of what the common and diverse thinking is around the subject matter. It's both exciting and engaging.

—**Michael, Leasing Consultant**

I think my biggest success was being able to connect to a key decision maker to discuss a job opportunity via a connection. While I didn't land the opportunity, it did lay the groundwork for establishing a connection that led me to a future opportunity that I landed.

—**Sean, Copywriter**

Participation and visibility on LinkedIn has led to qualified leads (10 to 12 within the past year), many of which I was able to close on the back end. As with many LinkedIn stories, it was not ME going after the leads. They came to me. At least 5 were from folks who lurked and watched my activity from a distance. Sometimes our activity on the networks feels like a waste of time. Just remember, people may still take notice without saying a word! You never know when they'll be ready to make contact!

—**Deana, Content Marketing Innovator**

My biggest success on LinkedIn is probably my starting as a freelance consultant. It was in 2008, and I received a contract on LinkedIn for eight months. I remember at that time that a few of my colleagues met difficult times and were out of work for several months. On my side, I had the eight-month contract, and so I faced the financial crisis without difficulties. We are still facing difficult and fragile times on the financial and economic levels, and LinkedIn remains an essential tool for freelance people like me.

—**Eric, Freelancer**

I joined LinkedIn a very long time ago to find businesses who would want to hire voice talent on my site Voice123. It took a lot of poking around and talking to related industry folks, but since July 2007 the job posting average on our site jumped from 700 to 1,500 monthly. The mere growth I found to be an amazing success.

—**Steven, Website Manager**

Finally, this note from Amnuai in Thailand who founded Thai Silk Magic and has had success promoting her company:

As a small handmade Thai silk business located in a remote Thai village, with most of us having very limited formal education or opportunities, LinkedIn has been essential to our success.

By sharing and helping people in various groups, I have had the pleasure to be invited to connect with people who can provide me with great advice and support. In quite a few cases they have arranged introductions to leaders in the textiles, fashion, and lifestyle industries.

This has resulted in some wonderful relationships that have led to five B2B partnerships. In addition, we have gained a wide range of advocates for what we are trying to do for our village. LinkedIn has given me and our Thai village business the opportunity to be able to very successfully compete in a worldwide market of Thai silk suppliers that has been dominated by large, well-established, and wealthier competitors.

People listen and become supporters of our mission of improving lifestyles and education opportunities for the children of our remote Thai village (we achieve this by sharing all profits). LinkedIn may well be for business professionals, but success for us is based on the fact that people buy people before anything else.

People Buy People

I could not agree more with her assessment. You see, people need to "buy in" to you. Then they will buy from you. If a woman in a small Thai village can use LinkedIn to create success, I believe it has the power to help anyone in the world achieve his or her goals. It comes down to a magic word: Ask!

Basically, you need to get active on LinkedIn and ask for what you want.

Ask for:

- Work from a potential client
- An introduction to someone who can assist you
- A job
- Advice
- Attendees for your event
- Publicity coverage
- Help with your book or movie

What else can you come up with? How about a yacht for your next party? The list is endless and is bounded only by your imagination and desires.

Asking goes hand-in-hand with another activity on LinkedIn, one that, as you have read, is responsible for many of the opportunities that come your way: give generously to your LinkedIn network!

Give by:

- Posting in your status updates helpful advice and links to great sites
- Joining group discussions with thoughtful replies
- Sending unsolicited recommendations
- Sharing important industry news and updates
- Helping out other users who need advice

So, it's a balance. Spend part of your time asking and part of your time giving.

Measure Your Success

After you've taken the time to grow your LinkedIn presence and you are marketing and branding your business and yourself, you should track your progress so you know your efforts are paying off. Since you are investing your time primarily, here are some ways you can tell if your work on LinkedIn is giving you some measure of return on your investment (ROI).

How big is your LinkedIn reach? You can measure your reach by looking at these statistics:

- The number of connections you have made
- The number of groups you have joined
- The number of groups you have started
- How many people have joined your groups
- How interactive your groups have become, with people discussing topics and responding on their own

How has your website traffic grown? Using Google analytics and other measuring services, see how many people are being referred to your site from LinkedIn:

- From your website links in your profile
- From Status Updates
- From other places you have put your website address on LinkedIn

Is that traffic growing?

How much new and potential business have you generated? Track your leads and sales by figuring out the following:

- How many business leads you have received
- How many phone calls you have generated
- How many face-to-face meetings you have generated
- How many deals you have closed

It's Up to You Now

You have all you need to begin the process of achieving maximum success on LinkedIn. Remember, what you put into the site you get out of it, so spend time every day getting to know LinkedIn and using it to accomplish whatever it is you want to accomplish. I wish you success in your LinkedIn journey!

For More Information

Visit http://www.linkedsuccess.com to:

- Download free resources
- Learn about LinkedIn training
- Watch video clips
- Read free LinkedIn articles
- Link to other resources from Dan

Connect with Dan at http://www.linkedin.com/in/ socialmediatrainer.

Join the conversation by becoming a member of Dan's LinkedIn groups, "Link Success with Dan Sherman" and "Tampa Bay Marketing Professionals."

Contact Dan at dan@linkedsuccess.com to learn more about the services he provides, including:

- Corporate sales training
- LinkedIn job search coaching
- Personalized sales coaching
- Keynotes and seminars

Index

About the Author

 Dan Sherman is a LinkedIn expert, social media marketing coach, author, and speaker whose focus is teaching business professionals how to leverage the incredible power of LinkedIn. Through his company, Linked Success, Dan shows entrepreneurs, business owners, and professionals how to get more customers, sell more products, build a powerful brand, and establish themselves as thought leaders by using LinkedIn every day.

Dan has more than 20 years of marketing management experience. He served as director of marketing for two Silicon Valley Internet companies, where he led marketing teams and developed innovative sales-generating programs. Dan was also a manager at Charles Schwab for eight years, where he created the marketing programs for the fastest-growing department in Schwab's history, which brought in $50 billion in assets. An avid entrepreneur, he built several successful Internet businesses after leaving the corporate world.

Dan is a highly rated speaker, and his social media and Internet marketing seminars receive top accolades from both new and veteran online marketers. He has been featured on CNN and NBC, as well as in business magazines such as *Entrepreneur* and *Selling Power*. He graduated from Tufts University with a BA in English with honors.

Dan's LinkedIn training site can be found at http://www.LinkedSuccess.com. His LinkedIn profile is at http://www.linkedin.com/in/socialmediatrainer. Dan's Twitter name is @DanLinkedinMan. Dan's two LinkedIn groups are "Tampa Bay Marketing Professionals" and "Link Success with Dan Sherman."

Also by Dan Sherman

You Can Be a Peak Performer:
10 Steps to Unlimited Success Which Anyone Can Take

"I think your ideas are wonderful, and I am sure your book will continue to prove very helpful to many people."
—Anthony Robbins, author, *Awaken the Giant Within*

"This remarkable book is a real springboard to greater success and achievement. It will change the way you think and everything you do. It's great."
—Brian Tracy, author, *Goals! How to Get Everything You Want—Faster than You Ever Thought Possible*

This book will show you how to apply the strategies of today's peak performers directly to your quest for success. From Bill Gates to Oprah Winfrey, from Charles Schwab to Debbie Fields, the secrets of over 80 peak performers—all millionaires and billionaires—are revealed. You'll learn how to:

- Think and act like a peak performer
- Push through any fears blocking your unlimited success
- Transform limiting beliefs into unstoppable self-confidence
- Turn obstacles into business opportunities
- Create million-dollar business ideas
- Live your dreams

If you have always wanted to be rich, you'll want to study the stories in this book about mega-wealthy individuals who started with nothing and became superstars. You'll learn that you can have that kind of success too. All you need to do is model the strategies of the world's most successful people described in this book, and with perseverance you too can create any kind of life you want.

Available from http://www.Amazon.com:
Paperback, 216 pages: $13.46
Kindle version: $9.00
ISBN-10: 1452879443
ISBN-13: 978-1452879444

Also by Dan Sherman

Linked for Work: Crack the Hidden Job Market with LinkedIn

Job hunting has changed since the Great Recession of 2008. Employers are now more selective and also more cautious. They can afford to be because there are so many highly qualified individuals looking for opportunities now. That means you have to change the way you look for work. So, think like an employer: if you needed to hire someone, you would most likely tap into your own network or the network of your colleagues. And that's why sending in résumés to a multitude of Internet job posting websites really won't help you land a great job. You need to network, and that's where LinkedIn comes in.

In this dynamic, one-of-a-kind home study video course, LinkedIn expert Dan Sherman shows you how to leverage LinkedIn to tap into the hidden job market by contacting hiring managers, recruiters, and "internal champions" at places you want to work. You'll learn how to create a "job magnet" profile that has you showing up high in LinkedIn search results, how to maximize groups to reach out and speak directly to the people who can hire you, how to build your brand as the go-to candidate for your dream job, and much more.

Job hunting has changed . . . and *Linked for Work* is your ticket to finding a great career fast.

Visit http://www.LinkedForWork.com.

Also by Dan Sherman

Linked Agent: Grow Your Real Estate Business Using LinkedIn

LinkedIn has the most educated, wealthiest, and most influential users of any website, and it's where you need to be right now to grow your real estate business exponentially. There are over 300 million professionals on LinkedIn who want to buy from you and partner with you!

Dan Sherman, LinkedIn expert and former Coldwell Banker real estate agent, will show you how to maximize LinkedIn in this in-depth video and e-book training program. You will learn how to:

- Optimize your profile with keywords so you come up on page 1 of LinkedIn searches as the go-to real estate agent in your town
- Learn what to say to attorneys, CPAs, and other referral partners so they send you hot leads
- Add listings to your LinkedIn profile so that buyers call you
- Start a LinkedIn company page that sends unlimited traffic to your site
- Add media mentions to your profile so you are seen as the industry expert
- Create a group that becomes your targeted mailing list, and use it to grow your business and promote offline events

You get a total of 19 videos, 19 MP3s, and seven e-books in this comprehensive home study course. Learn how to make more money working less time by leveraging the power of your LinkedIn network.

Visit http://www.LinkedAgent.net.

Also by Dan Sherman

Affiliate Wealth Today: Start Your Successful Internet Business Now

Every day people look at the tremendous growth of the Internet and wonder how they can get involved and make money. With over 2 billion people worldwide now online, Internet marketing is only getting bigger and bigger. If you want to learn how to generate income online with no product, no experience, and no investment, you need to consider affiliate marketing.

Affiliate marketing is *not* multi-level marketing (MLM) or network marketing. In affiliate marketing, you are an independent contractor marketing other people's products online. You work for yourself, and you don't recruit people or build an organization. You work in conjunction with leading companies whose products you market online. Affiliate marketing allows you to get into business for yourself with no start-up costs, to work with well-known companies and brand names, to choose your products, and to build an additional stream of income or full-time work.

Dan Sherman is an affiliate marketing expert, and he offers a home study course especially created for those new to affiliate and Internet marketing. It consists of over 20 videos and numerous e-books that are instantly available to you once you purchase the course. Learn at your own pace in the comfort of your home exactly how to start your own successful online business.

Visit http://www.AffiliateWealthToday.com.